John Parker, a writer all his working life, has authored three dozen books and published more than 75 editions worldwide in his long career, including many acclaimed military and investigative projects ranging from the Mafia to Northern Ireland. His previous military histories include BLACK WATCH, DESERT RATS, THE GURKHAS and the first officially approved history of the SPECIAL BOAT SERVICE.

Praise for John Parker's military titles:

Black Watch: 'A compelling account of an often heroic history'
The Scotsman

The Gurkhas: 'An incredible story of these most feared warriors'
Daily Mail

SBS: 'Even for one who should know the details already,
I was engrossed . . . an historical account linked with
personal recall which makes the story come alive'
former SBS Captain Len Holmes BEM

D1387777

ROYAL
MARINES
COMMANDOS
THE INSIDE STORY OF A FORCE FOR THE FUTURE

JOHN PARKER

headline
review

Copyright © 2006, 2007 John Parker

The right of John Parker to be identified as the Author
of the Work has been asserted by him in accordance with the
Copyright, Designs and Patents Act 1988.

First published in 2006
by HEADLINE PUBLISHING GROUP

First published in paperback in 2007
by HEADLINE REVIEW
an imprint of HEADLINE PUBLISHING GROUP

John Parker would be happy to hear from readers with their comments
on the book at the following e-mail address:
jv.parker@btinternet.com

9

Cataloguing in Publication Data is available from the British Library

ISBN 978 0 7553 1486 7

Typeset in Times New Roman by Palimpsest Book Production Limited,
Grangemouth, Stirlingshire

Printed and bound in Great Britain by
CPI Group (UK) Ltd, Croydon, CR0 4YY

Headline's policy is to use papers that are natural, renewable and recyclable products and
made from wood grown in sustainable forests. The logging and manufacturing processes are
expected to conform to the environmental regulations of the country of origin.

HEADLINE PUBLISHING GROUP
A division of Hachette Livre UK Ltd
338 Euston Road
London NW1 3BH

www.reviewbooks.co.uk
www.hodderheadline.com

Contents

PROLOGUE

Once a Marine ...

... always a Marine, so the saying goes. Although the title remains, the concept is changing fast. At the turn of the twenty-first century, with the Cold War over, the countdown began for the evolution of a multi-faceted, highly skilled, brilliantly equipped force whose *raison d'etre* began to move dramatically towards meeting the envisaged demands of an international scenario that is almost beyond comparison with what has gone before. The whole structure of the Royal Marines was to be finally and inexorably aligned to the single descriptive title of Commandos, although even that designation barely does justice to the planned rebirth of the Marines as a unique military outfit whose training and ethos, already classed as elite, begins to move to an even higher level in terms of both manpower skills and equipment.

As one of Britain's oldest military units, dating from 1664, the Royal Marines had a wealth of experience to draw on as they planned for the future. The planning, and the creation, is well under way with a vision of operational needs and equipment that will take Britain's greatest-ever amphibious force through to 2020. The revamping of the Marines around the core operations of 3 Commando Brigade builds on the 'go-anywhere' principle that has been the underlying theme of their activities for centuries, with a motto that boasted 'by land and sea' from the earliest times. Today, their reach is almost limitless, their firepower awesome, and much more is promised for the future in an intensely programmed restructuring now in progress under the title of Commando 21.

The project was launched at the turn of the century at a time when military units, emplacements and equipment of the major powers were being reviewed, analysed and pulled apart as it became clear that the Cold War was well and truly over. This event had been long awaited by the controllers of budgetary purse strings on both sides of the divide, where hopes of downsizing military spending were being welcomed with heady euphoria. In fact, it didn't and couldn't happen, at least not on the scale some had hoped, and the big boomers of the nuclear submarine fleets still populate our oceans, while smaller nations strive to equip themselves with weapons of mass destruction.

There was, however, a seismic shift in manner and location of emergencies that required the attention of ground forces which, in a curious way, were a throwback to earlier times, with echoes of the North-West Frontier, darkest Africa and the bloody uprisings of nationalist armies that fought to free their countries from imperial rule in the 1950s and 1960s. The great difference was that the new areas of conflict could no longer be settled by simply carting shiploads of troops and weaponry to a given situation and then relying on the might of that army to quell the opposing forces, with little regard for the resultant casualties.

The complexities of modern warfare combine the sophistication, and in some cases the simplicity, of new materiel with an underlying theme of terrorist activity so that no modern conflict can be resolved by a battle of wills. First, there emerged a far greater reliance on forward intelligence and the ongoing presence of Special Forces, clandestinely operating in dangerous territory long before the action and on a scale unmatched in any previous generation. There also arose the greater need for what in modern terminology is described as 'peace support' operations in the aftermath of war that have seen British forces involved in recent times in a plethora of diverse situations in the stamping grounds of old enmity around the globe.

Troops who fought in between those two extremities of any conflict were also confronted by new challenges, and it soon became apparent that their actions in support of global security frequently meant that units were destined for operations for which they had not originally been designed or trained. The need for greater force protection became of paramount importance. Former principles of sending light infantry units, such as the Commandos, to seize and hold key terrain by static defence, until armoured units or air forces manoeuvred to deliver the main strike, had to be re-examined, given the availability of long-range firepower that was a distant but devastating threat to invading troops. In safeguarding them from the mass slaughter of earlier times, greater intelligence and front-end input from Special Forces had to be developed along with a major rethink in the manner of troop deployment.

The British Naval Service's response to these requirements was a concept known as the Maritime Contribution to Joint Operations, which sought to enhance and combine the capabilities of the Maritime Forces to support a land campaign. One of the first innovations was the creation of the Amphibious Ready Group, which includes 3 Commando Brigade and which had already established itself as 'part of the lexicon of British defence diplomacy'. The structure of the Commandos themselves was also put under the microscope, and the result was the ending of the traditional platoon and company organisation, which has been the structure of infantry units since the end of the Second World War. The Commandos sought to increase substantially, in their own words, 'the operational tempo, getting them to hit harder, faster and more accurately', which in turn led to the Commandos being reorganised into a very special force that accommodates every aspect of their likely future roles, through logistics, close combat and fire support.

The rethink of operational concepts is to be matched by the introduction of a wide range of new equipment to meet immediate and future requirements planned for the first two decades of the twenty-first century based around their helicopter assault carrier *Ocean*, which has already proved herself in the 2003 Gulf War. The programme also includes the arrival of a suite of modern ships, aircraft, weapons and vehicles as well as an ongoing modernisation of ISTAR – Intelligence, Surveillance, Target Acquisition and Reconnaissance assets – that is also geared to Commando requirements. Other acquisitions already or soon to be introduced into the Commandos' inventory include new weapons, such as the long-range rifle, the heavy machine gun and the Light Forces Anti-Tank Guided Weapon (LFATGW), along with new land vehicles and an armoured all-terrain vehicle, the Viking, which will provide greater protection during mobility. Although the whole is geared to a 20-year plan, many of the improvements will be in place by 2010 to provide what the Commandos describe as a 'comprehensive, modern and highly effective range of capabilities that will take the UK Amphibious Force through to 2020 and beyond'.

But, of course, it is not simply a matter of powering up on equipment. The Royal Marines' planners are well advanced in their efforts to achieve maximum benefit from the new equipment which, in military-speak, will 'maximise the effectiveness of the Amphibious Force to deal with Defence Tasks assigned to it, and to evolve National and Nato operational concepts'. Over time, and moving notches of professionalism ever upwards, this will entail a training routine unsurpassed anywhere in the British military.

Ahead, then, lies a fascinating continuation of the Royal Marines' story, a future which nonetheless is based on the experience and traditions of the past . . .

CHAPTER ONE

The Treasure and the Rock

Captain Nemo was describing the scene: 'English vessels arrived in the Bay of Vigo on 22 October 1702. Despite his inferior forces, Admiral de Château-Renault [commanding a combined French and Spanish fleet of 23 vessels] fought courageously. But when he saw that [his] convoy's wealth was about to fall into enemy hands, he burned and scuttled the galleons, which went to the bottom with their immense treasures ... [well] we're actually in that Bay of Vigo, and all that's left is for you to probe the mysteries of the place' ... Around the *Nautilus* for a half-mile radius, the waters seemed saturated with electric light. The sandy bottom was clear and bright. Dressed in diving suits, crewmen were busy clearing away half-rotted barrels and disembowelled trunks in the midst of the dingy hulks of ships. Out of these trunks and kegs spilled ingots of gold and silver, cascades of jewels, pieces of eight. The sand was heaped with them. Then, laden with these valuable spoils, the men returned to the *Nautilus*, dropped off their burdens inside, and went to resume this inexhaustible fishing for silver and gold.

20,000 Leagues under the Sea (Part Two) by Jules Verne

The only fiction in the above account is Captain Nemo and *Nautilus*. Great treasures worth millions, part of one of the richest seaborne collections ever known, did go to the bottom in the Bay of Vigo on that very day as the French attempted to carry away their treasures and scuttle their fleet to prevent it falling into enemy hands. But not before hundreds of Marines from the incoming English fleet had swarmed aboard the ships to capture the spoils of battle, although for years there were rumours, perpetuated by Verne's novel, that some of the treasure still remains buried beneath the sand. It was without doubt one of the most spectacular and profitable events in the early history of the Royal Marines, and Jules Verne made the most of it, thus spreading the tale far and wide and forging an audacious plot in literary history that is indeed a factual reference point, enhanced though it is by the author's brilliant storytelling.

The Battle of Vigo Bay arose during the War of Spanish Succession when England and her European allies attempted to thwart French attempts to take control of the Spanish monarchy. The resultant power struggle that spread across Europe and the Americas lasted for almost 14 years and, while the attack on the treasure ships provided a spectacularly newsworthy opening, it was followed by an even greater achievement in which the Marines played a heroic and vital role, securing for Britain the greatest prize of all, Gibraltar, the ramifications of which repeatedly became apparent during the ensuing 300 years and is commemorated still on the insignia of the twenty-first-century Royal Marines Commandos.

These two historic events emerged in the early stages of the war when command of the Grand Fleet was handed to Sir George Rooke with orders to sail at once to gain possession of Cadiz, an important Spanish port that had been the scene of numerous clashes in the past, notably the burning of Spanish ships there by Sir Francis Drake. Now, it was the target again. On 10 June 1702 a fleet of 30 English and 20 Dutch ships of the line, with an army of 13,800 Marines and Foot under the Duke of Ormond on board, sailed in force, and by 12 August the ships were anchored outside the harbour of Cadiz.

The next day the governor of Cadiz was invited to surrender. He refused, and on 15 June the Duke of Ormond landed with his Marines and in a short time secured the forts of St Katherine and St Mary. However, progress was slow. The fleet was halted by strong opposition and eventually retreated. As they sailed back across the Gulf of Cadiz and on towards the safety of Portuguese waters, they happened upon some remarkable and diverting intelligence. Captain Hardy, in *Pembroke*, had gone ahead into Lagos on the southern coast of Portugal to arrange for the fleet to take on water and there learned that a Spanish treasure fleet, one of the richest ever assembled, had sailed from Cuba on 24 July bound for Cadiz. With the Anglo-Dutch fleet already heading in the same direction, a fast ship had been sent to warn the treasure fleet to divert to Vigo, just north of the Spanish border with Portugal. The galleons had arrived at the end of September under guard from a Franco-Spanish fleet of around 30 ships under the overall command of the French Admiral de Château-Renault.

Captain Hardy was later knighted for delivering this intelligence so promptly to Sir George Rooke, who in turn called a council of war, in which it was decided to sail at once for Vigo, to salvage something from the disaster at Cadiz. In fact, the French admiral was already one step ahead of the English. He had fortified the harbour and lined the approaches with guns, which had been rolled ashore from one of the ships. Rooke attacked on 23 October, and the following is an account of the action in the Bay of Vigo, published later in the *Naval Chronicle*:

The passage into the harbour was extremely narrow – both sides well defended by batteries – a strong boom, composed of a ship's yards and top-masts, fastened together with three-inch rope, and underneath with hawsers and cables, laid across the entrance, at each end of which was moored, with chains, a 74-gun ship, and within it five ships from 70 to 60 guns, with their broadsides to the sea. The depth of water not admitting the ships of first and second rates, Sir George and the other admirals shifted their flags into smaller ones. Fifteen English ships and ten Dutch ships with all the frigates, bomb-vessels and fire-ships were ordered in readiness to force the passage into the harbour, as soon as the troops landed under the Duke of Ormond [had taken] possession of the batteries. No sooner was the English flag seen flying than the ships advanced, and Vice-Admiral Hopson, in the *Torbay*, crowding all the sail he could, broke the boom, and the *Kent* and the rest of the squadron entered the harbour [and battle began, Marines swarming].

Of the galleons, the English took six and the Dutch five, who likewise sunk six. They had on board when they arrived 20 millions of pieces of eight, and merchandise estimated of equal value, the greater part of which had been landed previous to the arrival of our force. Four millions of plate were destroyed, with ten millions of merchandise; about two millions in silver, and five in goods were brought away. [It] was left by Sir George Rooke to bring away what [ships] he could, and to burn the rest. In the course of a week, he put the French men-of-war into the best condition possible, brought off 60 guns from the forts and batteries, took out 50 brass guns from the French ships that had been run on shore and on 24 October set fire to the ships that could not be brought away, and left Vigo to return home. In his passage thence to England, the weather was so boisterous that one of the galleons struck on a rock and foundered . . . and ultimately every ship of the squadron was separated, and though all in a shattered condition, afterwards reached home.

The Battle of Vigo Bay was a complete victory for Rooke in that all the Spanish and French ships were burned, sunk or captured. The French and Spanish lost 2,000 men, while 800 men from the English and Dutch force were killed. Back in England, the jubilant Queen Anne ordered the minting of guinea coins bearing the word 'Vigo' to commemorate the battle, and each regiment involved earned £561 prize money.

Two years into the war of succession, the second great drama, and such it was, began as an Anglo-Dutch fleet under the command of Sir George Rooke was returning from a fruitless expedition to Barcelona when the chief commander of the Alliance Army, Prince George of Hesse-Darmstadt, suggested that they might instead begin a new siege of Gibraltar, coupled with a demand for unconditional surrender and an oath of loyalty to the Habsburg pretender to the Spanish throne, Archduke Charles. Rooke agreed, but the Spanish Governor of Gibraltar, by now well used to such attempts on his city, had no intention of opening the gates. He refused this latest ultimatum point-blank, as the city had done on 11 previous occasions when a siege was threatened. Prince George prepared his troops to land on the Rock with 1,900 English and 400 Dutch Marines, and on the night of 3 August the fleet first launched the preliminaries with heavy bombardment. This onslaught and subsequent assault by the land forces was heavier than any previous attack, and the Governor eventually surrendered his city to Prince George, who accepted in the name of the Habsburg pretender.

However, according to the English version of events, Rooke arrived on the scene almost immediately after the Marines had secured their positions and ordered the British flag to be hoisted as he formally announced that he was taking possession of the Rock in the name of Queen Anne, quite ignoring Prince George's original intent with the raid, which was to receive a declaration of allegiance to the Habsburgs. This version has been hotly challenged through the ages by Spanish historians, who counterclaim that the only time the English flag was raised was when the Marines landed, to indicate their position so that they would not be hit by friendly fire from their own ships.

Rooke's claim of English sovereignty was the one that was ultimately accepted. The greater challenge, of course, was holding on to Gibraltar, as the Marines soon discovered. Within days of the arrival of the Anglo-Dutch force, large numbers of the town's residents packed up and left, along with the administrative council. They set up camp near the Chapel of San Roque, and eventually established a new town

9

of that name when it became apparent that the English would not easily give up possession of Gibraltar.

The first major challenge to the Anglo-Dutch forces emerged within a month, when a Spanish-French fleet appeared off Málaga apparently intent on regaining possession. They were met by Rooke's fleet with the Marines aboard, temporarily having been taken from the defence of Gibraltar. Although the French-Spanish ships were halted and turned, heavy losses were taken on both sides. To safeguard the Rock, Rooke landed 2,000 Marines together with 120 naval gunners, armourers and carpenters and six months' provisions, then promptly retired to England for the winter. Taking note of this remarkable development, a combined force of Spanish troops and French ships delivered 4,500 troops to Gibraltar to launch the twelfth Siege of Gibraltar, at a time when just the Anglo-Dutch administrative officials and the Marines were the only remaining people inside.

Heavily outnumbered, they were quickly reinforced with a further 400 Marines to ward off repeated attacks, launched in strength against alternative targets around the city. In one attempt, on 11 November, at least 500 French and Spanish grenadiers tried a surprise dawn raid on the Round Tower; according to contemporary reports, Captain Fisher, with just 17 Marines under command, successfully held them off until further Marines arrived to bolster defences in the tower.

The French moved even more troops in their attempts to break the stubborn steadfastness of the Marines, and further assaults came ever closer to penetration as the Marines were gradually reduced to fewer than 1,000 men, thinly spread and now desperately short of supplies. Just in time, supply ships arrived with ammunition and rations and in the following months returned with 2,000 reinforcements. Numerous additional attempts were launched as the siege dragged on into the New Year of 1705.

Even a new commander of the French-Spanish force was not able to bring the siege to a conclusion, and finally they gave up on 31 March 1705. The *Naval Chronicle* recorded that the Anglo-Dutch garrison had 'achieved more than could be humanly expected and the

English Marines gained immortal glory'. Given the long-term implications, there was no doubt about it. Major-General John Shrimpton was appointed Governor of Gibraltar, where he remained until the arrival of his successor, Roger Elliot, the first British Governor to be appointed by Queen Anne to rule over territory that was now classed as a British colony. At the end of the War of Spanish Succession, Spain formally ceded the territory to Britain in 1713 under the terms of the Treaties of Utrecht, which remains as contentious an issue in Spain today as it was then, and there were to be several attempts to reverse it, notably the Great Siege of Gibraltar of 1779 to 1783.

Perhaps more than any other seaborne activity at the time, the activities of the Marines and soldiers aboard the ships combined to form a vital role in the success of these operations in that they had to storm the defended positions, clambering over the fortified booms and defences and boarding the heavily manned and well-armed ships of the line – operations where sheer manpower was the key, rather like pirates in both deeds and appearance. From the outset they were singled out for such activity, to form a large body of men distributed among the English fleet to provide the muscle when, in the avenue of last resort, brute force was necessary. This also applied in administering security on board ship, quieting unruly pressed seamen and preventing them from deserting. Therein lay a poignant difference in their terms of service.

There was a popular misconception that the Marines were sailors. The fact that they served in ships and eventually came under the auspices of the Admiralty perpetuated that belief into modern times, but it was never the intention nor, in reality, the practice. Their role in naval life was to be ready to line the decks and forecastle to launch a hail of musket fire on to the enemy decks. They formed the line to repel boarders and, conversely, were at the front of boarding parties or in landing craft heading for shore emplacements. Once ashore, they fought in the manner of soldiers, usually in battalions.

For the most part they spent their time below decks, waiting for the action, although it is true that many did become skilled at sail craft, by necessity, when for decades they were used to strengthen ships' companies left short by the inadequacies of pressing men into service with the navy or by the rampant sickness that was inherent in all navies for centuries. Even so, they would be expected to do more menial tasks aboard, such as heaving around the capstan and keeping the ship clean. But although the lines of demarcation were blurred somewhat at various stages of their history, the Marines were always first and foremost soldiers, and designated as such in the original order for their formation on 28 October 1664.

On that day, King Charles II signed a warrant for the raising of a force of 1,200 soldiers who were to be prepared for 'sea service' and distributed among His Majesty's ships for soldiering activities in battles both at sea and on land. They were initially to form six companies of a single regiment, under one full colonel and one lieutenant-colonel, each company consisting of 200 soldiers, one captain, one lieutenant, one ensign, one drummer, four sergeants and four corporals. The earliest mention of them as Marines appeared in a 1667 report of a creditable involvement against the Dutch. Even so, for years hence they were regarded as the poor man's army, thoroughly dispensable in times of peace.

The true definition as to their precise role at that time also became somewhat indistinct, at least in public perception, in that the regiment was initially known as the Duke of York's Maritime Regiment of Foot. It became more commonly known as the Lord Admiral's Regiment because at the time James, Duke of York, was also the Lord High Admiral of the Fleet, although the regiment actually remained under the control of the army. The regiment's direct connections to high office further muddied the pond when the Duke of York succeeded to the throne as James II of England (James VII of Scotland) in 1685. Command of his Maritime Regiment passed to his son-in-law George, Prince of Denmark, whereon it then became known as the Prince's Regiment, albeit a short-lived acquisition.

The reign of the first Catholic monarch since Mary Tudor was welcomed with sedition and rebellion and within three years James II was forced to abdicate. The English Parliament handed the Crown to James's son-in-law, William of Orange, thus ensuring the end of the Stuart dynasty and the eventual arrival of the Hanoverian Georges and the present line of succession. The Prince's Regiment, still commanded by George of Denmark, remained loyal to James and was forced to disband within a year of this massive regal upheaval.

The irony of these events came to a head two years later when the sea-soldier concept was revived with two new regiments and they saw their first action in battles to thwart James's attempts – backed by the French, with Irish assistance – to regain the British Crown. The first of these naval encounters came with what became known as the Battle of Beachy Head on 30 June 1690 off the Sussex coast in what was the first War of the Grand Alliance, otherwise known as the Nine Years War. England, in league with the Dutch, sent out a 46-strong fleet under the Earl of Torrington against a far superior French force. The French had massed 70 ships and five frigates in ten-kilometre lines, too strong for the Dutch front line of 32 ships, backed up by a mere 12 from England covering the rear. The French weighed heavily against the lesser opposition, and the Anglo-Dutch force was roundly beaten. They failed to pursue their advantage by dealing an immediate knockout blow to the Anglo-Dutch fleet, but their victory clearly provided some belief in the possibility of destroying the allied fleet and landing an invading army to lead the way for James to regain the thrones of England and Scotland. Two years later, in May 1692, they tried again in the great naval battles of Barfleur and La Hogue in which Marines were again prominent. Spurred by their earlier victory, the French prepared a relatively modest fleet of 44 ships of the line fielding 3,132 guns to transport their army of Franco-Irish troops.

The fleet set off from Bertheaume Bay with their admirals in high spirits until they were met by the 7,154 guns of the Anglo-Dutch fleet – 99 ships in all – under the overall command of Admiral Edward Russell. Although heavily outnumbered, the French forged ahead and lodged early successes in attacking the Dutch line, forcing them to stand off, with two ships sunk and 5,000 men killed. Then the British fleet weighed in and the French were pushed back until they pulled out of battle and sought refuge in La Hogue. It was left to the Marines to finish the job. They sallied forth in 200 boats to attack and burn the ships at anchor.

During two days of fierce action, the Marines caused such mayhem that the French naval commanders summoned sword-wielding cavalry to assist by riding out into the sea in an attempt to ward off the incoming Marines. Dozens of the riders were, however, simply pulled off their horses by sailors and Marines armed with boathooks. In a further encounter six months later, the prize was even greater, and again the Marines were in the midst of the action when an Anglo-Dutch fleet, under Sir George Rooke in *Royal Oak*, defeated a French fleet off Lagos, Portugal, destroying or capturing 92 vessels.

These early adventures of the Marines, covering the first 30 years of their existence, were briefly interrupted by peace at the end of the Nine Years War. But they were back in action in the War of Spanish Succession following the death of Carlos II of Spain in 1701. France and Austria both laid claim to the throne, and England formed an alliance with the Dutch and the Austrians that led to the onset of wars on the European continent for decades. Although tens of thousands of troops had been released from duty at the end of the Nine Years War, the British Parliament authorised a rapid about-turn by ordering the formation of 18 new regiments, including six for the Marines.

Their first action was the attempt to secure Cadiz, which led subsequently to the Battle of Vigo Bay and the taking of Gibraltar, as described above. The Marines who achieved this feat were welcomed home as heroes, but acclaim for their work was not long in passing, given that the Utrecht peace treaty brought relative calm to Europe for some years hence. The heroes were cast out during the years of neglect of the armed forces that followed, most of them left penniless by an inconsiderate employer. Even during their sterling work in Gibraltar, the Marines went for long periods without pay, surviving on dire rations in unhealthy places.

When peace was established, cuts across the board meant the demise of all but two of the Marine regiments, which transferred into line regiments, and that remained the case for the next 25 years, when new regiments were formed specifically for a curious and long-running dispute with Spain in what was dubbed by the newspapers and politicians as the 'War of Jenkins' Ear'. It was the result of an incident in the 1730s when a Spanish ship patrolling the coast of Cuba boarded that of English privateer Captain Robert Jenkins, on his way to London. They tortured Jenkins and eventually a Spanish admiral sliced off his ear with his cutlass for impertinence and told him to take it to King George as a token of what they had in mind for the king. The ear was retained and pickled, although some time passed before Jenkins finally presented it to Parliament, apparently persuaded to do so by some troublemaking privateers who were getting a rough deal in the West Indies. Tension was already running high over territorial disputes with Spain in the region and in the colonies. Political and public opinion was so inflamed when Jenkins arrived in 1736 carrying his pickled ear that Walpole's government somewhat reluctantly declared war on Spain.

In the early months of 1740, the six new Marine regiments were rushed into service, ill-trained and with no battle experience. The gathering of so many men in the face of such competition from the army was no easy task and, in desperation, rules of age, height and general demeanour for potential recruits were relaxed. Volunteers might even be bribed into signing on with a bounty of four or five pounds. Many had the idea they would desert as soon as they were able; most did not live to try. Consequently, the quality of fighting men varied enormously. Many among them were green and scared teenagers or old men, bandy-legged, one-eyed or suffering from some other physical deficiency. The many gaps in the new Marine regiments were filled largely from other line regiments specifically for the purpose of launching a major attack on the Spanish Main. Life for the Marines, and indeed the sailors, became an appalling catalogue of disease and disaster. Regiments began to assemble on the Isle of Wight in April, and all was bustle and activity. John Fortescue, in his *History of the British Army*, wrote:

> There was not a little difficulty with these troops, for the new regiments of Marines were remarkable neither for drill nor discipline but by the energy of Brigadier-General [Thomas] Wentworth (commanding the land forces) they were licked into shape with creditable rapidity. Lord Cathcart, who had been selected for the chief command, was indefatigably vigilant, and indeed he had good cause, for the ignorance and stupidity of the authorities with whom he had to deal was almost incredible. Thus, for instance, the War Office, having depleted regiments of the Line to make up the new Corps of Marines, did not hesitate to order one of the regiments so depleted upon active service and that Cathcart, bound as he knew to a deadly climate in the heart of the tropics, found that part of the force allotted to him consisted of boys who had not strength to handle their arms.

There were many delays in the departure of the force from Spithead because of the shortage of manpower and the sheer physical effort of assembling what was to become the largest British naval task force ever mounted prior to the First World War, with 170 ships, led by 27 ships of the line, along with a trailing fleet that included frigates, hospital ships, cargo carriers, store ships, fire ships, bomb ketches and others carrying an incredible collection of 'warlike implements' – not to mention 15,000 seamen and 12,000 soldiers who included the six regiments of Marines. Another four regiments of Marines were to be raised in the American colonies, and known as Gooch's Marines, to join the main force at the first point of battle, planned for Cartagena, the headland to the Spanish holdings in South America, which is today in Colombia. It was a place heavily defended by fever-carrying mosquitoes. But men were already dying before they set off, as Fortescue recalled:

> [There were] vexatious delays, due partly to foul winds, partly to official blundering. Three times the ships got under way, the men cheering loudly at the prospect of sailing at last, and three times the wind failed them or turned foul. Cathcart grew more and more anxious. The favourable season was slipping away fast. The men had been cooped up in the transports for six weeks and had consumed most of the victuals intended for the voyage. Scorbutic sickness was seriously prevalent, and there had already been 60 deaths. 'Surely,' wrote the General, 'some fresh meat might be given to the troops,' but the authorities had given no thought to such matters. August passed away and September came, bringing with it the news that a Spanish fleet had put to sea, and that a French fleet also was about to sail from Brest. Such a contingency might have been foreseen, but it was not; so there was further delay while the British fleet was reinforced. Then, when the ships were ready, men could not be found to man them. Two old regiments of the line were turned over to the fleet to make up its complement but these were insufficient, and Cathcart was ordered to send 600 of his Marines also to the men-of-war. He obeyed, not without warning the Government that an infectious fever, which had already proved terribly fatal, was raging in the fleet; but his warning possibly in the pressure of business could not be heeded. So the days dragged on; the transports waited, and more men died . . .

The journey to the battle zone was bad enough, with the task force leaving England on 26 October 1740 for a rendezvous off Jamaica in early January before moving onwards to attack Cartagena. But the crossing was horrendous and a further 600 men died en route, largely from scurvy and dysentery, including the military commander-in-chief, Lord Cathcart. The toll rose dramatically as they moved out of the West Indies as the force began to be struck down by yellow fever. The 3,300 men travelling from the American colonies were equally badly hit, even as they moved through the southern reaches of Florida.

The Spanish, meantime, had been forewarned of this massive English force heading towards them and simply sank all their ships to form a defensive barrage in the mouth of the inner harbour to Cartagena, knowing full well that with further delays the English fleet would eventually be stalled by the April rains and the malarial atmosphere of the Cartagena swamps. Fortescue reported:

The fleet, however, quickly disposed of all these obstacles. A few broadsides cleared the beach for the disembarkation, and on 16 April Wentworth landed. He had begged hard for 5,000 men but had been answered curtly, though not unjustly, by the naval commanders that, while they were ready to land them if required, they thought 1,500 men quite sufficient, since time above all things was precious. So with 1,500 men Wentworth proceeded to the further task before him. There was now but one outwork between him and Cartagena, a fort standing on an eminence about 70 feet above the plain, and called Fort St Lazar. The approach to it from the head of the harbour lay through a narrow defile, at the mouth of which the Spaniards offered some light resistance. They soon gave way on the advance of the British, but poor Wentworth, always a general by the book, with his head full of ambuscades and other traps for the unwary, halted his men instead of pushing on boldly, or he would almost certainly have carried Fort St Lazar then and there. He advanced no further than to within a league of St Lazar, encamped, and pressed the admirals to send him the remainder of his men.

Admiral Vernon agreed to the request, but not without protest. 'I sent the men,' he wrote to Wentworth, 'but I still think such a number unnecessary. No time should be lost in cutting off the communication between the town and the surrounding country. We hope that you will be master of St Lazar to-morrow.' The advice was sound, but Wentworth failed to act on it for three days, and by then his men were falling fast from sickness. On the morning of 20 April the columns of attack were finally formed, first with an advance party of 50 men backed by 450 soldiers under Colonel Wynyard, then the two old regiments, the 15th and 24th, jointly 1,000 strong. A mixed company of the 34th and 36th Regiments came behind, followed by the American Marines with scaling ladders and 500 English Marines. The plan was to assault the north and south sides of St Lazar simultaneously, and at four o'clock the march towards the objectives began. They advanced slowly, firing steadily as flashes of cannon and musketry blazed over the parapet. Raked through by grapeshot and round shot, the soldiers stood without flinching for a moment, and loaded and fired as they had been taught, while the grenadiers lit the fuses coolly and hurled their hand grenades into the belt of flame before them only to discover that the grenades were faulty and only one in three of them burst. Wynyard ordered his column to continue firing, even though his men were being 'mown down like grass'.

The losses in the assault were heavy. Of the 1,500 English engaged, 43 officers and over 600 men were killed. Colonel Grant was picked up alive, but desperately wounded. 'The General ought to hang the guides and the king ought to hang the general,' he gasped out, and a few hours later he was dead. Wentworth, striving hard to put a good face on the disaster, ordered a battery to be erected against Fort St Lazar on that same evening, but by this time yellow fever gripped the force and by the following morning they were digging graves, not building batteries. In just four days the troops had dwindled from 6,600 to 3,200 combatants through fighting and sickness, until finally the fleet admirals grudgingly consented to blow up the defences of Boca Chica to enable an assault, and then for ten days the transports lay idle in the harbour of Cartagena with the troops crammed aboard. Men were kept between decks in the crowded vessels. It was a horrific scene, described by Fortescue:

They wallowed in filth; myriads of maggots were hatched in the putrefaction of their sores, which had no other dressing than that of being washed by themselves in their own allowance of brandy. Nothing was heard but groans and lamentations and the language of despair invoking death to deliver them from their miseries. So these poor fellows lay in this sickly, stifling atmosphere, with the raging thirst of fever on them, while the tropical sun burned fiercely overhead or the tropical rain poured down in a dense, grey stream, filling the air with that close clammy heat that even by a healthy man is grievous to be borne. So while the commanders quarrelled the soldiers perished. Officers died as fast as the men, all discipline on the transports came to an end, and the men gave themselves up to abandoned listlessness . . . Day after day the sailors rowed ashore to bury their boat-loads of corpses, for there was always order and discipline in the ships of war, but the raw soldiers simply dragged their dead comrades up on deck and dropped them overboard, without so much as a shroud to their bodies or a shot to their heels. Vernon railed furiously at this nastiness, as he called it, not reflecting that men untrained to the sea might know no better. So after a few hours the bodies that had sunk beneath the water came up again to the surface and floated, hideous and ghastly beyond description, about the transports, while schools of sharks jostled each other in the scramble to tear them limb from limb, and foul birds with ugly, ragged wings flapped heavily above them croaking for their share. Thus the air was still further poisoned, sickness increased, and the harbour became as a charnel-house. At length, on 5 May, it was resolved to return to Jamaica and two days later the fleet sailed away from the horrors of Cartagena. By that time the men nominally fit for service were reduced to seventeen hundred, of whom not above a thousand were in condition to be landed against an enemy.

It is widely acknowledged that of the original force only one in ten survived the expedition – a figure that fitted exactly the state of the 1st Regiment of Marines, which had left under the command of Colonel James Wolfe with 1,000 men and returned with just 96 of the original troops. The remaining regiments were combined and, back in Britain, briefly saw service in the Duke of Cumberland's army that put down the Jacobite Rebellion in 1745 at Culloden. But by then the Marines' days were already numbered – at least in the form that they had been managed for the past 80 years. In fact, it marked the end of an era.

CHAPTER TWO

Goodbye America, Hello Australia

The system of building regiments for wartime duty and then closing down come the peace was no way to run an army, but the system blighted the Marines for years. Certainly in the early days there was no continuation, no establishment and no loyalty or the passing on of spirit or tradition. Second-rate officers who could not afford to buy themselves a commission in the army were the norm. Mutinies among seamen were common over pay and disputed regimental accounts, which were the responsibility of the senior officers themselves. Many were found to have grave irregularities after service overseas, when a man's service might have to be traced through several ships' books before he could be paid. Many never received their money at all, even after several years' service. It was a wholly unsatisfactory situation, which was ongoing when the War of Austrian Succession ended in 1748, when all ten regiments of Marines, built up in the previous three years, were disbanded.

But all that was about to change, and in fact that would be the last time in their history that the Marines were paid off after conflict. After a long review of procedures, management and quality of recruits, they were to be re-established and reorganised, measures forced through by the new First Lord of the Admiralty, George Anson, who was appointed in 1751. He had long voiced his distrust and opposition to the existing system whereby officers 'owned' their command and the administration of it. When the Marines were re-formed on 3 April 1755, they did so under the auspices of the Admiralty with a new corps arrangement from which the present organisation of Royal Marines eventually emerged.

The Royal Navy took complete control of everything from uniforms to pay. This replaced the wholly unsatisfactory and corrupt system whereby senior officers and their agents took profit from the supply of clothing, and more important eliminated the possibility of men not receiving their monetary dues. In time, this new approach went far deeper, and Anson has long been credited with the fatherhood of modern Marines by establishing them on a firm footing, so that skills, traditions and history went hand in hand to provide an everlasting organisation in which pride of service became as important as the wages earned.

For too long, great ships had relied on a motley collection of seamen often drawn from the dregs of society, collected from jails or press-ganged into service and who were subsequently whipped and cajoled into handling cannon, rope and sail. The Marines were an integral part of that system in that apart from their role as fighting men they were also responsible for security aboard. As recruits to the navy were largely impressed men, no leave was granted to prevent 'running', and for much of their time on board Marines were used to keep order in dire conditions, although their own situation on the crowded below decks was no different. Only the upper deck enjoyed fresh air. The lower decks were all enclosed, and daylight and ventilation were by hatches and gun ports that could be opened only in fine weather. The ship's company was housed mainly on the gun decks, while midshipmen and other lesser crew members were on the lowest deck, which was below sea-level and had no ports. Extracts from the *Handbook for Royal Navy Medical Officers*, assessing causes of disease and death among sailors, provide a disturbing insight into conditions.

There was severe overcrowding between decks, and a space of only 36 centimetres was allowed between beds and hammocks. Rats were a constant nightmare. Punishments were appalling. The diet consisted chiefly of salt-beef or pork, oatmeal, biscuits, beer and occasionally cheese. There were no fresh provisions except on rare occasions, and after a short while much of the food became rancid, with the badness disguised by salt, and biscuits were alive with weevils. Water taken on board in casks rapidly became foul. Pay was negligible, and a levy of sixpence a month was demanded to the 'Chatham Chest' for the treatment of the sick and wounded. The experiences of Tobias Smollett, who served as surgeon's mate on HMS *Cumberland* in 1739, are recounted in the handbook, witnessed from his own accommodation on the lower deck among the holds for stores, rotting food and vegetable matter and bilges where foul stagnating water accumulated. Open braziers used in an attempt to dry the decks added fumes to the already poisoned atmosphere. The handbook quotes this description of life at sea in bad weather:

> During such furious storms the spray of the sea raised by the violence of the wind is dispersed over the whole ship; so that people breathe, as it were, in water for many weeks together. The tumultuous waves incessantly breaking upon the decks, and wetting those who are upon duty as if they had been drenched in the sea, are also continually sending down great quantities of water below; which makes it the most uncomfortable wet lodging imaginable; and from the labouring of the ship, it generally leaks down in many places, directly upon their beds. There being no fire or sun to dry or exhale the moisture, and the hatches necessarily kept shut, this most stagnating confined air below becomes most offensive and intolerable. When such weather continues long, attended with sleet and rain, as it generally is, we may easily figure to ourselves the condition of the

poor men; who are obliged to sleep in wet clothes and damp beds, the deck swimming with water below them; and there to remain only four hours at a time; till they are again called up to fresh fatigue, and hard labour, and again exposed to the washing of the sea and rains.

The overcrowding was often exacerbated by the need to carry extra fighting men in addition to the normal number of Marines carried aboard most ships and, even more, by the practice of taking extra numbers on board for longer journeys to allow for 'inevitable wastage' from sickness and death. A ship carrying 100 guns or more and varying from 2,000 to 6,000 tons might have a crew of nearly 1,000 men, while a 60- to 80-gun ship would have 750 men on board at the outset, of whom a quarter might fall victim to disease alone, not counting other causes of death at sea. Diseases of all kinds were rampant, many brought on board by men pressed into service or collected from prisons. Scurvy was the scourge of sailors right up to the end of the eighteenth century, and the cause and transmission of some diseases remained unresolved until early in the twentieth century.

Anson, as First Lord of the Admiralty from 1751 to 1762, attempted to tackle many of these problems. When he finally brought organisation to the Marines, he encouraged investigations into scurvy which caused huge losses among the men along with other common killer diseases, including malaria, dysentery and typhus, or jail fever, the last carried by the many men brought from prisons, lousy and in rags. Because no uniforms or clothing were issued by the navy and without any facilities for bodily cleanliness, disease spread rapidly. Many commanders were anxious to improve conditions so as to sail a relatively happy ship and build a crew that eventually moulded together, bound by loyalty to each other and a peculiar camaraderie, because at the end of the day the greatest loss of life came from the great battles at sea, broadside to broadside, when nerves and willpower were stretched to breaking point.

Anson's ideals for the Marines in particular would take years to come to fruition, and training remained a 'pick-it-up-as-you-go' arrangement for decades ahead. However, the navy's commitment to building up the Marines was apparent from the figures: from a starting point of 5,000 in 1755, the numbers had increased to more than 20,000 within eight years. The attractions for a career in the Marines were also improving, and a good deal was made of the potential for a decent income, especially in the way of prize money, although the Marines' share compared with the navy's was still abysmal. Naval officers could still make a fortune from capturing enemy ships.

However, in the long term these benefits were to cease, and there is little doubt that the 1755 edict for the formation of a new and permanent Marines establishment was serious, even to the point of forming three divisions based at Chatham, Portsmouth and Plymouth which were to remain intact for the next two centuries, providing a shore base, depots, stores and manpower for the fleet on demand, with detachments of between 20 and 100 men available for duty whenever and wherever they were required.

There now was a central point to which the Marines themselves could become attached, form bonds with their surroundings and with each other. It was, for the first time, a real step towards forging the loyalties and traditions that were already the lifeblood of many army regiments but which had been largely frittered away among Marines in the past by the constant pattern of neglect, corruption and disbandment by the hierarchy. Such bonding of the men could only be advantageous as the new structure more or less assured their presence at the start of major conflicts of the future, a fact that can be now viewed from their history.

The latest conflict would involve the Marines in virtually every zone of conflict. The Seven Years War (1756–63) – known in America as the French and Indian War – was the first war with worldwide implications, eventually drawing in most of the leading players in the international power game. English ships and transports carrying detachments of Marines of varying strength would be bound for destinations around the European coastlines, as well as India, Canada,

North America, South America and the West Indies. The widespread action saw far-flung historic battles and successes, including Clive's victory at Plessey, India (1757), Wolfe's capture of Quebec, Canada (1759) and Hawkes's naval victory at Quiberon Bay (1759), the last still regarded as one of the finest victories in the annals of the Royal Navy.

Tensions had been building between Britain and France for two years before the outbreak of the new war, particularly in relation to both their dealings with the colonies and their alliances in Europe. Hostilities in this round of conflict between the two nations first broke out in North America, and what became the Atlantic shuttle of troops began in earnest and was to continue for years hence. The French had been ambitiously increasing their colonising strengths, and the antagonism between the two nations in Europe was merely replicated in the jostling for position in the New World. Major territory deep in Canada and North America had fallen under French control during their massive fort-building enterprises, and in several areas the British began losing ground and their own fortified settlements.

In June 1756 a new British initiative was launched, urged on by William Pitt the Elder, who predicted that victory in North America was the supreme task in the worldwide struggle. But the British performance in the region thus far had been abysmal, largely because of the ineptitude and sheer lack of talent or courage of some of the senior officers in charge. In the summer of that year, Marines were part of a major military task force that sailed for New York to prepare for a confrontation with the French army, led by the famous Marquis de Montcalm. Many key British forts and much territory had already fallen before the British force commander, the Earl of Loudon, arrived to begin his task of regaining lost ground. Unfortunately, he proved to be a remarkably inept soldier, who seemed in no hurry to achieve his given objectives.

The troops were landed at Albany and were put to work immediately constructing a parade ground on a tract of rugged land and for the next month undergoing training. Fortunately, the incompetent earl's antics finally came to the notice of the high command in London and he was sacked, to be replaced by the ageing and corpulent General Sir Robert Abercrombie to whom a level of unwarranted responsibility was being handed somewhat late in life, and too late. The British had now amassed 30,000 troops, 16 ships of the line and numerous frigates and transports. Abercrombie planned an attack on the key French fort of Ticonderoga, which lay at the southern end of Lake Champlain, part of the long inland waterway that was the main route for a British land invasion of French Canada. In June 1758 a force of British regular and American provincial troops – 15,000 men in all – was assembled at the head of Lake George. The northern tip of Lake George was joined to the southern end of Lake Champlain by a five-mile strip of river, marked by rapids and morass. The French fort stood at the point where the river entered Lake Champlain. Montcalm's regular French battalions were positioned at various points along the river, but he planned a final hurdle to the British advance should it get that far. Montcalm ordered the building of a near-impenetrable mass of felled trees, branches and thorn in front of the fort. After an initial hesitation, Abercrombie decided to launch his attack, having first sent his engineer to reconnoitre the French position. He came back to report that the felled trees could be stormed by infantry assault. In fact, these defences proved to be insurmountable and the British withdrew, nursing heavy casualties.

It would be a further year before they could launch another attack, and a force was already being raised to perform the task, headed by the brilliant 32-year-old General James Wolfe. In 1759 he took command of the largest British naval force ever to cross the Atlantic, including a strong representation of Marines. The flotilla from England demonstrated to the French that this time they meant business. The formidable force comprised 49 men-of-war, almost a quarter of the Royal Navy's available ships, along with 200 transports and provision vessels. The attack was to be launched along the St Lawrence River towards Quebec.

Wolfe's great problem lay in getting his men across the river in sufficient strength to attack his enemy, safely hidden behind the natural fortress of steep cliffs stretching along the approaches to both sides of the city. General Montcalm believed his position to be impregnable to such an attack and had based his entire strategy on stalling the British until the winter, when enemy ships would have to pull out or be frozen solid. Wolfe, on the other hand, had to attempt to force the Canadians and their North American Indian allies to come out and fight.

On 13 September 1759 the general himself sailed in the lead with the Marines in flat-bottomed boats carrying his attacking force, utilising a specially selected troop of 24 men whose task was to kill or capture the sentries at the top of the path winding up the cliff face. The battle for Canada was finally under way, and by daylight almost 4,500 British and American troops had reached the clifftop to form up in open fields of the Plains of Abraham. Elements from five regiments took position in lines across the plains, with Wolfe himself leading from the front, on the right of the line. Montcalm was alerted too late.

The French commander saw before him the incredible sight of the infantrymen who had been secreted into position before dawn without a shot being fired, and there they stood, waiting for a fight. On the opposing side, Montcalm appeared on horseback ahead of his 5,000 troops, urging them to fight for all they were worth, then raised his sword to signal the advance. Montcalm's soldiers moved ahead in a formation three rows deep and held their fire until they were within a hundred yards of the British lines. Wolfe's troops stood their ground, refusing to fire yet, their only movement coming when soldiers ran to fill up the line when a comrade was felled. At 75 yards, the first rank of Wolfe's lines dropped to one knee and both ranks held their fire until the Canadians were 40 yards off, when Wolfe gave the order to fire. The scene was now a classic and intense killing contest, amid the screams and blood and gore of battle, as it reached close-quarters range, the last volley being fired by both lines at just a dozen yards before the bayonet charge. The French commander was hit twice but remained mounted on his horse. He rode back for treatment, but he died the following morning. His opponent, General Wolfe, also in the thick of the battle, was wounded as well; two grenadiers carried him from the field. He, too, died from his wounds, and his body was returned to England for a hero's funeral. Quebec had fallen, but the British had a long, harsh winter ahead before Canada was indisputably in their hands and the British flag waved over almost the whole of eastern North America.

During the fighting in Canada, India and the West Indies, however, France was under severe pressure in Europe. Apparently to resolve all these problems in one major diversionary effort, the French planned to land an army of 20,000 men in Scotland to be covered by a fleet of 21 ships of the line under Admiral Comte de Conflans. Sir Edward Hawke, with 23 ships, caught up with him off France's Biscay coast near St-Nazaire in November 1759. There, the French fleet was joined by a squadron from the West Indies. Hawke encountered them at dawn on 20 November heading towards the hazardous waters of Quiberon Bay. The British admiral followed them in, relying on the route picked out by the French themselves.

At two in the afternoon the vanguard of the British fleet was close enough to attack the rear of the French, and within the hour Marines clambered aboard the French ship *Formidable* and another three ships were disabled. The British lost two ships of their own, but the rout of the French was already well in hand, and only eight escaped to Rochefort. The battle, acclaimed as the most important victory of the war, had repercussions throughout the French colonial empire, which she was no longer able to defend, thus ending a year of victories immortalised in the song 'Hearts of Oak' composed to commemorate the Battle of Quiberon Bay.

Recognition was also won by the Marines in another famous battle in the same area three years later. Two battalions of Marines, under the command of Lieutenant-Colonel John McKenzie, served with great distinction at the siege of Belle Island in Quiberon Bay. With the 19th Regiment, these two units achieved their first successful seaborne landing in the face of stiff opposition. They took part in all subsequent fighting on the island. The Marine battalions gained great fame at the final storming of the redoubts in June. Of their conduct on this occasion the Annual Register for 1761 said: 'No action of greater spirit and gallantry has been performed during the whole war.' The laurel wreath borne on the colours and appointments of the Royal Marines is believed to have been chosen in honour of the achievement of the corps during this operation.

Next came the tidying up of unfinished business elsewhere in the colonies of France and Spain. With Canada secure, a considerable force was dispatched to the West Indies, totalling 17 regiments into transports and eight ships of the line under the command of Admiral Rodney to put some weight into the planned attack to break down a strongly held French position, not easily given up and which required bombardment and heavy fighting to achieve. Spain had supported France in the Seven Years War and continued to do so as the British sought to drive France out of the majority of her North American interests ahead of negotiations that would lead to the 1763 Treaty of Paris, under which the three nations would cede some of their territory to bring an era of supposed peace between them. Spain had control of Cuba, as well as parts of Florida and other linked interests to which the Caribbean was a tributary.

Havana, a hugely attractive city, was surrounded by a military presence that the Spanish believed to be impregnable. To continue the theme of Caribbean influence, the British mounted an attack through an expedition led by the Earl of Albemarle, who had under command a substantial fleet: 19 ships of the line, 18 frigates, 110 transports and an army of 11,000. Once again, the toll of the heat and disease on troops in the Caribbean was a heavy one during the four months of military actions: 694 died from illness, whereas 342 were killed in action. For those who survived, there was the reward of a share in the rich prize money, said to be worth more than £3 million.

George III's accession in 1760 brought changes in foreign policy, and in March 1762 secret peace negotiations were opened. When the final Treaty of Paris was signed in February 1763, Britain had acquired Quebec, Florida, Minorca and large additional parts of India, the West Indies and the Americas. For the first time, Britain was truly a world power, and where ships travelled, so went the Marines. For the British, however, spoils of war did not match the huge cost of achieving the victory – and in turn actually contributed the next war: that of American Independence.

The British government tried to relieve the burden of the national debt, running at £133 million, by increasing taxes and duties in America, which in turn brought about the Boston Tea Party a decade later. In the meantime, a swingeing round of cuts in military spending once again saw the Marines reduced in numbers, although this time – and for the first time at the end of any previous war – the corps was not closed down. They were maintained at just under 5,000 men at a time when the overall strength of the navy was at 16,000, the lowest for many years.

Numbers were still at around that level at the first encounter of the Revolutionary War in America, and it was the Marines who were thrust to the fore of the uprising. The 'tea party' signalled the start of it when, in 1773, Britain's East India Company was on the verge of bankruptcy, sitting on large stocks of tea that it could not sell in England. The British government passed the Tea Act, which gave the company the right to export its merchandise to the colonies without paying any of the taxes that were imposed on the colonial merchants. When preparations were made to land incoming cargoes in Boston, local patriots staged spectacular opposition. On 16 December 1773 three companies of 50 men each, masquerading as Mohawk Indians, passed through a tremendous crowd of spectators, went aboard the three ships, broke open the tea chests and dumped the contents into the harbour.

The rebellion spread and gathered pace until the first exchanges in what became the American War of Independence occurred in the village of Concord, 18 miles north-west of Boston. On 14 April 1775

General Thomas Gage, commander of the British garrison at Boston, received secret orders to proceed against the 'open rebellion' that existed in the colony and to take whatever action was necessary to stamp it out. He chose to send 700 Marines and grenadiers under Lieutenant-Colonel Francis Smith and Major John Pitcairn to attack and destroy the rebel militia's supply depot at Concord.

The battalion reached the village on the night of 18 April, but local patriots learned of the mission and sent Paul Revere and William Dawes by separate routes on their famous ride to raise the alarm. En route, the Marines successfully scattered a small force of rebels at Lexington and arrived at Concord to discover that this delaying tactic had allowed the Americans to carry off most of their stores and arms. The British destroyed the few remaining gun carriages, entrenching tools, flour and a liberty pole. News of this event had spread far and wide, and the local force had gathered at the North Bridge in Concord, where exchanges of fire broke out, each side blaming the other. Major Pitcairn was to carry the mantle of allegedly having shot dead the first American in the battle, thereby, according to some, lighting the blue touchpaper.

Fourteen casualties were inflicted on the British battalion, and about noon they were ordered to disengage, form up and begin the march back to Boston. It turned out to be a case of running the gauntlet, with farmers and patriots sniping from trees and behind every wall and from the cover of every barn. A further body of men from the 4th, 23rd and 47th Regiments under Colonel Lord Percy arrived just in time to help fight off the rebel attacks, but even so it was nightfall before the survivors reached the safety of their barracks in Boston, having lost 73 men killed and 200 wounded along the way. It was later alleged that some of the wounded were scalped or had their ears cut off by the former Indian fighters in the ranks of the patriots. American casualties totalled 95.

After retreating from Concord, the British remained cautiously inactive in Boston for several months while the build-up of reinforcements was under way, eventually to include a further 750 Marines and other regiments to provide a total force of around 6,500 men. Meanwhile, anti-British feeling continued to mount and the British generals decided to fortify nearby Dorchester Heights and Charlestown peninsulas, which provided a commanding view of the seaport and harbour and were vital to the security of the British base. As usual, with spies in every camp, the Americans gleaned advance knowledge of the plan and decided to take command of the Charlestown peninsula themselves, which they surmised might cause the British to leave Boston. On 16 June 1775, under the leadership of Major-General Putnam and Colonel Prescott, the American Continental Army stole out on to the Charlestown peninsula and established defensive positions on Bunker Hill and nearby Breed's Hill, which effectively put the British under siege. It was estimated that they mustered almost 4,000 men into position.

With three senior generals now in control of the British forces – Gage, Howe and Burgoyne – the troops were split into three sections. Howe's command of around 2,400 men, which included the 1st and 2nd Marine Battalions under Major Pitcairn, was to form the main assault force against the patriots' positions. The attack would then consolidate into an overall clearance of all the American positions that threatened the security of British operations. The troops took to the boats to begin their attack, watched by crowds of spectators who had clambered on to rooftops around Boston and gathered in carefully chosen vantage points to watch the ensuing battles. The British advanced in three lines through the long grass on the approaches to the hillsides and even as they did so came under fire from gunmen hidden in houses and other buildings in Charlestown.

The British commanders witnessing this called down red-hot shot fired from the British ships. Meanwhile, the patriot forces – partially hidden from the approaching troops – had instructions to hold their fire until 'whites of eyes' were visible. Twice the British were beaten back, and each time rallied by Major-General Howe. The third time, the 1st Marines and the 47th of Foot advanced and finally broke the Americans, charging forth with bayonets fixed.

The rebels retreated, leaving 441 dead, wounded or captured. British losses were far heavier: 226 killed, including 27 officers, and 828 wounded, including 63 officers. Major John Pitcairn of the Marines was among the dead, but a contemporary report stated:

The reputation of the Marines was never more nobly sustained. Their unshaken steadiness was conspicuous and their valour in closing with the enemy when part of the attacking column wavered gained them not only the admiration of their comrades but the commendation of their distinguished chief.

However, with 1,054 British casualties the whole business was to have immediate repercussions in terms of public opinion both in Britain and America. The outcome of the battle caused great consternation in Britain and had the opposite effect in America, where the infliction of a bloody nose on the British military was greeted with jubilation and national pride. British rule would never be the same again. Given the lack of substantive forces to cover all potential avenues of attack, Boston was certainly an unhealthy place, and the British abandoned the town and withdrew to Halifax, Nova Scotia. Howe moved to attack New York, taking the grenadier companies of the 1st and 2nd Marines, who fought in the campaign in New York and Philadelphia. The rest of the 1st and 2nd Marines remained to garrison Halifax.

As Britain was forced to send more and more troops to North America, the Royal Navy could barely keep pace with the requirements of the military in delivering men and equipment to the major points of conflict. The French, quick to realise that Britain was in trouble, declared war again in 1778, an enterprise in which they were to be joined by the Spanish and the Dutch in the coming months. With the Royal Navy in dire straits, Parliament voted additional funding to increase manning levels fourfold to almost 100,000, including 20,000 Marines, which would take years rather than months to implement. In the meantime, large numbers of men from army regiments were co-opted into the Marines as a temporary measure as enemy navies began threatening British coastlines. Further battles against the French, Spanish and Dutch fleets during the coming years also ran parallel to calls on the Marines for the American War of Independence, notably fighting ashore at New York, Savannah and Charleston, and never before had such numbers of Marines been in action.

Before moving on from this vital era of British history, two other significant events must be recorded, and in a curious way the Marines provide a link between them. The first concerns the voyages of discovery by Captain James Cook, who took Marines aboard each of the four ships associated with his historic journeys, which included his circumnavigation of New Zealand and the charting of the entire east coast of Australia (1768–79). Among the 82 Marines logged aboard the expedition vessels for Cook's most famous voyages was Captain Molesworth Phillips, who was wounded at the time Cook was killed by natives in the Sandwich Isles on 17 January 1779. Also with them was another Marine, John Ledyard, who later became a writer and noted traveller, and he provided his own account[*] of the death of Cook as he attempted to negotiate the return of the boat that had been purloined by a group of natives.

The link between Captain Cook and the second major event involving the Marines came in 1785, when the British, no longer able to send convicts to America, had to find a fresh location, far away, as the prime destination for the transportation of felons and convicts. The place selected – and there could be none further – was one of Cook's discoveries, Botany Bay, on the coast of what was to be called New South Wales. The first consignment of such prisoners, 775 in all, of whom 180 were women, were put aboard the boats under a Marine guard of 113 officers and men (with 40 wives) who, little did they realise it, were participating in the foundation of Australia.

Just before first light on 13 May 1787, the fleet of 11 relatively small ships weighed anchor off Portsmouth and sailed down the Solent

---

[*] Jared Spark's *Memoirs of Ledyard's Life and Travels*, published in 1828.

with, in total, 1,390 seamen, Marines and convicts on what was truly a journey into the unknown. They sailed via the Canary Islands, Rio de Janeiro, Brazil, and South Africa on a journey that took more than eight months before they anchored in Port Jackson, where they founded a settlement they called Sydney. The journey was all the more remarkable in that the ships were barely half the size of an average merchant ship of the East India Company, yet they arrived safely at Botany Bay within three days of each and lost only 48 people during the voyage, although the Second Transportation Fleet, which sailed from England at the end of 1789, lost 267 people en route.

The Marines were, then, the first units of the British military to land in Australia, and that association was to continue for decades hence. They would be joined over time by 25 regiments of British infantry who served in the colony between 1790 and 1870 along with units of engineers, artillery and mounted police. Although the original task was to provide security for the establishment of a penal colony, many military units became involved in building roads and accommodation. But it was a posting that few enjoyed. As Peter Stanley wrote in his account, *The Remote Garrison*:

> In buttressing the forces of order and at times ensuring the literal survival of the white settlement, British troops helped to determine the civilisation which would replace the culture of the Australian Aborigines. They fought in one of the most prolonged frontier wars in the history of the British Empire, and for the first half of their stay were probably more frequently in action than the garrison of any other colony besides that of southern Africa. The soldiers themselves were disinclined to consider their skirmishes with Aborigines or hunts for bushrangers as war. Their experience in the Australian bush certainly differed from the war which many had previously encountered . . . [and] Colonel Godfrey Mundy remarked that there was 'no colony . . . where British troops have been so thoroughly without opportunities of distinction'. For the British army, dazzled as it was

by notions of martial glory, probably did not heed the lessons of its fights on the Australian frontier: that war, and especially war waged against primitive peoples, is nasty and decidedly lacking in glory. This should not, however, diminish our interest in the British soldier in Australia, for these rather squalid skirmishes and the soldiers' service as jailers represent the beginnings of European military history in Australia.

The Marines continued to serve in Australia after 1870 and remained until 1913, stationed aboard Royal Naval vessels and shoreline bases at Sydney.

CHAPTER THREE

Red, Blue and Royal

Back in Europe, France was in a confrontational mood that subsequently turned to new conflicts with Britain and her allies which were to span more than 20 years. In the intervening peace, the Marines, in line with the rest of the Royal Navy, had been reduced in numbers to an establishment of just 4,495, a reduction that quickly proved an embarrassment as a new instalment of the French wars became inevitable in the 1790s. In fact, the deficiency in Marine numbers was glaringly apparent in preparations for what came to be known as the Battle of the Glorious First of June in 1794, so named because it was so far out in the Atlantic that it had to be identified by the date. Britain had been at war with Revolutionary France for 14 months. At the time, the French nation was in distress, facing the threat of starvation after a bad harvest and political unrest, so a convoy of 117 merchant ships was sent to Chesapeake Bay to carry back grain and other supplies.

Once loaded, the convoy set off for the return journey with an escort, linking up with a second squadron midway across the Atlantic and then finally falling under the protection of the French fleet, which would accompany them into port. Intelligence of these arrangements reached Britain in April, soon enough for Lord Howe, commander of the Channel fleet, to assemble his force at Spithead. There were to be 32 ships of the line with 15 frigates and support vessels. The shortage of Marines for the expected confrontation became something of an immediate crisis, and soldiers from seven infantry regiments were called on for seagoing duty, around 2,800 men in all to be distributed among the ships. The French convoy sailed on 11 April, and on 2 May Howe left Spithead with 26 ships of the line, having sent others out to reconnoitre the movement of the French fleet. On 19 May Howe received a report that the French fleet had sailed out of Brest, and he then moved to put his fleet in a position between the convoy and their covering force. The movement of the two fleets climaxed on 28 May, when the first exchanges began to the sound of lusty ships' bands playing 'Hearts of Oak' and continued until the culmination of an intense and bloody battle on 1 June. The convoy escaped capture, having passed over the spot on which the action of 28 May was fought, and it reached Brest on 3 June. Its safe arrival went far to console the French for their defeat. The Royal Navy had to suffice with victory over the French, who lost seven ships, with a further 13 badly damaged. They took a heavy toll in casualties, with 1,500 killed, 2,000 wounded and 3,000 captured, while the British had eight seriously damaged ships, 287 killed and 811 wounded.

Although the Glorious First of June rightly took its place among the Royal Navy's most famous battle honours, there remained an overhang in regard to the soldiers who filled the vacant berths of the Marines. Their presence caused considerable friction aboard the ships, because the soldiers remained under the control of the army and often refused to accept orders or punishment from naval officers or indeed participate in some of the shipboard roles normally undertaken by sailors and Marines. The Marines, on the other hand, had long accepted the blurring of the lines of demarcation, especially in times of emergency or difficulties. On a later occasion when army units were called in, Nelson himself pointedly spoke up: 'It would embitter my future days and expiring moments to hear of our Navy being sacrificed to the Army.' It was, as we will see, the cause of friction between the army, navy and Marines that would extend well into the twentieth century – especially in the early years of the Second World War.

The dash to recruit thousands more Marines resulted in a fourfold increase in manpower in double-quick time, many of the newcomers in their teens and most arriving for their shipboard service with modest ability. Marines, sailors and the military in general were about to be fully tested as Napoleon Bonaparte began his march to fame and fury. A series of spectacular victories in Italy as commander of the French army made him the idol of France. Next, he set his sights on what some conjectured was his ambition to become the new Alexander the Great. He launched an attack on Egypt in 1798 from where he could threaten key elements of the British and Turkish Empires, before finally marching his army through Persia and Afghanistan and on into India. Even the remotest possibility that he might succeed was enough for the British East India Company to call for urgent action from the British government.

Napoleon's expedition to Egypt did indeed have implications beyond military prowess in that he took with him many scientists and technical specialists, including a team of surveyors to study the feasibility of cutting a ship canal between the Red and Mediterranean Seas. Three weeks after his landing there, a British fleet of 14 ships, with Marines and troops aboard under Nelson, sighted the 17 French ships being used to support the invasion. Nelson promptly launched his famous and bloody assault on the French fleet anchored in Aboukir Bay on 1 August 1798, sinking or capturing 11 of Napoleon's 13 ships in the so-called Battle of the Nile in which the Marines were prominent. The French losses were as high as 1,700 dead and 3,000 captured. British casualties were put at 218 dead. John Nicol, aboard *Goliath*, left us this eyewitness account:

The *Goliath* led the van. There was a French frigate right in our way. Captain Foley cried, 'Sink that brute, what does he there?'

In a moment she went to the bottom and her crew were seen running into her rigging. My station was in the powder magazine with the gunner. As we entered the bay we stripped to our trousers, opened our ports, cleared, and every ship we passed [we] gave a broadside and three cheers. Any information we got was from the boys and women who carried the powder. The women behaved as well as the men, and got a present for their bravery. When the French Admiral's ship [*L'Orient*] blew up, the *Goliath* got such a shake we thought the after-part of her had blown up until the boys told us what it was. I was much indebted to the gunner's wife who gave her husband and me a drink of wine every now and then, which lessened our fatigue much. There were some of the women wounded, and one woman belonging to Leith died of her wounds and was buried on a small island in the bay. One woman bore a son in the heat of the action. She belonged to Edinburgh. When we ceased firing I went on deck to view the state of the fleets, and an awful sight it was. The whole bay was covered with dead bodies, mangled, wounded and scorched, not a bit of clothes on them except their trousers.[*]

Nelson was badly injured in the battle. He had barely recovered from the loss of his right arm during an attack on Tenerife the previous year and took a very severe wound to the head which his medics feared might kill him. But he recovered sufficiently to be helped back on deck to witness the latter stages of the battle. Regardless of the

[*] In the year 2000, Italian archaeologists found a burial site in Aboukir Bay containing the remains of sailors, officers, Marines, women and three infants. Subsequent work with British archaeologist Nick Slope confirmed that some of the graves dated from the battle, while others dated from another battle in 1801. Subsequently, on 18 April 2005, 30 of the British remains were given a military funeral in Alexandria, attended by the crew of the visiting HMS *Chatham*. Only one of the bodies, that of Commodore James Russell, who died during the 1801 battle, was positively identified. One of his descendants attended the ceremony and was presented with a flag.

carnage behind him, Napoleon had already moved on, marching 12,000 troops into Syria, with the potential to threaten Constantinople and beyond. He was halted at Acre by a combined Anglo-Turkish force reinforced by 800 Marines under the overall command of Sir Sydney Smith, an officer noted for his flair for guerrilla warfare for which he found Marines particularly useful.

Smith was frigate captain at the start of the French Revolutionary war and in 1795 was captured on the coast of France and imprisoned in Paris until early 1798 accused of espionage. He escaped through his fluent use of French and was sent immediately to the Mediterranean, where he was assigned to cooperate with the Turks to halt Napoleon's march. Under his leadership, the garrison at Acre held its own during a two-month siege until the French began their long march south. Napoleon reportedly later said of Smith: 'That man made me miss my destiny.' Nonetheless, Napoleon now abandoned his troops and headed back to Paris in the wake of political upheaval. In due course he appointed himself First Consul under a new constitution as his first step towards the role of dictator.

At the other end of the Mediterranean, one of Britain's most famous soldiers of the day, Sir Ralph Abercrombie, had arrived at Gibraltar – where the benefit of the garrison acquired by the Marines was once again so evident – to gather his army to link up with a Turkish contingent and ultimately launch a joint invasion of Egypt to defeat the remaining French forces. Many untrained Marines were aboard British ships ready for this new conflagration, and were greener still as numerous vessels were damaged by storms and had to put into the British naval dockyards at Valletta for repairs. By the time the convoy anchored in Marmorice Bay on the west coast of Turkey, large numbers of troops had been struck by illness.

Abercrombie's land forces amounted to 13,234 men and 630 artillery, but the efficient force, discounting those who were sick, was only 12,334. The fleet sailed in two divisions for Marmorice, the first arriving on 28 December 1799 and the second four days later. Having received the Turkish supplies, which were, it was noted, 'in every respect deficient', the fleet again got under way on 23 February, and on the morning of 1 March the white sandy coast of Egypt came into view.

The British task force immediately faced a violent gale that continued without let-up for six days until finally troops in 58 flat boats led in by Marines were on their way towards Aboukir Bay, an invasion planned and rehearsed in advance under the direction of Sir Sydney Smith. A battalion formed by Marines from the fleet marched to join the army. The next day it was recalled to attack Aboukir Castle while the main force pressed ahead to engage in heavy and bitter fighting in which Abercrombie himself was among the casualties. His army, however, made rapid advances, and by September the whole of Egypt was under British control and the threat to British interests there and in India for the time being ended. And it must be said that the newer Marines among the force had acquitted themselves well.

Throughout these difficult early years of the French wars, the Marines' battle honours were mounting and in 1802 they were afforded remarkable recognition for their much-improved prowess and versatility by being elevated to become 'Royal' Marines. In fact, it was Earl St Vincent who instigated the honour, which was normally reserved for the oldest and most distinguished British army regiments. The award was announced in April 1802, and it came with an instruction for the design of new uniforms apparently selected by King George III himself and modelled on that of the 1st Foot Guards. The uniforms were first worn at the king's birthday celebrations at Stonehouse, home of the Royal Marines' depot since 1784. To the last, Earl St Vincent remained a firm supporter of the Royal Marines and late in life went on record with this tribute: 'I never knew an appeal made to them for honour, courage or loyalty that they did not more than realise to my highest expectations. If ever the hour of real danger should come to England, they will be found the country's sheet anchor.'

The Royal Marines achieved well-deserved recognition, having managed to survive 150 years of uneven activity, alternating between heroics, mistreatment and disbandment. Their arrival at this state of enhanced respectability was also marked by the fact that in that year of 1802, when the French Revolutionary war was brought to an end with the Treaty of Amiens, the Royal Marines' establishment was held at its existing level of 12,119 – the first time in their history that the corps was not reduced at the end of a war. This was indeed a fortunate outcome, given that the treaty that promised 'peace, friendship, and good understanding' between the United Kingdom and the Republic of France did not hold and within a year the old enemy would soon be at daggers drawn in the Napoleonic Wars, which lasted until November 1815.

Other important changes were also signalled, one that saw the formation of the artillery companies which arose, finally, out of the realisation of the Marines' dependability. Artillery on ships was entirely new, and was started during the late eighteenth century when soldiers from the Royal Artillery were taken on ships in the 1790s at the time when there were insufficient Marines to man the ships. This, coupled with the invention of new, smaller and more manageable artillery pieces, notably by the French, provided the opportunity for introducing an additional dimension to shipboard firepower. The French navy had already established artillery gunners aboard ships, and the turn of the nineteenth century saw the senior navies experimenting with new weapons for ships of war, such as rockets and torpedoes.

Marines already had experience of artillery, manning a proportion of the guns when the need arose, although their principal role had always been to provide musket fire, the all-important secondary ingredient when the warships went broadside to broadside. Following the experience of having RA soldiers in ships, however, the decision was taken, and secured by Order in Council on 18 August 1804, to establish the Royal Marine Artillery. It was to be the beginning of a long and distinguished history of the Marines artillery and, to denote the RMA distinction, their uniforms were ordered in the blue of the Royal Artillery. Initially, one company of RMA was attached to each of the three divisions, consisting of nine officers, 21 NCOs and 62 gunners.

With these additions, the establishment of the Royal Marines was soon to reach in excess of 30,000, requiring a fourth division to be formed and based at Woolwich. More important, the arrival of these gunnery specialists was a landmark decision that held greater implications for the future than the present, at a time when the traditionalists among the naval hierarchy were yet to be convinced of their place in naval warfare. It was a short-sighted decision, especially in view of the newer weaponry becoming available. Rockets were used by the Royal Marine Artillery in the Battle of Trafalgar, in which the British fleet under Admiral Lord Nelson famously ranged against a combined French and Spanish armada.

Ninety-three officers and 2,600 other ranks of the Royal Marines fought at the Battle of Trafalgar of whom 146 from the Chatham Division, commanded by Captain Charles Adair, served on Nelson's ship, which took heavy casualties including, of course, the admiral himself. When Nelson was hit, he was carried below by Sergeant Secker and other Marines. The total RM casualties during the battle were four officers and 117 other ranks killed, with 14 officers and 226 other ranks wounded. Another noteworthy event at the end of the battle came when the French Admiral Villeneuve announced that he wished to surrender, and it was to an officer of the Marines, Captain James Atcherley, that he first offered his sword. The captain, thinking this was improper, declined and called his captain to accept it. The Royal Navy fleet of 27 ships of the line had faced an allied French and Spanish fleet of 33 ships of the line west of Cape Trafalgar in south-west Spain. The allies lost 22 ships; the British none. The victory confirmed Britain's naval supremacy, a fact that remained unchallenged until the rise of the Imperial German Navy a century later. However, it wasn't all plain sailing by any means.

Although the Battle of Trafalgar had been won, another ten years of fighting passed before the Duke of Wellington settled the issue at Waterloo. In the meantime, Marine detachments with the British fleet were in constant action in many of the smaller wars that occurred ashore and afloat as their area of operations expanded dramatically.

British expeditions took them on various assignments around Europe and the Baltic and to the French, Spanish and Dutch colonies.

Outstanding operations of this period came with the outbreak of the War of 1812 with the United States of America in which the British, still under pressure from the war in Europe, were forced into a series of battles in which mixed fortunes resulted. Although an overwhelming force of ships was available for the American mission now that the French threat at sea had subsided, the British were compelled to limit offensive action so that there would be no further demands on land forces. The principal areas of conflict therefore were confined to the eastern seaboard of America, the Great Lakes and the Canadian frontier, and the southern American states. Additional aggravation for the British came by way of extensive operations by American privateers.

By the autumn of 1812 the Royal Navy had no fewer than 97 vessels in American waters, led by 11 ships of the line and 34 frigates, all with their Marine detachments. Although the American navy had far fewer ships, their frigates generally carried more and bigger guns and were very heavily built compared with the 38-gun British frigates. To avoid a ground war, the British adopted a strategy of blockading major American ports, and over the ensuing two years numerous encounters occurred in which the British force, facing ships of greater size and larger guns, were hard pressed. The capture of three British frigates was a further blow to the British, forcing them to strengthen their grip on the eastern seaboard, and on 1 June 1813 the British frigate *Shannon* captured the American frigate *Chesapeake* as she attempted to leave Boston harbour.

Marines fought on the decks of the American ship to gain possession. As the blockade stiffened, the American ships could barely leave their ports without encountering the Royal Navy; as this superiority continued, the British were eventually able to land troops on the American mainland. In June 1813 the Royal Marines dispatched the 1st and 2nd Battalions each with an artillery company. They were involved in an attack on Hampton and in the defence of Montreal and saw action on Lakes Champlain and Ontario, where they manned some of the gunboats.

Then, as the war in Europe was being won, with Napoleon heading for exile, the British commander Sir George Prevost drew up plans for a dual invasion of the United States via New York for the lakes and Chesapeake Bay for Baltimore and Washington, the Americans believing that the former was the most likely target. But Prevost was on a mission to avenge the American burning of Toronto (then called York, Ontario). Marines were among his forces landing in Maryland for the march up to Washington, where American troops were defeated and the city torched. Baltimore was then attacked from the British base on Cumberland Island, and the Marines carried out raids to divert the American troops from the defence of Orleans while others landed in Louisiana and raised Creek and Choctaw Indians against the Americans. By then, the Americans had had enough, and Marines were released from the engagement and arrived back in England soon after the final battle at Waterloo.

In the years ahead, towards the arrival of Queen Victoria in 1837, Marines with the British Mediterranean Fleet undoubtedly saw the lion's share of remaining action. Numerous small conflicts required British attention, typical among them the enforcement of a peace treaty between Greece and Turkey. An allied force of 27 ships provided by Britain, France and Russia was sent to confront a Turkish-Egyptian fleet, which had been warned to stay away. What became known as the Battle of Navarino Bay in the autumn of 1827 culminated in fierce exchanges, resulting in over 600 allied casualties, killed or wounded. But the Turkish-Egyptian fleet was virtually wiped out, with more than 1,200 killed and 4,800 wounded. Their land forces in the Morea were unaffected, however, and although the Egyptian army retreated, the Ottomans stayed put and in control of five forts. Royal Marines joined French troops to clear out the remaining Turks and peace was restored, albeit temporarily. Less than a dozen years later, they were back in the region again, fighting alongside the Turks in their war with Egypt to reclaim Syria.

These confrontations were to become a more demanding feature of life in the Royal Marines as the empire-builders of Victoria's reign pressed ever outwards, gathering up nations and alliances and influence wherever they could be found, or won. For the Marines in particular, this became the era of imperial policing, which had as much to do with the expansion and protection of trade and commerce as the acquisition and supervision of British interests. There also emerged numerous smaller engagements for Marines that in many ways reflected some of the operations for which the Commandos were introduced in the early stages of the Second World War: smaller parties landed to raid or police a particular area and then to exit as soon as possible. Over the forthcoming half-century and beyond, the Marines traversed the globe in a succession of missions, often involving intense action, usually costly and generally much praised.

The Far East proved to be a successful initiation to such events when the fleet served in the First China War in the 1840s, when British shipping was threatened by fleets of Chinese war junks in the dispute over the East India Company's opium trade, resulting in threats to other British trade. As attacks on shipping in the Pearl River increased, Captain Ellis led 380 Marines in the capture of the Bogue Forts, guarding the approach to Canton, and occupied Hong Kong on 23 May 1841, which they held until a truce was declared. Elsewhere, 700 Marines fought minor actions at Chusan, Amoy and Shanghai, and a company of 200 Marines attacked the walled city of Chinkiang Foo. Further afield, RM detachments also fought ashore in the Maori Wars in New Zealand in 1845, while smaller groups were involved in operations in South America, Ireland and Burma.

The Crimea saw a large force engaged at various stages, with up to 4,500 Marines involved. The conflict resulted initially from a quarrel between Russian Orthodox monks and French Catholics over precedence at the Holy Places in Jerusalem and Nazareth. Tsar Nicholas I of Russia demanded the right to protect the Christian shrines in the Holy Land and made his move towards Turkey by crossing the borders of what is today Romania. The tsar's Black Sea

Fleet then sank a Turkish flotilla off Sinope, and war became a certainty when Britain, fearful of Russian domination of Constantinople, announced support for Turkey. The Emperor Louis Napoleon III of France, eager to show some of the military prowess displayed by his uncle Napoleon I, made clear his intention to defend French monks in Jerusalem and joined in on the side of the British and Turks.

It was an altogether murky background to a nasty conflict that formally began in March 1854; by the end of the summer the Franco-British expeditionary forces amounting to more than 50,000 would be engaged over time with 7,000 Turks. Four hundred Marines from the fleet covered the flanks of the initial landings, and after the armies had marched on Sebastopol a further 2,000 Marines and 2,400 seamen landed with 140 guns. Later, when installed in siege positions, known as Marine Heights, 26 guns of the RMA covered the charges of both the Heavy and the Light Brigades, while 300 Marines under Captain Hopkins took part in the Battle of Inkerman. As they approached, they came under fire from enemy sharpshooters who were picking off officers and gunners from the cover of a series of caves, while a frigate in the harbour 'thinned the British ranks' whenever they showed themselves on an alternative route.

On 5 November 1854 a division under Sergeant Richards and Corporal Prettyjohns was sent out to clear the caves, and they had all but completed the task when they began to run out of ammunition. As the shooting momentarily cooled, a fresh batch of enemy soldiers was seen heading towards them up the hillside in single file. Sergeant Turner filed this account of what happened next:

> Prettyjohns, a strong West Countryman, said, 'Well lads, we are just in for a warming, and it will be every man for himself in a few minutes. Look alive, my hearties, and collect all the stones handy, and pile them on the ridge in front of you. When I grip the front man, you let go the biggest stones upon those fellows behind.' As soon as the first man stood on the level, Prettyjohns gripped him and threw him over upon the men following, and

a shower of stones from the others knocked the leaders over. Away they went, tumbling one over the other, down the incline; we gave them a parting volley, and retired out of sight to load; they made off and left us, although there was sufficient to have eaten us up. Later in the day we were recalled, and to keep clear of the frigate's fire had to keep to our left, passing over the field of slaughter. On being mustered, if my memory is not at fault, 21 had been killed and disabled and we felt proud . . .

For his actions, Corporal Prettyjohns was awarded Britain's newest and highest military honour, the Victoria Cross – the first of three Royal Marines to be decorated with this coveted award during the Crimean War. Next came 23-year-old Thomas Wilkinson, a bombardier in the RMA who received the award for his courageous actions at Sebastopol on 7 June 1855, when, while working with the advanced batteries, he continued to repair depleted defences with heavy sandbags while 'under the most galling fire' which he managed to survive.

A third Victoria Cross was won on 13 July 1855, when RMA Lieutenant G. D. Dowell, aged 24, was at the Fort of Viborg when an explosion occurred in one of the rocket boats. Under intense enemy fire and the risk of explosion, Dowell took three volunteers to rescue the crew of the cutter. Having made sure the entire crew had been brought to safety, he then towed the stricken boat out of enemy gun range.

In the wake of the Crimean War, 1855 was a year that saw a change in the structure of the Royal Marines, in that an Order in Council was issued designating the infantry as a 'Light Corps' and henceforth to be known as the Royal Marine Light Infantry, whose uniform would be red. They therefore became widely referred to as the Red Marines, while the RMA were known as the Blue Marines. A recruiting depot was opened at Deal, in Kent, as demands on their services continued to occur in both greater numbers and diversity, with famous-name engagements drawing on them for the rest of the century. They were seldom out of action, and while a detailed account is beyond the scope of this work, a summary of their activities provides a worthwhile excursion into the demand on their increasing skills and importance in the British military effort around the Empire.

In the Indian Mutiny, they landed in small parties and were in action at Cawnpore and took part in the Relief of Lucknow. Two battalions were formed in England and sent out to the Second China War, later to be joined by a third battalion, 300 strong, under Lieutenant-Colonel Thomas Lemon, from India where it had been garrisoned in Calcutta. In June 1857 Marines were involved in the Battle of Fatshan Creek and later were sent to attack the Taku Forts which guarded the mouth of the Pei-ho River. Despite heavy losses, they occupied the vast city of Canton in January 1858 and were engaged in considerable action across the Far East during the following decade. This included a long spell in Japan when an RMLI battalion was sent to reinforce the Legation Guard at Yokohama, under siege from the Samurai. A second battalion went to Yokohama in 1870 and remained there for five years, dealing with internal strife.

In the early 1870s the Ashanti wars in East Africa attracted a mixed contingent of RMA, with two mountain guns and 200 war rockets, and 110 RMLI. They were dispatched to join other Marines and seamen from the fleet in a taut struggle against 2,000 Ashanti warriors. As the battles went on, most of the British force had been struck down with fever by the end of July and were replaced by 200 Marines shipped in from the UK. Further action against the Ashanti followed before the Marines were relieved – or more accurately replaced – so that they could attend other emergencies elsewhere.

Royal Navy ships' detachments also served ashore with naval brigades in Malaya in 1874–5, in Zanzibar in 1875, the Congo in 1875–6, in Samoa in 1876, on the Niger in 1876–7 and afloat in the constant task of policing the high seas for ships carrying slaves. Other interests that demanded their attention included short, sharp engagements on Cyprus, in Alexandria and Port Said, and at the Suez

Canal and Tel el-Kebir. In the last, the RMLI Battalion was first to storm the defences and, in another ferocious battle, lost 13 killed and 54 wounded, but the Egyptians were routed.

They were back in African actions in the early 1880s at El Teb on the Red Sea coast and at Tamai, where Osman Digma's famous 'fuzzy-wuzzies' gave the Marines a run for their money. At El Teb 380 Marines positioned on the left flank carried out a daring flanking movement, only to see thousands of Dervishes suddenly rise up and charge down the hill at the main square of troops, but they were cut down with the loss of 3,000 of their 6,000 men. An RMLI company also served with the Guards Camel Regiment in the Desert Column in the attempt to relieve Khartoum, while other units were variously in action in East and West Africa between 1891 and 1896, in Sierra Leone and Zanzibar in 1896, and Burma and Crete during the same period – all destinations, incidentally, that would figure strongly in the Marines' curriculum vitae of the twentieth century.

The last days of the nineteenth century saw a party of Marines in the line for the Second Boer War, when they made up shortfalls in field artillery by bringing ships' guns ashore on improvised carriages. Simultaneously, on the east coast of Africa a naval brigade was formed from ships at Durban with navy guns providing artillery support for the advance on Ladysmith.

Across the world, another Victoria Cross was about to be won in an international drama in China, which eventually became the subject of a film, *55 Days in Peking*, starring a host of Hollywood stars including Charlton Heston, Ava Gardner and David Niven. In May 1900 the Boxer rebellion was spiralling into an orgy of massacres of Chinese Christians and anti-Western riots. A riot in Pao Ting Fu led to the death of two British missionaries, prompting Western diplomats in Peking to issue an ultimatum to the Chinese that unless they 'put down the Boxers' in 24 hours they would use force themselves and call up troops, which they did. A party of RMLI and Marines from British ships, including bandsmen, were joined by smaller groups of German and US Marines – 340 in all – to form a protection squad for the foreign legation. By then, the Western compounds had been surrounded by the Boxers in what was the beginning of a bloody siege.

The Chinese established themselves around the perimeter of the international settlement and made constant forays, burning buildings and tempting the troops inside into fire fights. When the Boxers began the systematic massacre of Chinese Christians, the Marines formed a raiding party of 30 British and German Marines, led by Captain Lewis Halliday, and succeeded in rescuing several hundred Christians from the Catholic Mission after a bloody battle in which 300 Boxers were killed. Captain Halliday was seriously wounded, but he carried on fighting, killing four of his attackers amid desperate hand-to-hand fighting by his group. For his gallantry Halliday was awarded the Victoria Cross, and a CGM and five DCMs were awarded to other British Marines in his detachment. The assaults continued throughout July and August until the siege was lifted on 14 August, when a large international relief force arrived to clear the Boxers from the area.

CHAPTER FOUR

Ironclads and Technocrats

Technology had moved at a rapid pace in the late nineteenth century, and it brought with it another threat to the existence of the Royal Marines. In spite of the many operations described above, questions were being asked as to the reality or need of running amphibious operations from the giant ships now rolling out of the shipyards, and there was little doubt that many of the original tasks of the corps were gradually fading away in the face of classic gunboat diplomacy. Whereas navy action under sail had inevitably been close and brutal encounters, under steam and with more powerful armoury there would be miles of water between the ships. Britain's first iron-hull ship was Queen Victoria's pride and joy, HMS *Warrior*, which some claimed had the ability to defeat an enemy fleet single-handedly. Commissioned in 1861, *Warrior* was the first ship of the industrial age, bringing together technological innovations such as the use of iron and steel and the introduction of steam power, albeit on a limited basis because of the shortage of coaling points and the restricted distance a ship could travel before needing to take on more fuel.

Even so, the steam age advanced so quickly that *Warrior* was obsolete within a decade. With her unrivalled lead in the Industrial Revolution, Britain pressed ahead with replacing all her wooden-hull ships with ironclads, progressively using thicker armour and bigger guns, which were now mounted on revolving turrets shielded by slabs of metal. Whereas once the navy relied on manpower and gallantry, machines were fast replacing human contact. Boarding parties became a thing of the past as bows were strengthened to enable the greater use of ramming tactics, although it also led to a number of serious peacetime disasters in which ships were accidentally rammed – in fog, for example – and sunk. The standardised introduction of steel for armour for battleships also gave rise to the appearance of large armoured cruisers of almost equal size to battleships, but faster and more powerful, and all in all new shipboard technology required the recruitment of men capable of accepting new skills.

Initially, there was a real commitment that the Royal Marines would at last be trained specifically for roles that now included the protection of Britain's vast network of trade routes and her massively enhanced merchant fleet as well as the formation of a protective cordon around Britain's multitude of foreign naval stations. But as the march of improvements hastened, questions were asked as to what exactly the Marines would do in ships that could attack an enemy by firing their guns at targets over a distant horizon. New weaponry that allowed battles to be fought from great distances eliminated their traditional roles, and it became apparent that naval officers were in fact using the Marines aboard their ships for lesser tasks.

So much so that the Admiralty had to issue firm instructions that RM gunners were not to be used as stokers and that where possible a number of the guns should be manned entirely by Marines. Some captains concurred with the instruction, but others did not, and the old issue of 'soldiers' involved in shipboard operations still arose, as illustrated by the words of Admiral Sir Thomas Maitland in the Journal of the Royal United Services Institute in 1883. He reckoned that experienced Marines were being 'thrown away' on board ship because 'if we get a seaman capable of being captain of a gun, we put him to it because we do not like guns of the navy being taken out of our hands'.

The technology and innovative design of both warships and merchant vessels had put the nation well ahead of her rivals on virtually every level. Even so, a political pact between Russia and France exposed a weakness – and indeed complacency – among the navy of Queen Victoria, in that the joint navies of those two countries exceeded the power of the British fleet. The naval hierarchy took flak from commentators, who criticised their lack of intelligence about opposing navies and accused them of snobbery and smugness resulting from several decades of relatively unchallenged dominance that was also, in part, responsible for the neglect in establishing a more definitive role for the Marines. In the end, the British government ordered a review and in 1889 passed the Naval Defence Act, authorising a massive building programme to put the Royal Navy on comparable terms with the world's next two largest navies, although ironically when the time came for action it would not be the French who were the enemy.

A complete revamp of naval thinking was called for which again seriously affected the operations of both the artillery and infantry elements of the Royal Marines in that the increased size of the navy would make it impossible to man the guns of the fleet from naval manpower alone, and the expanding Royal Navy had to resort to formally instructing ships' captains to employ Marines on their guns and to ensure that regular training routines were instigated. Initially, only first-class battleships carried RMA detachments, although over the coming decade the situation altered considerably: all Marines would be routinely trained in gunnery, as the workload increased with heavier guns and massive shells to be humped. By the early 1900s Marines were expected to be capable of manning a main armoury turret and secondary guns in all battleships and cruisers, and the extra pay previously paid to those trained in gunnery was discontinued. But still the questions remained as to whether, in this way, the Marines were simply fulfilling the role normally undertaken by sailors.

However, their contribution was clearly evident at the great demonstration of Britain's naval power staged to celebrate Queen Victoria's Diamond Jubilee in 1897. Without withdrawing a single vessel from any of Britain's overseas stations, more than 150 warships were mustered for this spectacular display: four lines of ships, stretching for 25 miles, including 22 battleships and 42 cruisers, all of which required the presence of Marines. The Germans were already taking action to match this fleet of steel.

Sir John Fisher, a renowned technocrat among the naval hierarchy, was a leading figure in the surge towards this great British achievement, but conversely he proved to be no friend of the Marines. Born in Ceylon in 1841, he entered the navy at the age of 13 on board HMS *Victory* at Portsmouth. He was a midshipman in the Crimean War and in China (1859–60), where he took part in the capture of Canton. Promoted to captain (1874), he commanded various ships and the gunnery school and took a prominent part in the bombardment of Alexandria (1882) as commander of the battleship *Inflexible*. He was commandant of HMS *Excellent* when the future king, 20-year-old Prince George, joined his company.

On his elevation to First Sea Lord in 1904, he made no secret of his determination to shake the navy to its foundations, with modernisation at every level, and he became the hero of the lower decks by insisting on making life more acceptable down below. But in submitting his proposals for that thorough shake-up, he, too, began to question the organisation of the Royal Marines as presently constituted – and many agreed with him. There is little doubt that once again the training and diversity of deployment of the Royal Marines were badly neglected in favour of them supplying the big ships with men to fill the predetermined numbers, to the point where many Marines themselves preferred a shore base to being at sea.

Apart from assignments that arose in far-flung posts of the Empire, Marine officers, especially, were considered by Fisher and others to be a redundant level of administration in ships, especially as the practice of using Marines to deploy to enemy coasts was now considered virtually impossible in the face of the modern threat of mines, rockets and submarines – even if there was a need for it. This debate was to be ongoing, well into the twentieth century; as will be seen, it re-emerged just prior to the battle for the Falklands in 1982, when once and for all the issue was finally settled.

Fisher also questioned the age-old system of keeping a garrison of Marines on Gibraltar and of having a Marine general as Governor. He wrote in October 1905:

> Nothing would induce me personally to agree to [that]. It must be . . . solely under the Admiralty. The Marine Officer can't be loyal! Just look at that statue outside the Admiralty in honour of the Marines, recently put up by them. It has its back turned on the Admiralty and it's looking at the War Office! Damn the Army! Another reason! If we had 3,000 Marines locked up in Gibraltar, we would want another 3,000 Marines at home as their relief and then the total number of Marines would be so great they would cease to be Marines as they would have no sea service, hardly. Even at present only 30 per cent of their whole service is on board ship and most of that often in a harbour ship.[*]

This kind of antagonism towards the Marines, dating from their historical connection with the British army, had clearly never been completely expunged from the naval hierarchy even though the Marines had long since come under Admiralty control. Indeed, it seemed as rampant as ever and must surely have had some sort of effect on the general consensus among the admirals and captains as to how, exactly, the Marines should be deployed. At the same time, the British army was expanding, in cost and in numbers, and so from that standpoint the government of the day was supposedly recruiting sufficient soldiers – and in real terms Marines were still soldiers – to meet any forthcoming

[*] Fisher papers, Navy Records Society.

emergency. In fact, even the need for such an expansion of the army was controversially challenged, not least by the new Member of Parliament for Oldham (in 1901), Mr Winston Churchill, in the first of many speeches he made on the theme:

There has been great demand for army reform and I am pledged to it up to the hilt. Either it means a bigger army for the same money or the same army for less money. What I pledged myself to ... was a better, not a bigger army, value for our money and not more of the same old bad bargain. Any danger that comes to Britain would not be on land; it would come on the sea. In regard to our military system, we must be prepared to deal with all the little wars which occur continually on the frontiers of the Empire. We cannot expect to meet great wars; we can only assure ourselves that ultimately we shall be able to realise the entire forces of the Empire ... [and] I think our game essentially is to be a naval and commercial power. I cannot look upon the army as anything but an adjunct to the navy. I hope we will not be drawn from our true policy, which is to preserve command of the sea.

The need for a 'great army' would, of course, arise soon enough. But as war approached, the Royal Marines were positioned somewhere between a rock and a hard place, performing duties on board ship that were tantamount to playing second fiddle to the sailors while at the same time being bereft of a more precisely defined role or training for eventualities that had a nasty habit of occurring when least expected. Attempts were made at training Marines for full-blown amphibious operations to meet modern requirements, but the navy clearly had no enthusiasm for them and the result was by all accounts unconvincing.

Consequently, in the years immediately prior to the First World War, there seemed no urgency to train Marines of either Blue and Red persuasion in anything other than the principal disciplines of gunnery or infantry. The Marines were scattered across the world before, during and after the First World War, aboard the main elements of the British fleet, covering virtually every ocean or garrisoned in land bases in faraway places. But when the time came for the new conflict, it would become apparent as the war progressed that the Royal Marines steadfastly met every eventuality that came along, not least in providing all the reinforcements the Royal Navy needed in key roles aboard ship, as well as providing personnel in all other areas of the war.

When the British fleet was mobilised a week before Britain declared war on Germany on 4 August 1914, there were 10,047 Marines at sea, either with the Grand Fleet or elsewhere in the world. In total, however, there were more than 18,000 Marines, of whom 13,425 were RMLI, 3,393 RMA and 1,442 Royal Marines Band, which had units aboard the larger ships, and whose men doubled in various other roles in times of battle. An additional 8,000 men, former Marines and pensioners, in the Royal Fleet Reserve were also available, and all those who were fit and under the age of 55 were mobilised. Further recruitment in the coming months came by way of volunteers, many from Kitchener's famous appeal, which bolstered the numbers in the Royal Marines units, although they were, of course, no different from the tens of thousands who offered themselves for military service in the forthcoming desperate years, untrained and unprepared for the horrors that lay ahead.

Dealing first in this narrative of the early operations at sea during the First World War, there was a full complement of Marines aboard when the crews of 32 battleships and battle cruisers and 20 cruisers, along with 50 destroyers of the Home Fleet, moved out through the Strait of Dover heading north to its war base at Scapa Flow. The initial encounter between the German and British navies came on 28 August 1914, when a British force made up of the cruisers *Fearless* and *Arethusa*, 31 destroyers and six submarines prepared a mission towards the German home waters off Heligoland Bight. The British surface contingent, known as the Harwich Force, set out to raid German shipping located close to the German naval base at Heligoland.

The 1st Battle Cruiser Squadron was sent to give further weight to the attack, sailing from the naval base at Scapa Flow under the command of Vice-Admiral Sir David Beatty. His squadron consisted of the battleships *New Zealand* and *Invincible*, plus three battle cruisers and cruisers. The Harwich Force began the action by sinking two German torpedo boats, but the Germans responded by rapidly deploying six light cruisers whose joint firepower left the Harwich ships substantially outgunned and under incessant fire. With *Arethusa* heavily damaged, the Harwich commander signalled for assistance from Beatty's squadron, then some 25 miles to the north.

Beatty arrived within the hour and immediately opened fire, sinking three German cruisers – *Mainz*, *Köln* and *Ariadne* – and damaging three others. In fact, the Germans were outclassed in terms of firing in what was something of an historic event, as pointed out by RMA Corporal Albert Saunders:

> . . . the firing was controlled. That meant that a certain turret would be detailed to fire a round or two to get the range. Then came the order Rapid Independent and for a few moments fury was let loose. Crash upon crash rent the air and right and left swing those great turrets and guns as those 13.5-inch [guns] spoke for the first time in angry tone. Then came a long continuous ringing: the captain's ceasefire. The first naval engagement for over a century had been fought and won.

The remaining German ships turned and sailed for cover in the mist, with 1,200 of their men dead or captured against just 35 British fatalities. The Admiralty was delighted with the result of this first battle of the war and issued a directive that each ship engaged in the action in the Heligoland Bight, whether damaged or not, should have the words 'Heligoland August 28th 1914' painted in gold letters in some convenient place along with a plaque for the Royal Marines. This congratulatory action, however, hid the fact that the whole operation was seriously undermined by weaknesses in planning and communication among the hierarchy.

The outcome of the battle had the desired effect. The Germans were somewhat reluctant to expose their big ships, sending out only hit-and-run squadrons until their submarine fleet was large enough to spearhead the U-boat assault that was soon to wreak such havoc around the British sea lanes, giving sufficient leeway for the British Expeditionary Force to be ferried across the English Channel to France with barely a hitch. It was this uninterrupted service, protected and managed by the Royal Navy and the Royal Marines, that Winston Churchill highlighted as a major contributing factor to the eventual allied victory over the Germans, although for tens of thousands of parents and wives it represented a moving platform along which their sons and husbands were being herded to the horror of the trenches as the land war ground on to one of appalling attrition.

By early autumn the Germans began to see success through U-boat attacks and their policy of mass dispersal of mines. On 22 September a single submarine sank three British cruisers within an hour off the Netherlands. Hundreds of seamen and Marines survived this first initial attack, but no sooner had they been picked from the water by a cruiser that had escaped destruction than she, too, was sunk by a torpedo, throwing them into the sea again, with heavy losses. The mining of the seas around Britain was also hitting shipping routes badly. The light cruiser *Amphion* was the first British warship to be hit, on 6 August, but Britain's biggest loss to mines in the North Sea occurred on 27 October when one of the navy's newest battleships, *Audacious*, was sunk. She was a *King George V*-class super-dreadnought and had only completed her sea trials a few months earlier, carrying the latest powerful 13.5-inch guns.

There was an appalling accidental tragedy, too, destroying *Bulwark*, a 15,000-ton twin-screw armoured battleship, launched in 1899 and once commanded by Captain R. F. Scott, who later came to fame as the Antarctic explorer. She exploded while taking on ammunition off

Sheerness on 26 November 1914. There were only 12 survivors from a ship's company of 750. The explosion shocked a nervous British public, who were being warned to expect the possibility of aerial bombing from Zeppelin attacks, but in fact the next move by the Germans was totally unexpected and brought panic down the east coast of England.

On 15 December three battle cruisers of the German High Seas Fleet set off on a sortie across the North Sea under the command of Rear-Admiral Franz von Hipper. Evading the Royal Navy's protective shield, they loomed out of the mist and began bombarding the seaside towns of Scarborough, Whitby and Hartlepool. Over 200 shells rained down on the towns, killing more than 100 civilians and injuring 400 others. Two destroyers in the British flotilla arrived to drive the Germans off but were also hit, with several seamen killed. In the following month Hipper set out on a similar mission, but this time his sortie was intercepted by the British in what became known as the Battle of Dogger Bank.

Hipper led his force comprising the armoured cruiser *Blücher*, which was claimed to be the most powerful in the world, four light cruisers and a number of torpedo boats. Their intentions were uncovered by the British Admiralty's deciphering service, 'Room 40', and the Harwich Force of light cruisers and destroyers under Commodore Tyrwhitt was sent to intercept from the south, and Vice-Admiral Sir David Beatty came from the north with his battle cruiser group consisting of his own ship *Lion* followed by *Tiger*, *Princess Royal* and, bringing up the rear, the older *New Zealand* and *Indomitable*. At daybreak on 24 January, the German flotilla was spotted off the coast of Great Yarmouth, and the Harwich Force moved in. The Germans squared for battle when their light cruiser *Kolberg* signalled the sighting of the British light cruiser *Aurora*. Both opened fire and took a couple of hits. The German commander was convinced that the British opposition consisted of the light enemy units from Harwich and had already turned to engage them when Beatty's battle cruisers appeared on the northern horizon.

Hipper decided to make a quick exit, and a running battle developed across the North Sea with Beatty's battle cruisers pursuing at a fast pace, reaching 27 knots, while the Germans were held back by the slower *Blücher*, which eventually dropped out of the line and fell within range of the British guns and torpedoes. The Germans returned fire and nominated Beatty's ship as the prime target and scored a dozen hits in quick succession. *Lion* was out of the fight and dropped back. The damage to Beatty's ship was so severe that he had no power or wireless contact. A signalling error during the transmission of his orders to the rest of his ships sent them in the wrong direction, allowing the rest of Hipper's flotilla to make a run for it. *Blücher*, meanwhile, had taken heavy punishment and was further hammered until the battle cruiser rolled over and capsized on Dogger Bank. Unfortunately, the British rescue operation to collect survivors had to be called off when a Zeppelin and a seaplane appeared overhead and began bombing the British ships. The Germans suffered almost 1,000 casualties and 189 captured, while the British recorded losses of 15 killed and 32 wounded.

During the engagement, well over 1,100 shells were fired by the British group, yet fewer than half a dozen hits were recorded against ships other than *Blücher*. These, then, were the developments in home waters, but there was even more dramatic action abroad on the high seas involving the Germans' most powerful surface force under one of their highly revered naval officers, Admiral Graf Maximilian von Spee. He was leading a squadron of Germany's fastest and most powerful cruisers, including *Scharnhorst*, *Gneisenau* and *Nürnberg*, which had been operating in the eastern waters of South-East Asia. Spee's group moved without serious challenge across the Pacific Ocean, and another of Germany's fastest ships, *Emden*, joined the squadron in August 1914 but later moved on to cause havoc in the Indian Ocean.

For months, these cruisers were a threat to merchant shipping on the British trade routes and to troopships on their way to Europe or the Middle East from India, New Zealand or Australia. Then, Admiral von Spee moved across the Pacific in September towards the South American coast for his transport vessels to take on supplies and coal. Off the Chilean coast, the group was joined by two additional cruisers, *Leipzig* and *Dresden*, an accumulation of five exceedingly potent ships under Spee's command. The Admiralty in London decided to send the only squadron available in that region, the West Indies patrol group under Sir Christopher Cradock, which at that time was in the Atlantic patrolling the eastern coastline of South America. Cradock was not, at that time, told of the strength of Spee's force and was undoubtedly given the impression that he could take the Germans on, but as he would soon discover his squadron of old ships was hopelessly outclassed. Cradock's own flagship was the ageing cruiser *Good Hope*, which had just come out of the reserve fleet and was manned by an inexperienced crew. He had the armoured cruiser *Monmouth*, which was notoriously underarmed for a ship of her size, and the armed merchant cruiser *Otranto*, which was a converted liner with very visible vast smokestacks, was also short on gunnery strength. Only the light cruiser *Glasgow* was up to date and well equipped and carried a well-trained crew.

To strengthen this totally outgunned force, the Admiralty sent another ancient battleship, *Canopus*, also from the reserve stock, entirely manned by reservists who, courageous though they were, had never fired the ship's guns in anger. Worse, *Canopus* developed engine trouble on the way and could travel at only 12 knots. One other armoured cruiser, *Defence*, was also supposedly on her way to join the patrol, but in fact never arrived at the rendezvous point in the Falkland Islands. On 1 November Cradock sailed to make his challenge, a fool's errand that would surely end in the sacrifice of his brave sailors and Marines. Just off the coastal town of Coronel, 300 miles south of Valparaiso, they made contact and Cradock formed his line of ships, which comprised his own inaptly named *Good Hope* along with *Monmouth*, *Glasgow* and *Otranto*. *Canopus* was still limping behind. When he spotted the opposition, Spee had formed a battle line of *Scharnhorst*, *Gneisenau*,

Leipzig and *Dresden*. His fifth, *Nürnberg*, was still some 30 miles north.

The British line turned towards the Germans and found themselves silhouetted against the setting sun. They made the approach, but at 11,500 yards the German armoured cruisers opened fire. *Scharnhorst* hit the British flagship with her third salvo and a wall of flame shot skywards. *Monmouth* was also hit immediately by *Gneisenau*'s guns. Shell after shell hit the two British cruisers, while *Leipzig* and *Glasgow* also engaged and *Dresden* took on *Otranto*. The last realised the hopelessness of the situation and pulled back out of the line, leaving *Dresden* free to join the onslaught elsewhere. Just 20 minutes after the battle began, Cradock's *Good Hope* was wrecked by a magazine explosion. She went down in minutes without survivors. *Monmouth* was also crippled and listing to port. She was already beyond help when *Nürnberg* arrived to join the battle, and five more shells finished her off. She, too, sank without survivors. *Glasgow*, meanwhile, had taken half a dozen hits but was still operational and pulled out to fight another day. Slowcoach *Canopus* was also warned to turn back, and so three ships were saved. The cost of this mismatched mission, known in history as the Battle of Coronel, was 1,600 British lives, including 200 Marines, a bloody nightmare for the seamen – and the Royal Navy's first major defeat for almost a century.

The shock in London was immense, and immediately a revenge attack was planned, with First Sea Lord Fisher and Churchill, as First Lord of the Admiralty, personally involved. A British force, strong enough to hunt down and sink the German squadron, was ordered to prepare immediately under the leadership of the eminent and – this time – more aptly named Rear-Admiral Sir Doveton Sturdee. He would take two modern battle cruisers, *Invincible* and *Inflexible*, each equipped with eight 12-inch guns, and no fewer than six other cruisers. All were to rendezvous off the Brazilian coast and then sail south to the Falkland Islands. It was an impressive sight: *Invincible*, *Inflexible* and the cruisers HMS *Bristol*, *Carnarvon*, *Cornwall* and *Kent*. To these were added the remains of Cradock's squadron, *Glasgow* and *Canopus*, already at Port Stanley, as well as the armed merchant cruiser *Macedonia*.

Apparently unaware of the strength of the newly arrived British force, Admiral von Spee was already moving south towards the Falklands to perform what he believed would be a second great victory. Sturdee's squadron arrived at the Falkland Islands on the evening of 7 December 1914. Coaling was commenced at once so that the ships would be ready to begin the search for the enemy the next day. At 8 a.m. on the following day a signal was received from a station on shore that a four-funnel and two-funnel man-of-war, in sight from Sapper Hill, were steering northwards. The recollections of Captain I. D. Allen, on *Kent*, provide a commentary of the opening stages of a battle that was to last over 12 hours:

Just under half an hour after the signal was received, *Kent* was under way and steaming down the harbour past the flagship. A general signal had been made for all ships to raise steam for full speed. The flagship signalled to *Kent* to proceed to the entrance to the harbour and wait there for further orders. From aloft we could now see over the land ... the German cruisers *Gneisenau* and *Nürnberg* approaching the harbour. We hoisted three ensigns, including the silk ensign and Union Jack, which had been presented to *Kent* by the ladies of the county of Kent and which we had promised to hoist if ever we went into action.

Gneisenau and *Nürnberg* came steadily on towards the harbour until they were only 14,000 yards from *Kent*... Suddenly we heard *Canopus* open fire on them with her 12-inch guns across the land, and we saw the shell strike the water a few hundred yards short of the German ships. This must have surprised them, as *Canopus* was hidden behind the land. Presently *Glasgow* came along at full speed and passed us, then out came *Invincible* and *Inflexible*, sending up great columns of black smoke, then *Carnarvon* and *Cornwall*. It was a magnificent sight. It was a glorious day, just like a fine spring day in England, a smooth sea, a bright sun, a light breeze from the north-west. Right ahead of us we could see the masts, funnels and smoke of the five German cruisers, all in line abreast and steaming straight away from us. At 10.20 a.m. the signal was made for a general chase, and off we all went as hard as we could go. It was only a question of who could steam the fastest. *Invincible* and *Inflexible* were increasing speed every minute, and soon passed *Kent*. They were now steaming at 25 knots and were rapidly gaining on the enemy ...

A formal report of the ensuing action by Rear-Admiral Doveton Sturdee to London provided dramatic reading. The two leading ships of the enemy, *Gneisenau* and *Nürnberg*, with guns trained on the wireless station, came within range of *Canopus*, which opened fire at them across the low land at a range of 11,000 yards. The enemy at once hoisted their colours and turned away. At this time the masts and smoke of the enemy were visible from the upper bridge of *Invincible* at a range of approximately 17,000 yards across the low lands to the south of Port William. A few minutes later the two cruisers altered course to port, as though to close *Kent* at the entrance to the harbour, but at about this time it seems that *Invincible* and *Inflexible* were seen over the land, as the enemy at once altered course and increased speed to join their consorts.

The signal for a general chase was made, and after almost two hours of cat-and-mouse manoeuvres the action finally developed into three separate encounters. The fire of the British battle cruisers was directed on *Scharnhorst* and *Gneisenau*. The effect was quickly seen, and after a battle lasting almost 90 minutes *Scharnhorst* caught fire and *Gneisenau* was badly hit. The drastic damage to *Scharnhorst* soon became apparent. There was a large shell hole in her side, through which could be seen a dull red glow of flame. At 4.40 p.m. *Scharnhorst*, whose flag remained flying to the last, suddenly listed heavily to port and within a few minutes disappeared. *Gneisenau* continued a determined effort to fight the two battle cruisers, but at

5.08 p.m. the forward funnel was knocked over and her fire slackened. At 5.15 p.m. one of *Gneisenau*'s shells struck *Invincible*, which proved to be a final effort. She turned with a heavy list to starboard, and, with steam pouring from her escape-pipes and smoke rising everywhere, the British battle commander gave the order to cease fire. *Gneisenau* made one final effort before keeling over suddenly, with men gathered on her decks and then walking on her side as she lay a minute on her beam ends before sinking. With 600 men already killed or wounded, the survivors were ordered to prepare to take to the water.

When the ship capsized and sank there were probably some 200 survivors in the water, but many were drowned within sight of the British rescue boats and ships owing to the shock of the cold water. *Invincible* alone pulled 108 men from the water, 14 of whom were dead and were buried at sea the following day with full military honours.

The light cruisers *Dresden*, *Nürnberg* and *Leipzig* had already made their move to escape, but the British force gave chase and *Nürnberg* and Leipzig were sunk and fewer than a dozen men from the two ships were pulled alive from the water. *Dresden* managed to get ahead of the action due to her superior speed and, in the fading light and closing weather, escaped, for the time being at least. She was eventually caught and sunk off the Juan Fernandez Islands on 14 March 1915, and her demise also marked a virtual end to Germany's attacks on British trading routes using surface vessels. British casualties from the entire operation this time numbered just 25.

For the Royal Marines and navy gunners in their turrets, these battles saw the real-life action that they had trained for come to fruition in abundance. RMLI Captain (later Major) Robert Sinclair, who was second-in-command of an RM gun turret on *Inflexible*, wrote home:

> . . . my station in action is in the turret superintending the loading
> of the guns so I am shut in behind armour and unable to see

what is going on outside ... the only information we inside
could get was from the gun-layers at their telescopes and from
the major at his periscope and they ... are so busy that they
could not tell us much. It was our first sensation under fire and,
speaking for myself, I felt quite normal and not the least excited,
but then I was behind armour and hardly realised anyone was
firing at us. The men in the turret were the same and I think
far cooler than in battle practice, when there is usually some
tension and extreme anxiety. Now we are doing the real thing
for which we have been practising for so long, and the only
fault I could find was that the men were inclined to talk and
joke – there's enough noise in the turret without that.

The job was done and the Marines came through these early tests at
sea with flying colours. The German fleet seldom ventured into the
open after the destruction of Admiral von Spee's squadron in the
Battle of the Falklands, which proved to be the last major naval action
until the Battle of Jutland.

CHAPTER FIVE

The Antwerp Affair and Gallipoli

Early operations in the ground war did not augur well as British Expeditionary Force divisions began to disembark across the Channel to join the allies against the German invasion of the Low Countries and France. This was not due to a lack of steadfastness or enthusiasm on the part of the troops and the thousands volunteering for service. Quite the reverse. But the fact remained that the British army had long been employed policing the Empire and dealing with manageable minor wars. By August 1914 there were approximately 400,000 under arms but fewer than 80,000 were ready for war, and the BEF, made up of seven divisions and sent to Mons, was small compared with the armies of Germany and France.

The vast expenditure lavished on the Royal Navy in recent years ensured protection for the British Isles – up to a point – but the one great sea battle, a repeat of Trafalgar, no less, that so many had said would end the war before it really began just did not happen. Thus, an army constructed principally for the defence of Britain and her Empire was actually well short of the vast requirements that would soon become necessary when the British government agreed to send its troops across the Channel to join the allies in attempting to halt the Germans. But then, the carnage that was soon to unfold had never been even hinted at in the projections of military analysts.

Enthusiastic recruits were being drawn in at all levels, but the whole fabric for training and equipping them was demonstrably inadequate. Among the newer fellows straining at the leash for action was eighteen-year-old Lieutenant Arthur Chater (later to become Major-General), who had been in training for almost a year but discovered himself ill prepared for what lay ahead:

. . . 21 young men of 17 or 18 arrived at the Royal Naval College, Greenwich, on first appointment as Probationary Second Lieutenants in the Royal Marines. We were all rather pleased with ourselves in our new uniforms, which we wore very badly. To us at that time, wars seemed very far away. Little did we think that within two years four of us would be killed in battle. In the mess one night I drank with Richard Foote to 'the first time we would be under fire'. Within a bare year he had been killed, and I had been wounded.

After nine months at Greenwich, wasted in acquiring knowledge which we never used, we moved to Deal, where our military training began. July 1914 was a perfect summer month. The AGRM carried out his annual inspection of the depot RM. As the days passed by, excitement in the events in Europe increased. We awoke on Thursday 30 July to be told that many of the trained soldiers were to leave the depot that day for their mobilisation stations. On Saturday, a cricket match was being played on the South Green when between two overs, about 4 p.m., an orderly came across the field and gave a message to the staff officer, who was keeping wicket. This was the order for the navy to mobilise. Within a few minutes, buglers were sounding the general assembly around the town. Many of the staff and senior recruits left Deal that evening. Church on Sunday morning was a moving and, for some, a very sorrowful service.

Immediately after lunch, the 21 Second Lieutenants were called to the commandant's office and told that we were to leave that evening to join our RM divisions.

By 22 August elements of the BEF had taken up position in the allied counterplan just across the Belgian border to place themselves in front of the German armies moving westwards with a massive force, making a wide sweep with their right flank, which was streaming through Belgium at a fast pace heading towards Mons. It was there that the British planned to make their stand in accordance with an agreement with the French prior to the war. Despite brave efforts to hold the line at Mons, the British troops faced double their own numbers and were eventually forced into a fighting retreat. In due course the allies halted the German push towards Paris, at which point the gruesome and catastrophic trench warfare began, fed by a conveyor belt of human sacrifice, devouring millions of men in the course of the next four years.

With the BEF suffering severe casualties at Mons, the Marine Brigade under Brigadier-General Sir George Aston was ordered to Ostend after reports of German patrols supposedly sighted near the town on 24 August, thus threatening the Royal Naval Air Service base nearby. The Marines hastily gathered up 200 tons of gear and embarked on the morning of 26 August on four Channel Fleet battleships with the light cruiser *Proserpine*, six destroyers and three monitors covering the movement. Unusually bad weather and delays in the port meant that the brigade was unable to land fully until two days later. Then, without any form of transport, the troops marched to defensive positions around Ostend to stage an albeit limited show of activity, although they were grossly ill equipped to meet any German advance. Apart from the deficiency of transport, they had little food, no supply chain and carried with them the only ammunition they would have available. They also had to stay close to the coast to receive artillery from the naval guns of the 7th Battle Squadron, which had carried the force across the Channel.

Aston led his force to trenches on the perimeter of the town to deploy along a seven-mile front, with only bicycle patrols to link the positions. The point of this was to demonstrate to the Germans that Ostend would not be easily occupied. The Marines were reinforced by a tired and bedraggled battalion of Belgian troops on 31 August, but on the same night Aston received orders to up sticks and return to England immediately, the German threat to Ostend having apparently diminished. Thus, four days after landing and settling into their position, the baggage and 200 tons of stores had to be uploaded on to their ships, a task they completed in just over 12 hours.

However, it would clearly not be long before the Marines were required to strengthen the BEF as part of a newly created Royal Naval Division of infantry, initially a grouping of navy reservists, Territorials, Royal Marines and a large intake of raw recruits, ill equipped and untrained as a group. From this inauspicious beginning, the division grew into a highly regarded organisation that achieved fame and plaudits in the years ahead, but at the time it was a rather make-do-and-mend affair. The division and each of the RN brigades were to be staffed by a command of officers from the navy, RMLI or Foot Guards, although by the very nature of their constitution many navy officers with little or no experience found themselves at the helm in the battalions, and, indeed, junior officers in the RN division came mostly from the Royal Naval Volunteer Reserve. That is not to detract from the men's courage and dedication, but in the matters that faced them they clearly had little experience – but then who had?

With the majority of regular Marines afloat and many of the remaining RMA units seconded into army artillery, which had commandeered all available 18-pounder guns, the RND battalions had initially been filled with ageing regulars, reservists and even pensioners, along with – for the first time in RM history – short-service recruits for both officers and men. The Royal Marines Brigade, which became the 3rd Brigade RN Division, consisted of four battalions, one each formed from the RMA, and the Chatham, Portsmouth and Plymouth RM divisions, although the RMA unit was later withdrawn and formed into two Artillery Brigades for service in France. As with many elements of the British land forces at that time, there was time for only limited training as a unit before the men went to war. They were needed for another urgent mission. Arthur Chater was sent from his training location to Chatham:

> We found the whole [Chatham] division on parade under arms, as though expecting an invasion, although war was not declared until over 24 hours later. Our early days at Chatham were spent watching elderly reservists being kitted up and doing a little spasmodic training. When the RM Brigade was formed to go to Ostend, we were first put under orders to go with it, and then – to our bitter grief – we were taken out again. But when after only a few days the Brigade returned and was reformed, we were appointed to it and told to provide ourselves with khaki uniform and camp kit. I was proud to be in command of No. 1 Platoon of A Company. I was 18. My company commander, a 'dug-out' major, was 35 years older than me. On 12 September the RM Brigade concentrated for training in camp near St Margaret's Bay. We had been there just a week and training had barely started when on 19 September we marched to Dover and embarked for France.

With Antwerp threatened, a real possibility emerged of the Germans securing Dunkirk and Calais, thus cutting off the BEF supply line. On 20 September the Marines arrived ahead of the brigades of the Royal Naval Division, whose men were largely untrained and unready for battle. They did, however, have some transport – a collection of London buses, whose drivers had been hurriedly enlisted as Royal Marines at Chatham – and the support of a small force of armoured cars belonging to the RNAS. These were manned by 200 Marines recruited for the purpose from the RMA and RMLI under Major Armstrong, RMLI, and who were eventually given the nickname of 'the motor bandits'.

They began by carrying out wide-ranging patrols and had been operating independently under Commander Samson at Dunkirk since 12 September and now came under Aston's command. The employment of armoured cars proved to be a successful new departure for patrolling and intelligence-gathering, and even the buses were to remain in France attached to the army until the winter of 1915, thus pioneering the army bus companies. There was one immediate deficiency for the brigade in that the Portsmouth Battalion was dispatched to Lille to meet an urgent request of the French to cover the withdrawal of a number of isolated French detachments. Then Aston himself was invalided out at the end of the month and replaced by General Archibald Paris, RMA, who came with orders to move the brigade headquarters to Cassel, and there concentrated all three battalions of his brigade, minus 678 raw recruits whom he left at Dunkirk.

Cassel was well placed for the operations that lay ahead as, by the end of the month, the Germans were closing on Antwerp. Arthur Chater recalled:

From Cassel we carried out patrolling – in the buses. On 3 October the brigade entrained at short notice, and it became known that we were on the way to Antwerp. We detrained at Vieux Dieu late that evening, and slept the remainder of the night in billets. Early next morning we started marching along a typical straight Belgian road with tall poplars on either side. Also typical of those days, the men were made to carry more than was humanly possible. Some men threw away the blankets they were carrying in addition to full marching order with packs. During a halt, when we were fallen out under the trees on the right of the road, we saw our first enemy shell bursts – shrapnel burst in the air. Just then we were ordered to fall in facing the road, as the First Lord of the Admiralty was coming to look at us. When Mr Winston Churchill reached me he asked how old I was. I had to answer 'eighteen' in front of my platoon, and so thought this a tactless question. About noon, we reached the town of Lierre, and were ordered to take over from a Belgian unit and hold the line of the Petit Nethe which runs through the town. A Company was allotted the main street, the bridge in front of us having been blown up by the Belgians My platoon was mostly in a trench dug by Belgians straight across the road. We sent a party over the river to demolish the nearest buildings, which would give cover to the enemy. The town seemed to be deserted, but an old woman arrived with a shawl over her head, and carrying her possessions in a basket on her arm. The Marines took pity on the poor old thing and ferried her across the river and sent her on her way. We heard later that she was a young German spy and that she had been shot by the Belgians. The officers dined well that night, for their Marine servants cooked some chickens they found running around and produced a bottle of wine from the cellar of a deserted casino. Towards dawn there were two or three explosions in the road behind us for which we could not account. We found later that in the dark the Germans had mounted a gun in the street only some 300 yards in front of us and were firing ranging shots. We stood to before dawn. As it was getting lighter, the German gun opened fire. I was looking over the top of the parapet. A shell burst in front of me and spattered me in the face. I rolled over and could see nothing but was able to tell my platoon sergeant to take over the platoon. I was dragged into a house and bandaged up. Although I could not see, I could walk, and so I was led away to the rear, where I was examined by Dr Louis Greig, who sent me to hospital in Antwerp. Some days later it was decided to evacuate Antwerp. I was lucky to be taken over by the British Field Hospital for the Belgians, who took me by car to Ostend, and thence to London. My eyes were examined, and it was found that I had partially lost the sight of one eye.

Winston Churchill had impressed on Paris the need to hold the Germans on the line of the Nethe until the 7th Division and expected

French divisions could link up on the west of Antwerp and attack the flank of the besieging army. But those units were delayed or diverted and in fact never arrived. As the Germans built their own forces, General Paris had no alternative but to fall back and then retire from the Nethe line, unaware then that the naval brigades had finally landed at Dunkirk, although in the event they were, as one described them, 'a slender asset from a military point of view'. No khaki uniforms were available for those who did not already possess them, and 80 per cent of the force did not have basic equipment such as packs, mess tins or water bottles. There was also a shortage of bandoliers and haversacks; those who did not receive them had to carry their allotment of 120 rounds of ammunition in their pockets. Some were armed with old converted charger-loading rifles, which they received just three days before embarking. The men were also dog-tired. After a long march to Dover, the brigades had loaded their own stores and had travelled in transports so overcrowded that most of the men had to remain standing for the entire journey – and then had to wait 12 hours before they could get into Dunkirk harbour.

In spite of these early difficulties, the naval brigades and the Marines joined troops of Belgium and France to stage a remarkably staunch defence of the city against tremendous odds before being forced into a fighting retreat that ultimately fell into disarray, and 1,479 members of the RND brigades were to seek refuge in neutral Netherlands, where they were promptly interned. There were also 198 casualties in the fighting, and 936 were taken prisoner. In the overall position in France at that time, the operations of the Royal Naval Division were a minor event, especially set alongside the concurrent disaster for the BEF at Mons. But the experience had to be quickly dismissed, and the RN Division was quickly reorganised ahead of a new area of emerging conflict that would engage both the Royal Marines at sea in British ships and those assigned to the RND. Dead ahead for them now lay the catastrophe of Gallipoli.

* * *

First Sea Lord Fisher was brought out of retirement at 74 to resume his administration of the Royal Navy. He was to have a serious falling out with his great friend the First Lord of the Admiralty, Winston Churchill, over invasion plans for the Dardanelles – an impending disaster that caused the rift and, at its climax, brought a temporary halt to Churchill's career. Fisher had angrily told the First Lord: 'Damn the Dardanelles. It will be our grave.' No one listened, and it would indeed become the place that saw half a million allied and enemy casualties in what was one of the most ill-conceived campaigns of the war, although there were quite a few contenders for the title.

Britain had shown little interest in the Dardanelles prior to the war until the Turks signed a treaty with Germany that gave them control of the Dardanelles, a long and narrow strait linking the Aegean and the Sea of Marmara, which is connected to the Black Sea by the Bosporus. In return, Turkey received German military advisers, weapons and two brand-new ships, *Breslau*, a light cruiser, and a battle cruiser of 22,600 tons, *Goeben*. The German experts began mining the strait, effectively blockading all the Russian Black Sea ports to imports of necessary war supplies and halting exports of wheat to Europe and the United Kingdom.

More than 120 allied merchant ships were locked up in the Black Sea when the Turks sealed access to the Sea of Marmara and in turn into the Mediterranean through the Dardanelles strait and Aegean. The British War Cabinet agreed that if Russia were strengthened, it would help the allies to overcome the stalemate on the Western Front and set free the grain-carrying ships bound for Britain.

An operation to open the Dardanelles was approved by the British government with the proviso that only a strong Royal Navy force should be used. At first Churchill did not like the plan, but later he fell in behind the others. First Sea Lord Fisher did not. He foresaw huge dangers to his ships as they attempted to run the gauntlet of the heavily defended approach to the Marmara Sea from the Aegean.

For centuries the strait had provided the Turks with a natural defence to Constantinople. No attacking enemy craft had successfully negotiated the Dardanelles for a hundred years. The easily defended passage was 40 miles long, running south out of the Marmara at the Gallipoli peninsula into the Aegean Sea and on to the Mediterranean. Although several miles from shore to shore at its widest points, the Dardanelles formed into a natural rat-run 12 miles upstream from the Aegean known as the Narrows. The rocky banks of the strait were strewn with forts and fortified bunkers containing around 150 guns from six to 14 inches in calibre ranged on the waters below. There were shore-mounted torpedo launchers, mobile howitzers, floating and fixed mine-fields and huge anti-submarine nets. In December 1914 a large flotilla of British and French ships assembled off the Greek island of Limnos.

The navy force, with Royal Marines detachments aboard all the major ships, consisted of the new super-dreadnought *Queen Elizabeth*, 16 pre-dreadnought battleships, a battle cruiser, five cruisers, 22 destroyers, 32 minesweeping trawlers, a seaplane carrier and initially six submarines, although more would arrive later to perform great heroics. In all, it sounded an impressive force, but given that the capital ships required constant protection, 22 destroyers were barely enough to go round, and there was already a shortage of ammunition, given the need to keep up supplies to the disastrous events on the Western Front.

The allies' ships arrived on 19 February 1915 and fired the opening salvoes ahead of the assault proper. It began with a long-range bombardment followed by heavy fire at closer range, and as the navy flotilla edged closer the outer forts were abandoned by the Turks as the shells began crashing into the masonry. In fact, the opening barrage did little more than cause panic among the Turks, until, that is, three British ships struck mines and sank. Henry Denham, aboard *Agamemnon*, a battleship that had four 12-inch, ten 9.2-inch guns and a secondary armament, two converted anti-aircraft guns and half a dozen torpedo tubes, saw the Turkish resolve change swiftly:

We were bombarding either gun placements or enemy troops and we had a wonderful view of the targets. We could see the

fall of shot, which is what I was there for on my lookout post.
We travelled up the strait towards the Narrows, which was as
far as we could get. There were mines all over the place, and
there was not a great deal of room to manoeuvre. From what I
could see, the bombardment was quite effective, but also there
was a lot which was rather wasted. We also took a great deal
of incoming fire from the enemy, and had quite a few people
killed. We were hit about 50 times in all, and the ship was very
badly damaged. There was always fear of enemy submarines,
very much so. Torpedoes were in use, and several ships were
sunk by torpedo.

Bad weather delayed progress, and it was 25 February before the
outer forts overlooking the Dardanelles were silenced by the navy
bombardment. Those further inland were simply out of range of the
ships' guns, and withering enemy fire continued to disrupt
minesweeping operations. This aspect alone was to prove fatal to a
third of the Royal Navy's ships preparing to make a major thrust into
the Dardanelles as London grew impatient for swifter action.

Admiral Carden, the navy's operational commander, had a nervous
breakdown in the second week of March and was replaced by his
deputy, Vice-Admiral Sir John de Robeck. He immediately responded
to Churchill's demands for action and ordered the allied fleet to prepare
for an immediate attempt to force the Dardanelles by sheer weight
of firepower. Two days after he took over, 18 ships entered the strait,
including *Queen Elizabeth*, *Lord Nelson*, *Agamemnon*, *Inflexible*,
Ocean, *Irresistible*, *Prince George* and *Majestic* from Britain and the
Gaulois, *Bouvet* and *Suffren* from France. Henry Denham in
Agamemnon recalled:

We set out full of enthusiasm. It was a terrific sight, these
huge ships making a lot of smoke and blasting away at the
shoreline batteries and troop positions. We made fairly good
progress and then the first tragedy occurred. The French ship

Bouvet hit a mine, which blew a hole in her port side, and she just keeled over, capsized and disappeared in a great cloud of smoke and steam. Soon afterwards, another two went down, both victims of mines: first *Irresistible* and then *Ocean*, which had been standing by to take on survivors. But it was a double hit for *Ocean*. After she struck a mine, almost immediately she was hit by shelling, and this giant of a ship went down very quickly.

In the same squadron, *Goliath* was also sunk and *Albion* had to retire from action, all hit within the space of two hours with more than 700 casualties. In London, Fisher was still pressing for the whole operation to be abandoned. He was convinced that the Dardanelles was a suicidal place to be for the Royal Navy, and it would be worse for the troops, especially in the flyblown heat of the coming summer. But Lord Kitchener had already initiated a plan for a mass invasion to secure the region, and colonial forces and Royal Marines were already on their way.

Churchill had been against the idea from the beginning, but the War Cabinet approved it and he later concurred. Leaders of the Greek army implored the British to reconsider. They told Kitchener personally that the task would be a murderous one for the troops, and they would face extremes of climate. They warned that it would need an army of at least 150,000 men; Kitchener said he could take the Gallipoli peninsula with half that number, and he was given approval to go ahead and launch the final act in this great military tragedy. Back in England, Arthur Chater, despite his eye injury was still raring to go and recalled that the RM brigades were among the first to head for Gallipoli:

Tropical helmets were suddenly issued. Next morning we embarked at Plymouth and sailed under sealed orders. The next day was my nineteenth birthday. I was so seasick that for the first time in my life I forgot all about it. We passed Gibraltar and called at Malta. On 21 February, in very murky weather, we arrived at the entrance to the Dardanelles, where we met the fleet withdrawing from the bombardment of the strait of that day. We withdrew to Mudros Bay, but were off to the Dardanelles again on 4 March when the Plymouth Battalion landed on both sides of the entrance and the Chatham Battalion stood by to land, but were not called in. The two battalions then went to Port Said, where the whole of the division was disembarked and encamped. After some days in camp, during which we were inspected by General Sir Ian Hamilton, the RN division re-embarked and on 8 April sailed to Mudros Bay, where there was a mighty army being assembled in transports.

The invasion force was led by the 29th Division, consisting of three infantry brigades each of four battalions and an additional regiment of artillery. Next came the Royal Naval Division, now consisting of only two naval brigades and the RM Brigade, without the Deal Battalion, which had been lent to another under-strength division of infantry. Next came two divisions of the Australian and New Zealand Army Corps (ANZAC) and finally the French Corps Expéditionnaire d'Orient, with just two brigades of French Colonial and Foreign Legion troops, and eight batteries of 75-millimetre quick-firing guns. Later a further 20,000 troops were brought in, including the 29th Brigade of Gurkhas, but it would prove to be nowhere near enough, and as allied casualties began to mount horrendously the equivalent of five more divisions were pulled in from around the Mediterranean, the Middle East and Britain.

Their arrival came as no surprise to the Turks, who by then had managed to get 60,000 men strategically placed to meet them, positioned on the high grounds above the landing points, all in place long before the allies had even attempted to land their main body of men. Allied troops would have to climb treacherous terrain, with sheer rock, deep ravines and dense jungle growth, while above them, protected by rocky outcrops, the Turks began picking them off as if at a duck shoot. The Royal Navy, with the Marine detachments, had the task of ferrying in the invasion army, whose intention was to capture the Gallipoli peninsula, while at the same time continuing its bombardment of gunnery positions. Shipping in the men was no straightforward task: the navy had to equip itself with suitable landing craft to handle a massive supply chain for the land army as well as shifting more than 5,000 mules and horses, 2,500 vehicles and 2,000 artillery pieces over the coming months, and the Royal Marines posted on the ships and in the landing craft made a substantial contribution to their safe arrival. It was no easy task, as Henry Denham recalled:

> We took many, many casualties in the landing [of troops], which was supposedly going to solve everything. But, of course, it did not. When we came close in, we were under heavy fire, but the steel plating protection was very good. Even so, there was no lack of spirit, either on our part or the men going in.

The landings were all straight on to open beaches, often at night because there were no protections or jetties and the men had to wade ashore from up to their waist, totally exposed, while being shot at. There were vivid scenes, especially at what became known as Anzac Cove, where the Australian and New Zealand forces were landing. Arthur Chater again:

> With the exception of the Plymouth Battalion RM, the RN division did not take part in the initial landings on the Gallipoli peninsula on 25 April but carried out a feint landing up the Gulf of Xeros. Then, on the afternoon of 28 April, we were ordered to land in support of the Australians, who had landed near Gaba Tepe [later known as Anzac Cove]. Landing in horse boats on the open beach at dusk, we were led by an Australian guide up the bottom of a deep ravine. This was our first experience of being in enemy country. It was all rather eerie. In the darkness, the guide lost the way, which led to countermarching and some

confusion. He eventually found the right path, which as dawn was breaking brought us to a very steep slope at the top of which the Australians were entrenched only a few yards from the edge of the ravine. We took over the trenches and they withdrew into rest. For four days the battalion held this precarious line wholly devoid of depth against spasmodic attacks and suffered grievous casualties.

During 2 May the battalion was again relieved in the line by Australians, and we were told that we would have a rest. But this was not to be. During the night of 2 to 3 May, an Australian unit captured a vital crest line, which commanded the greater part of the Anzac position. The enemy counterattacked to retake the crest. At dawn on 3 May the battalion was aroused and ordered to move at speed to reinforce the Australians. As we moved up the ravine, HMS *Bacchante* opened fire on the crest and began to shell the Australians out of their newly won trenches. Signalling was slow and uncertain, and information that the position had been taken during the night had not reached the ship. As the battalion reached the foot of the slope to the crest, A Company was for some reason diverted to the right. From our position we watched the remainder of the battalion struggling up the steep slope. As the leading waves reached the crest, they were caught by machine-gun fire from the flank. Many of the bodies rolled back down the hill they had so laboriously climbed; some lay where they fell until two days later we went out in darkness and pulled them down. Monday 3 May was a black day for the Chatham Battalion, [suffering] 200 casualties, including our adjutant, Captain Richards. To my amazement, [our CO] sent for me and told me to take over the duties of adjutant. During the remainder of our time at Anzac, the two RMLI battalions and the 4th Australian Brigade held a sector of the defence, all under command of our brigade commander, Brigadier-General Trotman, RM. The 4th Australian Brigade was commanded by Lieutenant-Colonel Monash, who was to become one of Australia's great generals. Two incidents remain in my mind. The first occurred when I was sent on a mission by the CO and had to run the gauntlet of a sniper whose deadly fire was holding up movement in the ravine. His bullet passed in just above the belt of my jacket and out through my breeches. On the afternoon of 12 May, the RM brigade was relieved at Anzac by the Australian Light Horse, who had been dismounted and left their horses in Egypt. In the dark, the Chatham Battalion re-embarked our ship. The old captain was shocked when told the numbers of our casualties and the names of the officers killed. During those two weeks, the battalion had lost 11 officers and over 300 other ranks.

From day one, the Gallipoli adventure looked ill-judged and doomed to failure, although one of the outstanding features of this campaign – the high morale and courage of the men themselves – was evident from the beginning. Incidents of great heroism became daily occurrences as the fighting intensified, as illustrated by a letter to his family from Private R. Bush, of the RMLI, who was among those badly wounded and evacuated to hospital in Plymouth:

No artist can ever paint a picture that would disclose the true horrors of that memorable landing of our troops under a perfect torrent of fire from forts and trenches hidden from our view, with enemy snipers covering us and sending our gallant lads to their doom whenever we showed ourselves for a moment. The terrible scenes will for ever live in the memory of all who took part in this fierce engagement. Our biggest reverse was in landing from the boats to a shell- and bullet-swept shore. While we were doing our utmost to overcome the wire entanglements, the enemy poured bullets into our midst at a fearful rate, accounting for a great number of our lads, who dropped back into the sea lifeless, without even setting foot on shore. From nowhere, it seemed to us, they picked us off, while shrapnel burst in the heavens, and when at last we landed on the beach, which was devoid of cover, we were simply facing death. Eventually we got a footing, and from that time we did nothing but advance into the territory that had been won at such terrible cost.

From the first day of the landings, casualty figures were appalling, and there were many acts of heroism by sailors and Marines who had the task of taking the troops ashore. In one ship alone – HMS *River Clyde* – five members of crew were each awarded the Victoria Cross for heroic action rescuing wounded men at what was known as V Beach. Another Victoria Cross was also awarded to Lance-Corporal Walter Richard Parker, 33, of the RMLI, for heroic action on the night of 30 April, when he volunteered as a stretcher-bearer at Gaba Tepe and went out with a party of NCOs and men to take vital supplies to an isolated trench. Several men had already been killed in an attempt to reach the trench, and after crossing an area of about 400 yards swept by machine-gun and rifle fire, Lance-Corporal Parker was alone, the rest of the party having been killed or wounded. On his arrival he gave assistance to the wounded, and when the trench was finally evacuated he helped to remove and attend the casualties, although he himself was seriously hurt.

In London, First Sea Lord Fisher came under increasing pressure to order his battleship fleet positioned in the Aegean to resume their efforts to force the Dardanelles. He refused point-blank to override the decisions of his admirals on the spot and subsequently resigned on 14 May 1915. The Royal Navy battleships did not resume attempts to force the strait but kept up bombardment in support of the troops. Instead, the battle commanders brought in their most modern submarines, which went on to make many sorties through the Narrows and into the Sea of Marmara, causing havoc among Turkish shipping. Their efforts in the Dardanelles were one of the few bright spots in an appalling conflict.

By the end of August the allies had lost over 40,000 men, and the situation grew worse by the day as the winter set in. Casualties through disease and sickness as the battles dragged on into October and November were almost as high as those wounded and killed. Literally hundreds were drowned in their trenches, many simply froze to death and dozens lost one or both feet through frostbite, while the stalemate of battle remained solid. The Royal Marines' casualties in this drama amounted to 100 officers and 3,000 other ranks killed or wounded.

In October General Hamilton, who had directed this ground war from the outset, was relieved of his post and was replaced by General Sir Charles Munro. He personally toured all three fronts where battle continued and was appalled by what he saw. He made an immediate recommendation that the Gallipoli expedition should be halted and the allied army evacuated. In London, his report instigated immediate political upheaval. Winston Churchill resigned as First Lord of the Admiralty. Newspapers reported that he was bitter 'about not having clear guidance from the admirals before launching the attempt to force the Dardanelles'. Asquith's Liberal government was replaced by a coalition, and an end to the Gallipoli fiasco was finally in sight. After almost nine months of incredible bravery and heroism on the part of all concerned, the evacuation at the end of 1915 had to be planned; it went very successfully – unbelievably so. The final act to retrieve the remaining 90,000 men, 4,000 animals, 1,700 vehicles and 200 guns turned out to be one of the great successes of the whole campaign. What seemed a logistical nightmare to its planners was carried out to perfection and with few casualties under the noses of the Turkish forces. The evacuation of all allied personnel began on 7 December and was carried out at night, while by day the activity ceased and the naval fleet gave the impression that they were still operating as normal. At night, the evacuation continued while a line of ships turned searchlights on the enemy trenches. The last of the men left Helles on 9 January 1916.

Almost half a million allied troops had been drawn into the Gallipoli campaign, and losses had been heartbreaking. The British suffered 205,000 casualties, of whom 43,000 were killed; there were 33,600

Anzac casualties, with more than 12,000 killed, and 47,000 French casualties, of whom 4,800 died. Turkish casualties were estimated at around 280,000, with 65,000 killed. If there was any defence for the ridiculously high cost of the campaign, it could be seen in other areas, in that the action distracted the Germans from opening another offensive in France and weakened the Turks enough to help the British seizure of Palestine in 1917. British submariners had also kept up the pressure, and the effect on Turkish supply lines was catastrophic, seriously affecting Turkey's capacity elsewhere in other theatres.

On the night of 9 January 1916, Royal Marines oversaw the final act of this drama, as ever first in and last out. The four Marine battalions had been reduced to two, and for the time being the Royal Naval Division was split by their distribution to other tasks. There was talk of disbandment, but RND commander General Archibald Paris, RMA, was fighting a strong rearguard action and won a reprieve. The division was to be re-formed and made up, ready to be shipped to France in May 1916.

CHAPTER SIX

Jutland, the Somme and Zeebrugge

While the Royal Marines brigades, along with virtually every other available infantry and artillery unit from Britain, were experiencing the traumas of the war on the front lines, there were thousands who had spent 18 months virtually locked up on the big ships. They were the RM detachments and sailors aboard the vessels of the Grand Fleet bottled up in Scapa Flow, waiting for action since their last encounter with the Germans at the Battle of Dogger Bank. Just short of 6,000 RMLI and RMA officers and men were aboard the 67 battleships, battle cruisers and cruisers. They had spent most of that time at the naval base in the Orkneys, with patrols in the North Sea, although these were limited by ever-increasing U-boat activity. For the men, endless exercises, polishing the brass, swabbing the decks and trips ashore to a temporary bar and sports facilities set up by the navy in the otherwise barren landscape of the Orkneys became routine. Friction between the Marines and sailors became inevitable, especially on some of the larger ships where neither group was permitted to go ashore for weeks on end. There were occasional fights and a general unease as tempers grew shorter as the wait grew longer.

The fleet commanders, meanwhile, kept their ships on alert, training and exercising for the big event, if it ever came, that had been billed as the greatest naval engagement of all time: a shoot-out between the opposing dreadnoughts, hurling one-ton shells at each other. Moves towards the confrontation began to unfold on the afternoon of 30 May 1916 when Admiral Reinhard Scheer, commander-in-chief of the German High Seas Fleet, led his ships forwards. The Germans had devised a plan to entice elements of the British fleet into a manoeuvre through which they could achieve a separation from the Grand Fleet under the overall command of Admiral Sir John Jellicoe and by such a division could go on to victory. When that prospect finally moved towards reality, Robert Shaw was sitting on a gun turret of his ship, *Hercules*, steaming towards the scrap that became known as the Battle of Jutland:

There was a real sense of occasion, because the Grand Fleet had not been in direct action at all and we all hoped that this was going to be a modern Trafalgar. When we came close to action, my station was in a gun turret. There was considerable speculation about how we would fare. Sailing south, as the fleet was, we were all thrilled with the idea of going into action. As we approached Jutland itself, we were all closed up at action stations and I was sitting on top of the turret at the time. In the distance, which was a bit misty, I saw a flash of gunfire on the horizon and thought, Oh dear, something's happening now, and didn't worry very much until within a few seconds there was the most enormous splash alongside the ship. We had been near-missed, and I quickly ran down the turret. A few splinters came on board, and within minutes we were firing ourselves at the German fleet in the distance.

The target for separation was Admiral Sir David Beatty's squadron of battle cruisers, then operating from Rosyth out of the Firth of Forth. It was to be achieved by sending five German battle cruisers and four light cruisers from Wilhelmshaven under the command of Rear-Admiral Franz von Hipper, who last encountered Beatty at the Battle of Dogger Bank. This advance party was intended to lure Beatty into a chase across the North Sea and into the hands of Scheer, who had positioned the rest of his fleet off the southern coast of Norway. If all had gone to plan, Beatty would have been trapped and sunk. As the German ships moved to take up their positions late in the afternoon of 30 May, the British intercepted a signal, only partly decoded, which alerted them to some kind of German movement, although the precise details were still not clear. Jellicoe reacted immediately, and by midnight the entire British Grand Fleet was at sea heading for a confrontation off the south-west coast of Norway.

The Grand Fleet, sailing from Scapa Flow, was still 50 miles away to the north on the afternoon of 31 May when Beatty, joined by four *Queen Elizabeth*-class battleships of the 5th Battle Squadron, realised he was closing on the enemy. But he dashed into the fight without waiting for the slower battleships. His battle cruisers were also faster than the enemy's, and his guns had a longer range. He was presented with a choice: at 19,000 yards he could have bombarded Hipper's ships but instead chose to move in to 14,000 before opening fire. But in the running battle that developed, dangerous ammunition handling practices in all the British battle cruisers led to first *Indefatigable* and then *Queen Mary* blowing up as soon as they took a hit. Having pursued Hipper almost to the point of contact with Scheer's High Seas Fleet, Beatty turned northwards to lead the Germans towards Admiral Jellicoe's oncoming Grand Fleet. As they steamed to meet head on, the Grand Fleet switched to its battle formation, as Robert Shaw explained:

It was after six in the evening ... The fleet, which had been approaching in six lines, re-formed into a single line abreast, ships end to end, under Admiral Jellicoe. It was getting dark and misty, and there was a great deal of confusion. Those of us closed up down below had no real idea of what was going on.

Through the manoeuvre of turning his battle fleet into an end-to-end line, Jellicoe calculated that he would be firing broadside-on with all guns blazing towards the German ships while they could only return fire with the forward guns of their leading ships. Even with this advantage, the British were unable to make the most of what was described in a later analysis as a 'lambs-to-the-slaughter' situation. The inferior quality of the British shells and the superior strength of the German ships allowed the enemy to turn without far greater wounds than were in fact inflicted.

The ships of the two fleets blasted away at each other, almost 600 heavy guns between them, with the Germans outnumbered in average weight of firepower by almost two to one. Scheer's fleet faced annihilation, and soon after 6.30 p.m. he decided to pull back to escape the British onslaught. He ordered all his ships to make a 180-degree turn, a difficult manoeuvre in an exercise let alone under heavy fire, but it was completed with incredible precision to allow the great escape to take place into a smoke screen laid by German destroyers steaming across their rear. At 6.45 p.m. Jellicoe's fleet had lost contact, but Scheer's troubles were not over yet.

The British fleet now lay between the German fleet and their home ports, and so just before 7 p.m. Scheer made another sharp detour, hoping to get past the British fleet. Instead he ran straight into a fresh bombardment and was forced to re-engage. The flagship *Lützow* sustained fatal damage in a duel to the death with the British battle cruiser *Invincible*, which later also blew up when one of the German salvoes hit a gun turret. Many other ships on both sides were sunk or damaged at this time, and in desperation Scheer at one point ordered his cruisers and destroyers ahead to mount a line-abreast charge against the British ships.

Behind them, Scheer's battleships fell into a state of confusion amid the smoke and gunfire, and by 7.45 p.m. the two battle fleets had drawn apart at a combined speed of around 35 knots, at which point the Germans made a dash for home – and there they stayed. Behind them, the scene at the Battle of Jutland was one of smouldering desolation and death. A newspaper commentator of the day described it thus:

> All the theories of a century's peace were being put to the test amid the roar of battle and the flashes of the most powerful guns ever fired in anger at sea. Tonight, the sea is reported to be awash with bodies. One steamer alone spotted 500, but there are many tales of heroism . . .

Indeed there were, and many that never became known, because in the heat of battle, although thousands of men were killed outright, many others simply drowned because of the impossibility of launching rescue parties. A number of the actions were of such merit as to receive the highest accolade, the Victoria Cross. Among them, RN seaman John Cornwell, aged 16, became the youngest-ever posthumous recipient of the VC for his heroic stand as part of a gun crew on HMS *Chester*. Although severely wounded early in the battle, he remained alone at a most exposed post with the gun's crew dead and wounded around him. He continued firing virtually to the end of the action and was then himself killed.

On Beatty's flagship, *Lion*, RMLI Major Francis John William Harvey, 43, was awarded a posthumous Victoria Cross. He was in command of the Marines' Q turret, one of the four twin 13.5-inch gun turrets ranged from bow to stern along the ship. The turret had just fired its twelfth shell at the *Lützow* around 13,000 yards away, and the guns were being reloaded when an 11-inch shell from that ship hit the turret. The explosion killed almost everyone in the gunhouse, peeled back the armoured roof and started a serious fire. Although he had lost both his legs, Major Harvey used the voice pipe to order the doors of the magazine below gunhouse to be closed and the cordite magazine flooded with seawater to make sure the fire did not spread. He died shortly afterwards.

The way in which the battle ended aroused controversy that would last for years as to who exactly won. Britain declared herself the victor because it was the Germans who gave up and ran for home. In fact, Jellicoe's fleet suffered greater losses: three battle cruisers, three cruisers and eight destroyers sunk, with 6,094 officers and men killed (of whom 538 were Marines). The Germans lost one battleship, one battle cruiser, four light cruisers, five destroyers and 2,545 officers and men.

The general opinion, outside Germany, was that the Grand Fleet emerged in better shape and retained supremacy in the oceans of the world, and Germany did not feel inclined to challenge that proposition again throughout the remainder of the First World War. As one commentator wrote, the 'High Seas Fleet has assaulted its jailer but is still in jail'. It was a painful exercise on the part of the jailer, and the British fleet accepted that there had been many failings, not least of which was the tendency of the battle cruisers to blow up on taking a hit that might otherwise not be of a crippling nature. Robert Shaw said:

> Our large number of losses was [self-inflicted] because of poor protection between the gun and magazines. Magazines blew up due to the trail of cordite from the turret down to the magazine. The Germans had already dealt with that problem, but it was only after Jutland that all magazines on British ships were given another layer of protection, and in fact when that was being done in *Hercules* one of the bulkheads near one of the magazines got warm through a fire in the engine room and preparations were made to flood the magazine in case the ship blew. There were at least two ships which had blown up in harbour.

The German High Seas Fleet did not venture out again for battle, and instead the German navy concentrated heavily on submarine warfare as its main arm of attack at sea and redirected its efforts against the merchant fleet in a bid to starve Britain of vital supplies and food. This action was further enhanced when the United States entered the war in April 1917, to which Germany reacted by reinforcing its policy of unrestricted submarine warfare – in other words, any ship was fair game in areas Germany declared to be a war zone – from which it had pulled back after the sinking of *Lusitania* in 1915.

While the shipboard Marines were being tested at sea, the RMLI and RMA in their various guises were destined for participation in some of the great land battles of the First World War, although, of course, their numbers were small compared with the overall manpower by then being deployed on the Western Front. The interesting footnote to that statement, however, is that this smaller percentage of Marines who made up the RMLI battalions and the RMA on the Western Front saw far more fighting than the rest of the corps.

The brigades had to be heavily replenished after Gallipoli and never fully recovered from the losses. There was another discomfort affecting troops of the Royal Naval Division when they arrived for battle in France. It was caused by the ongoing rumblings and rivalries between the army and the navy about this hybrid organisation that the War Office still did not much like, especially since its formation was originally at the behest of the then First Lord of the Admiralty, Winston Churchill.

However, in such desperate times these historical personality clashes between army and navy could barely be a consideration, but they were. The RND became the 63rd Division and, for the first time, found itself under the direct control of the British army, which the navy people did not much like but got on with the job. It is not difficult to understand the causes of some of the conflict that arose around this naval division that acted as infantry, and there was ample evidence that the age-old difficulties vis-à-vis the army and navy still existed even in the most critical of times. The Marines themselves sat uncomfortably in the middle, as soldiers aligned to a naval command, which was itself subordinate to an army command, as Winston Churchill himself highlighted:

When the division went to France in the spring of 1916 a new set of difficulties began to assail it and even to menace its

101

existence. It was a naval division. It had different rates of pay, different ranks, different customs, different methods, different traditions from those of the British Expeditionary Army. Its officers and men used consistently the naval parlance on every possible occasion. To leave their camps, in which the White Ensign flew and bells recorded the passage of time, men requested 'leave to go ashore'; when they returned they 'came aboard' and . . . for sergeants and lance-corporals they had petty officers and leading seamen. Anchors were stencilled on their limbers and emblazoned on their company flags, and their regimental badges were in the form of the crests of the admirals whose names their battalions bore. When ill or wounded they attended 'sick bay'; field kitchens were the 'galley'; the king's health was drunk sitting in the 'wardroom', where officers wanting salt are even reported to have been heard asking their neighbours to 'give it a fair wind'; many of the men and some of the officers requested 'leave to grow', and paraded creditable beards in the faces of a clean-chinned army. It need scarcely be said that these manifestations inspired in a certain type of military mind feelings of the liveliest alarm. To this type of mind anything which diverged in the slightest degree from absolute uniformity according to the sealed pattern was inexpressibly painful.[*]

The naval battalions were reduced from three to two and renamed the 189th Brigade. Two battalions of Royal Marines, 1RM and 2RM, were conjoined with two RNVR battalions to form the 188th Brigade. An army brigade consisting of four infantry battalions was also assigned to the 63rd Division, which remained under the overall command of Major-General Paris, who was, of course, a Marine. The brigades were regrouped after a period of consolidation on the return

[*] Winston S. Churchill, introduction to *The Royal Naval Division* by Douglas Jerrold, Hutchinson & Co., London, 1923.

from Gallipoli and underwent extensive training to acclimatise them to the vast change of conditions they would now have to face, although given the vagaries of the Turkish situation they had already gone through the mill in that regard.

On 4 October the division became part of what was to be the final phase of the 1916 Battle of the Somme, an assault north of the River Ancre. But Paris was far from happy with his overall complement, and Julian Thompson quotes a memorandum from him which bemoaned the state of his division:

> I wonder if the time will come when this division will run on ball bearings. We were to have had volunteers from the army as the Admiralty wouldn't enlist any more. The only hitch is that there are no volunteers! Then the Admiralty have stolen men by the hundred. All who go on leave never return and some thousands are hidden in ships. It doesn't make it easy. Here, the army say we are fighting the navy as well as the Hun. The last kick by our AG – 'no more proper Marine officers or men are to be allowed to drain away to the army'. What is an improper Marine?

Paris was by now the father-like figure to the division he had commanded since Antwerp, and to his Marines in particular, since the bulk of his officer career had been with them. He led his troops immediately to the Somme sector to begin training, but on 13 October, while visiting the 190th Brigade, a shell exploded close to him and to his staff officer, RMLI Major Sketchley. Paris lost a leg in the explosion and Sketchley was killed. Major-General Shute, an army officer, was appointed divisional commander, much to the chagrin of his naval subordinates, who saw it as an attempt to standardise discipline and general procedures to bring the division 'into line with the army command structure'. That, Winston Churchill wrote after the war, was precisely the aim:

An army officer [Shute], with unexceptionable credentials for the task, was placed in command. For six months in 1916 he laboured to force the officers and men of the Royal Navy Division to amend their ways ... to forget their naval tradition. Army officers selected for this express purpose were placed in command of many of the battalions over the heads of those who had won their way to these situations by continued promotion under the fire of the enemy. But so stubborn was the resisting power which all ranks developed in a perfectly obedient and respectful manner, and so high was their conduct in action, that after six months the essential character of the division was unchanged.

To begin an upheaval of such matters at the very moment that the brigades were lining up for the great battles ahead in France was, to say the least, unfortunate. Shute received the operational orders on 23 October, although it was 13 November before they were finally moved into position after several changes of mind. It was at this point that the division was given a role in the final stages of this infamous struggle, which had raged since 1 July and ultimately claimed more than a million casualties as British and French forces attempted to break the Germans' stand across a 25-mile front north and south of the River Somme. The original object of the battle was to relieve the French at Verdun by drawing German forces away. But in the end the losses on the Somme far exceeded those at Verdun, a catastrophe signalled on the very first day, which became the bloodiest and most costly in British military history when they suffered 57,470 casualties, of whom 19,240 were killed.

The two battalions of Royal Marines fought as part of the 63rd Division from 13 to 16 November along the River Ancre. There was also now a strong RM presence at the helm in that the commanding officers of the division's Anson, Drake, Nelson and Hawke Battalions were now all lieutenant-colonels of the Royal Marines. Five previous attempts had been made to secure the position, all rebuffed. An attack was planned for either side of the Ancre, a small tributary of the Somme flowing through the northern sector of the battlefield. South of the Ancre was the village of Thiepval, which had been recently captured by the British, and St-Pierre-Divion, still held by the Germans. To the north of the river were the villages of Beaumont-Hamel and Beaucourt-sur-Ancre, which had not seen any fighting since the Somme operations began in July. Now five divisions were brought forward to lead what amounted to a last-ditch attempt to secure the Somme before the winter set in. The 63rd Division was opposing the north bank, with the 51st Highland Division. To the left of them, between Beaumont-Hamel and Serre, was the 3rd Division, and furthest north was the 31st Division in front of Serre. There was to be an attack south of the Ancre by the 19th Division to run alongside the attack of the RND.

The 51st took Beaumont-Hamel and the 63rd captured Beaucourt; in doing so, one of the 63rd Division's commanders, Lieutenant-Colonel Bernard Freyberg, won a Victoria Cross. One of New Zealand's most famous soldiers in this war and the Second World War, Freyberg rose to prominence during the Gallipoli landings when he swam ashore with lighting flares to distract the enemy, for which he received his first Distinguished Service Order. He was badly wounded several times and left the peninsula when his division was evacuated in January 1916.

After carrying the initial attack through the enemy's front system of trenches, Freyberg's troops were badly spread out and disorganised. As he fought to restore order, he led from the front on a successful assault of the second objective and was wounded twice in the process. When reinforced the next morning, he attacked and captured a strongly fortified village, taking 500 prisoners. He was wounded twice more, the second time badly, but he refused to leave the line until he had issued final instructions.

A further VC was awarded to RMA Major Frederick William Lumsden, 44, following his courageous action at Francilly, France, in April 1917, when he undertook to bring in six captured enemy field guns that had been left in dug-in positions 300 yards ahead of the Marines' position. The Germans were raking the area with murderous fire as Major Lumsden led four artillery teams and a party of infantry in an attempt to collect the guns. Despite heavy casualties, Lumsden made three journeys to the guns and then remained with them, directing operations, until the last gun had been taken back. Sadly, he was later killed in action, near Arras, on 4 June 1918, having amassed further honours, with a CB, DSO with three bars and the Croix de Guerre (France).

The 63rd Division had again taken heavy casualties in the Battle of the Somme, which ended officially on 19 November, although the division returned to the Ancre for further operations between the beginning of January and early March in what proved to be the coldest winter of the entire war. By April, they were in the thick of it, fighting through two of the phases of the Battle of Arras, and towards the end of the year transferring to Ypres in time to participate in the Second Battle of Passchendaele, the latest in the long line of horrendous scenes in that section spanning 38 months. To isolate the Marines' contribution to these ongoing engagements under the banner of the 63rd is beyond the scope of this work, but there can be no better way of recalling those appalling days than by using the words of Douglas Jerrold, who was there and wrote these words in relation to Passchendaele:

The chief tactical features on the intended front of attack were the Paddebeek, a flooded streamlet running parallel to our front at a distance of some 500 yards, and some higher ground 1,000 yards to the right front, on which stood the ruins known as Tournant Farm. This side of the Paddebeek, the main enemy posts were believed to be in five groups of ruins and pillboxes known as Berks House, Bray Farm, Banff House, Sourd Farm and Varlet Farm, and in an isolated trench, near our junction with the Canadians, known as Source Trench. Across the stream to our right were Source Farm and Tournant Farm, and on the right a number of isolated pillboxes and fortified shell holes. The first objective of the 188th Brigade included all the enemy positions this side of the Paddebeek except Sourd Farm; the second objective comprised the remaining position, as far as a line drawn north-west through Tournant Farm. The first objective was to be attacked by the Anson Battalion on the right and the 1st RM Battalion on the left. Through these battalions, the Howe and the 2nd RM Battalions were to advance across the Paddebeek to the second objective. The attack was fixed for dawn on the 26th.

That night, the inevitable rain had continued steadily and, when the time came for the advance, the ground was as impassable as had been expected. They pushed ahead on a very wide front, with the 1st Marines having a frontage of nearly 900 yards. Each battalion adopted much the same formation: two thin lines of skirmishers went in front, and behind them were small columns of sections or platoons according to the objective to which each was detailed. Two platoons from each battalion were required for duty as stretcher-bearers, the normal complement being inadequate to the nature of the fighting. At 5.45, in heavy rain, the advance began across ground pocked with deep shell holes flooded to a depth of several feet; between them a path had to be picked over ground only less impassable. Despite these difficulties, the first waves kept fairly well up to the barrage and, especially on the left (the 1st Marine Battalion), substantial gains were recorded. Banff House (the last objective of the 1st Marine Battalion) was reported at 7.20 a.m. as having been captured by Lieutenant Careless, RM. The enemy machine-gun fire from across the Paddebeek was extremely severe, and almost all the company commanders of the attacking battalions had become casualties. Jerrold went on:

One of the finest exploits of this second stage of the attack was the crossing of the Paddebeek by Captain Ligertwood's A

Company of the 2nd Marines. The platoons of this company had gone into action under their own flags, strips of red canvas nailed to a stick cut from the woods where the company had done their training, solemnly blessed by the battalion chaplain, Father Davey, and taken into action with honour and reverence. These flags were carried through the battle. Captain Ligertwood, three times wounded, led his company to within sight of their goal, when he fell mortally wounded, to rise only once to direct his men to their objective. But on this front and at this time success was denied even to the bravest. This company, staying on their objective throughout the entire day, were powerless to lift a finger to assist the main battle still being fought on the first objective where the enemy centre held their ground . . .

Temporary confusion on the left flank was characteristic of the prevailing conditions. Many men were lost through mistaking enemy posts for our own; only investigation could show the truth; many, it is feared, reached their objective and were cut off because no one knew of their success. Only under cover of darkness could communications, inevitably severed in a daylight advance, be re-established. Yet without the maintenance of communications, enabling local success to be exploited, nothing could in the prevailing conditions enable us to reach and consolidate our objectives. Nevertheless, the line finally won by the relieving battalions comprised at least five strongly fortified enemy posts and represented an advance of from 300 to 400 yards from our old front; and this in spite of the fact that, in the words of Sir Hubert Gough, 'no troops could have had to face worse conditions'. Success achieved under such conditions had to be bought dearly, and the four assaulting battalions lost heavily in officers and men.

The final act in this drama of the RND was described by Churchill himself as follows:

At last 1918 ... its difficult and exhausting retreat leading up to the brilliantly sustained engagements of 25 March when at Les Boeufs, at High Wood and at Courcelette the Naval Division stood in the van of the 5th Corps and saved the line of the Ancre, and so all through the long summer struggle till the victorious advance ... still the division is in the forefront, taking part in the storming of the redoubtable Drocourt-Queant switch of the Hindenburg Line (3 September) with the Anson and the Marines on the flank of the Canadian advance, and [then] thrusting forward to Pronville and opening the way to the banks of the Canal du Nord. On 30 September begins that astonishing advance of the division towards Cambrai ... when we see them forcing the passage of the Canal du Nord, carrying Anneux and Graincourt, storming the almost impassable defences of the St-Quentin Canal, capturing the village of Niergnies and repelling with a captured field gun and captured German anti-tank rifles a German counterattack made with captured British tanks – an extraordinary inversion. They were fighting still in the neighbourhood of Mons when 11 o'clock struck on the morning of 11 November, and the annals of the Royal Naval Division came in honour to a close. Long may the record of their achievements be preserved, and long may their memory be respected by those for whom they fought.

There were many stories, too many to recount. One more, however, must be added and that is the famous Zeebrugge mission in which the Marines had a part. In 1918 British and American minelayers put out more than 60,000 mines over a 200-mile passage of the North Sea to block U-boat access from Germany into the Atlantic. At the same time, Admiral Roger Keyes took command of the Dover Patrol of fast boats equipped with searchlights to harass U-boats using the English Channel. These were very effective measures in combating the U-boat campaign around the British Isles, but there remained one other area where the U-boat could gain sustenance, and it centred on the Belgian coastal town of Zeebrugge, which in turn led to a submarine base at Bruges, reached by an eight-mile-long canal. The access point at Zeebrugge was a heavily defended mole, a curving wall 40 feet high and 80 yards wide stretching one and a half miles out into the sea brimming with German guns. The base provided a perfect haven for ocean-bound U-boats, and in 1917 U-boat commanders began using the Zeebrugge hideaway, thus dodging the North Sea minefields.

On his arrival to command the Dover Patrol, Keyes was presented with the urgent task of tackling the Zeebrugge problem. His answer was an ambitious and risky plan to take a large force across the English Channel and, while Marines launched a diversionary assault on the German fortifications, three ancient cruisers, *Thetis*, *Intrepid* and *Iphigenia*, filled with concrete would be scuttled in the Bruges Canal, thereby blocking German access. Meanwhile, an equally ancient submarine packed with explosives would be steered to a point close to a viaduct connecting the Zeebrugge mole to the mainland. At a given point, the five-man crew would evacuate in a skiff, leaving the boat to sally forth on automatic pilot, with a timer set to detonate the explosives and blow the construction to pieces to prevent the Germans from reinforcing their troops at the mole once the fighting had begun. The key to the success of the whole operation was the landing of the diversionary force at the Zeebrugge mole. The raiding party would be ferried in aboard a fourth redundant cruiser, *Vindictive*, engage the German defenders and withdraw as soon as the cruisers had been scuttled. Around this main body of ships would be a flurry of smaller craft laying smoke screens.

The plan, which would not be out of place in later Commando operations, sounded too far-fetched for many of Keyes's senior officers at the Admiralty, but in the end he won approval and set about gathering his force, drawn from the Royal Navy, the Royal Marines and the submarine service. Admiral David Beatty, who by then had succeeded Jellicoe as commander of the British Grand Fleet, was only too willing to participate. Almost two years had passed since the Battle of Jutland, and his ships had been waiting in vain at Scapa Flow for the German High Seas Fleet to venture out.

Beatty sent 200 volunteers, young, unmarried sailors with no dependants, who were to be joined by the 4th Battalion Royal Marines, which had been quickly reorganised at Deal to join the expedition. They spent three weeks training while Keyes put together his mini-fleet for the operation. For troop carriers, Keyes borrowed *Royal Daffodil* and *Royal Iris II*, which for years had been carrying passengers across the River Mersey in Liverpool. The three old cruisers, *Thetis*, *Intrepid* and *Iphigenia*, were stripped and filled with concrete. Then came two submarines, *C1* and *C3*, which were to be modified to take the explosive charges and which were to be operated by skeleton crews.

Another crucial addition was the assembling of a posse of fast motorboats from the Dover Patrol whose task was to lay dense smoke screens using a new concoction developed by Commander Brock of the Brock Firework Company. The boats would also remain on hand to pick up survivors from the attack. The whole group assembled north of Harwich, ready to sail at 5 p.m. on 22 April 1918, a motley collection of 76 vessels, including the new destroyer *Warwick* with Admiral Keyes aboard, and in total carrying 1,760 men.

The ships were spotted immediately and the Germans sent up a series of star shells, which lit up the skies over the whole area covered by the incoming attackers. Undaunted, they sailed on into murderously heavy shellfire from the German positions, which killed a number of men even before they had reached the landing point. *Vindictive* bombarded the emplacements, but the German guns on the mole were presented with easy targets. Even so, *Vindictive* arrived alongside the mole just after midnight on St George's Day but had difficulty getting into position. Four hundred yards off the landing area, she was met with the full force of enemy guns on the mole, and the Marines and sailors designated to attack the shore batteries went into action. *Vindictive* berthed 300 yards from her planned position. As *Daffodil* moved alongside to hold her steady, German shells exploded in her engine room. *Daffodil's* engineers managed to keep her coal-fired boilers burning, allowing the assault team on *Vindictive* to disembark. Because of her position, the team had to drop down 16 feet to the level of the mole under heavy fire, covered by the gunners on the ships, who also remained under heavy fire. RMA Sergeant Norman Finch was second-in-command of the team on the pom-poms and Lewis gun in the foretop of *Vindictive* and the men kept up continuous fire until two heavy shells made direct hits, killing or disabling everyone except Sergeant Finch. Although seriously wounded himself, he remained in his battered and exposed position firing the Lewis gun and harassing the enemy on the mole until the foretop received another direct hit, putting the gun out of action. Finch was subsequently awarded the Victoria Cross by ballot (see below).

During this action, *Vindictive* took another direct hit, which killed or wounded half the assault force as they prepared to attack. Those on *Daffodil* herself were also unable to disembark and none took part in the raid. Those aboard *Iris* did get ashore relatively unscathed, and the weakened force stormed off towards its objectives, the first task being to silence the guns mounted on the end of the mole. However, the raiding party suffered heavy casualties from the very beginning and had been unable to achieve several of its goals simply because they did not have enough fighting men.

Even so, they had completed what they set out to do, which was to stage a massive diversion while the three old cruisers were moved towards the entrance to the canal, where they were to be scuttled. Unfortunately, one of them hit an obstruction before entering the mouth of the canal, and the remaining two ships were too small to make a complete blockage. Nonetheless the sunken ships provided a sufficient hazard to make the canal unusable by the U-boats, and after the war it took a salvage company almost a year to clear the wreckage.

As they began to sink, their crews were picked up by the fast launches. Meanwhile, the two old submarines *C1* and *C3*, packed with explosives, also hit problems. They were to be towed by destroyers towards a rendezvous point five miles from the viaduct, but *C1* came adrift and was delayed, so Lieutenant Richard Sandford, commander of *C3*, went on alone. Discarding the use of the automatic pilot, he and his crew gingerly steered a course to the viaduct. As he neared the viaduct, star shells burst overhead, providing the German gunners with near-daylight conditions to take range and fire. Sandford held a steady course and made it to the target, ramming the bows of the submarine into the side of the masonry.

Overhead there were howls of laughter as German troops on the viaduct mistakenly believed that the submarine had become accidentally stuck. Those who survived the next few minutes would know differently. With the time fuse set, Sandford led his five crew members out into the motor-driven skiff to make their escape. As they did so, they came under a hail of fire. Sandford took two bullets, and three of the others were also wounded. The skiff's motor was also hit, so they had to paddle their way out until they were picked up by a picket boat driven by Sandford's brother. As they clambered aboard the mother ship, they witnessed the satisfying blinding flash as their exploding submarine brought down the centre struts of the viaduct, which then collapsed.

The assault team was also to make its escape, called back to the ships by a Morse code 'K' sounding on *Daffodil*'s siren. The men were allowed ten minutes, and those who didn't make it were left behind to be taken into captivity or to be buried. The whole operation from the time *Vindictive* pulled in to her moving out took 70 minutes. Even as they drew away, they took heavy fire from the Germans. In all, 176 men were killed in the operation, 75 of them by a single shell, which hit the ferry *Iris* as she pulled away from the mole. A further 28 died later from their injuries, 386 were wounded, 16 others were reported missing and 13 were taken prisoner.

Back at Dover, the survivors of the raid were greeted with a heroes' welcome. King George sent Roger Keyes a telegram: 'I most heartily congratulate you and the forces under your command who carried out last night's operation with such success. The splendid gallantry displayed by all under exceptionally hazardous circumstances fills me with pride and admiration.'

Keyes was awarded a knighthood and given a grant of £10,000 by Parliament. An unprecedented number of medals was awarded to the men, including eight VCs, but even more remarkable was the method of selection. Keyes argued that there were so many deserving examples of heroism that he wished to invoke the little-used Clause 13 of the Victoria Cross Warrant, which allowed members of a particular unit to nominate one of their colleagues to be awarded the VC to represent them all. This was to be achieved by applying the social divisions in the Royal Navy at that time, which allowed officers to vote for their own candidates and the naval ratings and Marines to do the same.

Four nominees were named under this procedure, and Keyes himself selected four other VC candidates, along with a recommendation for the award of 21 DSOs, 29 DSCs, 16 medals for Conspicuous Gallantry, 143 medals for Distinguished Service and 283 names to be Mentioned in Dispatches. He also submitted 56 names for immediate promotion for service in action. The extent of his list of awards sent the hierarchy at the Admiralty into apoplexy. They objected to the selection by ballot and retorted that never had such a large number of awards been suggested for an operation of such duration. Some even made the point that with the huge numbers of deaths occurring in France and elsewhere in land-based actions of great importance, this might be felt as an extravagant gesture. Keyes stood his ground and wrote back complaining of the Admiralty's 'infernal rudeness'. The upshot was that most of the awards he requested were granted. After the war the Anglo-Belgian Union erected a memorial at the shore end of the Zeebrugge mole in the form of a figure of St George and the Dragon on the top of a tall column. People from all over England, Belgium and France subscribed to the memorial, which was unveiled by the King and Queen of Belgium on St George's Day in 1925.

There was also one poignant end to the story for the Royal Marines involving the second recipient of the Victoria Cross awarded by ballot in this operation to 30-year-old RMLI Captain (later Major) Edward Bamford. He had landed on the mole from *Vindictive* with three platoons of the Royal Marines from Portsmouth Company, storming ahead under heavy fire. The citation records that he commanded his company with total disregard of personal danger and 'showed a magnificent example to his men'. He first established a strong point on the right of the disembarkation and, when satisfied that it was safe, led an assault on a battery to the left. Edward, who already possessed the DSO for his gallantry aboard *Chester* at the Battle of Jutland, died in 1928 aboard *Cumberland* en route to Hong Kong and was buried in the Bubbling Wells Road Cemetery in Shanghai. Unfortunately, during the Cultural Revolution memorials to 'foreigners' were destroyed and a shopping centre was subsequently built on the site. However, a memorial to Edward Bamford was established at Depot Church in Deal, and in 2004 the Royal Marines presented a plaque in his memory to the town of Zeebrugge. As a further mark of respect to Bamford and Finch, no future RM battalion would be numbered the 4th.

CHAPTER SEVEN

Special Force or None at All?

In the immediate aftermath of the war, one more task arose for the embarked Royal Marines which was to have an unexpected and dramatic conclusion. One of the conditions in the Armistice demanded by the allies in the provisional terms of agreement placed before the Germans on 11 November 1918 was the surrender of their High Seas Fleet of 71 warships into the hands of the British to await dispersal among the allies. The ships were among the vast quantities of hardware, including aircraft, submarines, lorries and guns, that were to be handed over.

A reinforced detachment of Marines was aboard every ship and on fast-moving patrol boats weaving in and out as Admiral Sir David Beatty, commander of the British Grand Fleet, sailed to escort the ships into internment until the peace agreement – still subject to much haggling between the two sides, and between the allies themselves – was signed. Beatty was to accept the surrender of the German fleet on 21 November 1919 and then accompany the ships to internment at Scapa Flow. It was an event that caused great interest among the British public, not least for the sheer spectacle of it. Naval historian H. W. Wilson captured the moment aboard HMS *Royal Sovereign*:

In the Grand Fleet there was a general doubt whether some officers or some ships might not try a last stroke and prefer to perish in smoke and fire rather than accept this end of ignoble submission. There will always be desperate men to be reckoned with; therefore very special precautions were taken. The Grand Fleet was to approach the Germans with cruisers and fast craft ahead. It was to be formed up in two immense lines six miles apart, and between them the Germans were to proceed to internment exactly as two policemen, one on either side, conduct a malefactor to the police station.

Overhead, watching the Germans, the aeroplane squadrons from local stations were directed to fly. Thus provision was made against surprise and treachery. The whole [available] strength of the Grand Fleet was to be employed, [along with] five lattice-towered American super-dreadnoughts there under Rear-Admiral Rodman. There were two squadrons of battle cruisers and six of light cruisers, with eight flotillas of destroyers, a gigantic force overwhelming in its superiority. The order in which the Germans were to meet us was [they were to be in a single line with intervals of 600 yards between each ship's bow and the next astern]: nine battleships, five battle cruisers, seven light cruisers and 50 destroyers. The German ships were ordered to have their guns in the fore-and-aft position, in which they could not be trained upon our ships without attracting instant attention. Two examinations of them were to be carried out – the first by a small number of officers to make certain that their magazines were empty; the second, a complete and careful search as a precaution against booby traps and tricks of any kind, a work necessarily demanding hours of attention, as every compartment would have to be thoroughly inspected. The return of the fleet with its prizes to the Firth was one of the most splendid spectacles which man can imagine ... for miles the lines of British ships crossed the sea, moving with exquisite precision, with paint and brass work ... sparkling in the sun, with the glorious White Ensign flying and the signalmen busy with their rainbow hoists of signal flags. The ships of the First Battle Squadron, and the *Royal Sovereign* among them, cheered Admiral Beatty as they passed his flagship, the immense *Queen Elizabeth*, and he stood there in the evening sun waving his hand in this last ceremony of the Grand Fleet.

On arrival at Scapa Flow, the ships were anchored and skeleton crews, numbering upwards of 3,000 men, were kept aboard the interned ships for care and maintenance while the rest were sent back to Germany in transport vessels. And while the future of the ships was being determined – or so the allies thought – the British kept watch. Robert Shaw on *Royal Sovereign* found himself at the epicentre of dramatic events soon to unfold at Scapa Flow:

There were no British guards on the German boats, but there were usually a few patrol boats and other ships of the Grand Fleet that stood guard because the ships were interned rather than captured vessels. They would remain so until the Armistice was ratified and the peace agreement signed, and although we did not know it then, this would take months to achieve. Parties from our fleet went aboard each ship. They were in a pretty messy state, I must say, but then the ships' companies had not been used to living on board because in their home ports they generally had onshore accommodation. As the weeks passed, rats and cockroaches flourished, and quite a few sailors became ill. It was a pretty desperate time for all concerned.

Seven months passed while the allies argued over the terms of the Armistice treaty and their share of the spoils. The French wanted Germany partitioned, while British Prime Minister Lloyd George, fighting a general election at home, was demanding financial reparation 'to squeeze the German lemon until the pips squeak'. But even he felt the final resolution 'so harsh that we shall have to fight another war again in 25 years' time at three times the cost'. His words, of course, proved to be an exceedingly accurate assessment. Finally, in the third week of June 1919, terms were agreed and then, incredibly, the entire British Grand Fleet left Scapa Flow on 21 June for exercises in the North Sea, leaving just two destroyers and the smaller patrol vessels on guard duty. What happened next caused mayhem among the Admiralty hierarchy.

German Rear-Admiral von Reuter, in command of the interned fleet, watched the British fleet disappear over the horizon and then moved rapidly to an action that shocked the world. He signalled from his flagship *Emden* to the rest of his fleet a single word: 'Scuttle'. The skeleton crews, well aware of what was now expected of them, dashed to their prearranged stations and opened all sea cocks, portholes, torpedo ports and internal doors and in some ships laid explosive charges. They then made for their boats and headed for the nearest land.

Within an hour the scene was one of staggering desolation, with ships sinking in clouds of steam, foam and spray. Robert Shaw was among the few witnesses to the events:

I was left behind with the trawler patrolling the fleet, and we were embarking coal ready to go out when one of the destroyers left behind rushed by and said: 'Look what's going on.' I was horrified to see that the German ships were starting to sink. It was an incredible sight. . . . Some sank more quickly than others. It had to be done in a hurry, all the holes, so to speak, down below, such as the torpedo ports and so on, had to be opened up to fill the ships so that they'd sink. Then the crews took to their boats and made for the nearest land.

The Grand Fleet was alerted and made an immediate about-turn and raced back to Scapa Flow, arriving soon after 2 p.m. on 21 June.

Beatty quickly realised that there was little they could do to halt the scuttling of their charges, said to be worth £70 million. There were angry scenes as German crews were picked up, and nine Germans were killed that day and 10 others wounded, becoming the last casualties of the war as the Royal Marines led the task of rounding up the fleeing sailors. In all, five battle cruisers, ten battleships, five cruisers and 31 other ships were sunk, thus providing the British salvage industry with a decade of employment.

In a way, this event helped draw attention to the Royal Marines at a time when drastic cuts in the whole of the British military were under way. With 6,200 or more men still aboard the British fleet, the obvious questions were being asked. Where were they? Why did the fleet not remain until all possibilities with regard to the handover of the ships had been exhausted? But, of course, that was a general criticism, and not one that could be laid at the door of the Marines anyhow. In fact, it is quite evident from diaries, articles and histories of that period relating to the Royal Marines – in their own words – that they were equally unhappy about their presence at sea in peacetime. Being on the ships with no action in sight, as many noted, could become boring, but the navy insisted on maintaining a full complement of embarked Marines, regardless of what was happening in the outside world. Everything pointed to a need for reorganisation, a definitive policy of who they were and where the Marines should be deployed, with, importantly, the introduction of a career structure. But with Britain facing financial meltdown, the Treasury, trying to balance the horrendous state of the books, came up with its own solution: scrap the Royal Marines entirely.

After all, hadn't this been the 'war to end wars'? Supporters of the Marines, on the other hand, called for a clear and precise policy for the future that provided the RM detachments on ships with clearly defined roles, and, additionally, said that training should be introduced for those ashore for them to become the Royal Navy's 'strike force', to be deployed as and when needed in tasks that arose in faraway places in the British Empire with predictable regularity. But, outside of the ship, many admitted that a definitive role for the Marines was difficult to justify during that period of drastic cuts across all the armed forces. The Royal Marines themselves had been reduced after post-war demobilisation from a total of 55,000 to a corps strength of around 16,000.

The army, too, had quickly reverted to being the 'police force of the Empire' with a suitable reduction in manpower. The immediate effect on the Marines was the amalgamation of RMA and RMLI in 1923, which appeared to indicate that the top brass had come to the conclusion that the Royal Marines should no longer serve specifically as either gunners or infantry, and that their role should be in that of an all-embracing force with potential for amphibious operations about which there had been much talk but little action.

Their talent and availability for such operations was recognised and strongly recommended as early as 1924 by a committee of review of the Royal Marines appointed under the chairmanship of the much-respected Admiral Sir Charles Madden. His brief was to more or less predict the future role of the Marines in operations by sea or land. But he supported the view of the Committee of Imperial Defence that, despite the calls for reconsideration, in order for the navy to maintain its strength to meet all possibilities, the Marines should continue to be embarked on ships for naval gunnery but that the rest of the corps should be expanded to develop an independent striking force to undertake smaller-scale operations to seize and defend temporary bases or in raids on enemy coastal installations.

Further, as an indication towards Madden's favourable view of Combined Operations, the Marines, as part of the navy's overall commitment, would take part in landing an army on a hostile shore. Looking back, these recommendations came close to suggesting a form of seaborne Commando raiders, although the word was not used, nor would it be by anyone connected to the Royal Navy or the Marines at that time. Commandos (a word that can be applied to individuals or to units) were historically, as in the Boer War, army units and so, while the Marines might well not have objected to the use of the term, the Royal Navy certainly would have.

The definitions aside, Madden had drawn his evidence from a detailed examination of military disasters of the First World War and, specifically as far as the Marines were concerned, the huge losses suffered during amphibious troop landings at Gallipoli. Madden proposed that a 3,000-strong Royal Marines brigade should be set up to 'undertake raids on enemy coastlines and bases'. Anyway, this great opportunity to create a substantial unit in the style of Madden's suggestion came to naught, even though the Admiralty accepted the proposal for the formation of what it termed an 'independent striking force' of brigade strength for amphibious operations. They also accepted Madden's recommendation that a training centre be established for the new force, and that it should carry out exercises with the fleet. But that's as far as it went.

The reasons were twofold: memories of Gallipoli were still invoked when amphibious operations were discussed. Many of the old men at the top remained nervous at the prospect. Second, there had been great concern in a number of operations immediately after the war in which battalions of Royal Marines were formed from ship detachments run by officers who had spent their entire careers embarked on ships, and thus did not possess the management skills required for action on shore. These were serious considerations. Limited experimental amphibious training was carried out by the Marines, but the navy claimed then that they had neither the capability nor need for such an adjunct to the service, and there the matter rested for the time being. Certainly, the Royal Navy did not attempt to form any offensive amphibious capability, and that remained the case well into the early stages of the Second World War, when Commando-style formations were being muted, a void – as we will see – that was initially filled by the army.

There were, in fact, few occasions in the 1920s where such forces were required. Seven battalions had been formed specifically for clearing-up operations at the end of the war, while the 8th Battalion was mustered for duty in Ireland at the time of the Troubles to protect coastguard and signal stations around the coast and sensitive sites inland. A four-year assignment there prior to the Anglo-Irish Treaty was completed in 1923. On mainland Britain, the 9th and 10th Battalions were formed at the time of the 1921 miners' strike, deployed at strategic installations. Then, the 11th Battalion and detachments from Marines embarked in the Mediterranean Fleet, amounting to 3,600 men in all, landed in Constantinople to put themselves between the Turks and Greeks at various stages between mid-1920 to October 1922. The battalion, under Lieutenant-Colonel J. A. M. A. Clark, RMLI, included an RMA Heavy Batteries company. This time, the Turkish expedition claimed only one casualty, from malaria.

Later in the decade, the Royal Marines became part of the 20,000-strong Shanghai Defence Force, sent to China when the British government judged that British economic interests and communities were under threat from warlords and Bolsheviks led by Chiang Kai-shek. Troops were gathered up by British ships from various stations en route, but by the time they reached China after a rapid deployment in 1927 the emergency was over. Chiang fell out with the Bolsheviks and became an ally of the UK instead. So the force found it had little to do.

Consequently, whereas the inter-war years could have been used to create and train a seriously efficient Special Operations force within the existing Marines, they instead became years of wasted opportunities for which the Royal Navy itself and the then Committee for Imperial Defence, which drew up defence policy for government approval, shared the blame. Even by 1938 – already too late, anyway – the Chief of Imperial General Staff (CIGS) stated categorically that there were no plans to create any kind of Combined Operations' organisation using ships and landing craft to deliver soldiers or Marines against an opposing force on shore. In fact, in the late 1930s the Royal Navy possessed fewer than a dozen flat-bottomed landing craft, and neither RN commanders nor the CIGS showed any enthusiasm for reviving talk of offensive amphibious operations of a joint nature. A change of mind would soon become necessary.

The decision might well have been influenced by the lack of any such action that called for Combined Operations. The only other serious activity of the 1930s involving the Marines proved to be one of the building blocks of the Second World War, when Mussolini was embarking on his mission to create the second Roman Empire. The flexing of Italian muscle in the Mediterranean and Africa in 1935 was perceived as a potential threat to Britain's most vital naval bases in Malta and Alexandria and onwards to the Suez Canal. This was really a precursor to what followed four years later, but for the time being the Royal Marines combined with a show of naval strength in Alexandria, while at the same time the government offered a controversial hand of friendship to Mussolini the following year.

There was already little doubt by then that Hitler and Mussolini were about to form a double act, or the possibility that Japan would complete the Axis. But the Chamberlain government, desperate to avoid a war for which the nation was ill-equipped, was pursuing a policy of appeasement. Only modest forces were maintained on Malta, including a Royal Marines detachment of just 250 men and three officers, while the 1st Royal Marines Anti-Aircraft Battery boosted defences in Alexandria in 1939. Just across the water, Mussolini had assembled a large and capable air force, a fine navy and a powerful submarine and torpedo-boat fleet with which to cause trouble. Behind him were the beady eyes of Hitler.

The notion was that this British activity, in addition to the (hugely underequipped) Western Desert Force, would be sufficient to deter Mussolini from pursuing his ambitions into British-held territory following his invasion of Ethiopia. It wasn't. But, of course, Mussolini's adventures in East Africa were already overshadowed by developments across Europe, culminating in Hitler's march into Poland, and when war came the Royal Marines were left in a kind of time warp – i.e. 1914 all over again – with dual demands on their manpower, underequipped and with no clear and precise direction for immediate action. Were they to be gunners on the nation's ships or infantry and artillery ashore or would they turn themselves into Special Forces in Combined Operations? The age-old question remained, as did the animosity between army and navy, with the Marines as ever caught in the middle. There is little doubt that initially the organisation of the Marines into their wartime roles was far from satisfactory.

At the outbreak of war, the Royal Marines immediately became the chief provider of gunnery manpower for the Royal Navy, which had first call on them to provide a detachment and an RM band for every major British warship, from cruisers and aircraft carriers to capital ships, and in the Fleet Air Arm some Marines even trained as pilots. In that first month of September 1939, the total number of regular Marines was fewer than 14,000, although 1,000 retirees and reservists were already being recalled. The task from the outset was far more daunting, in that Marines were also called on to man the gunnery systems on defensively equipped merchant ships; although volunteers and conscripts began arriving in force for the army and Royal Air Force, the Marines had a far smaller intake.

The challenges were already emerging. As the so-called 'phoney war' on land played out in the months prior to Germany's blitzkrieg across Europe, it was a different story at sea, and for the first months of the war it was the embarked, seagoing Marines who were to see the most prolific action in several oceans, beginning with their covering the transfer of the British Expeditionary Force to France in October.

The British fleet was once again based in Scapa Flow, and this time the war of the waves was a very different story, with Germany ready to send out her fine new warships and, more crucially, her U-boats, which were soon out in force around the British Isles from the onset of the conflict. The Royal Navy was short of ships and aircraft, and many of its major vessels dated from before the First World War. The Germans were well aware of this, and in the first few months of the war engagements at sea bore the brunt of the exchanges between the two sides; consequently, the names of men of the Royal Navy and the Royal Marines filled the early lists of casualties.

The first major loss was one of Britain's four aircraft carriers, *Courageous*, victim of the Germans' ability to intercept and decode Royal Navy radio messages, a facility that they enjoyed until early

1943. At this stage of the war, very few British ships were equipped with radar, and submarines were difficult to spot on the surface, especially at night. *Courageous*, commissioned in January 1917 as a large light cruiser, was converted into a carrier and operated as such from May 1928. On 17 September 1939 Kapitän-Leutnant Otto Schuhart in the U-boat *U29* torpedoed and sank the carrier in the south-west approaches, 150 nautical miles off Mizen Head, Ireland. She went down in only 20 minutes, and 518 of her 1,200 crew went with her, including her commander, Captain W. T. Makeig-Jones.

Barely a month later, the Royal Navy suffered another shocking and humiliating loss when a U-boat famously achieved the 'impossible' and managed to get inside the supposedly impregnable naval harbour of Scapa Flow. Intelligence had provided the information that the entire British fleet was anchored there, and Kapitän-Leutnant Günther Prien in *U47* had been awarded the honour of attempting to hit the ships in their own domain, an idea that the Japanese usurped for their attack on Pearl Harbor. It was sheer good fortune that only a few days before Prien entered Scapa Flow, the entire fleet of Britain's finest had moved north to a safer haven because of the threat of aerial attack from German bombers, leaving only *Royal Oak*, flagship of the 2nd Battle Squadron, to act as an anti-aircraft guard for Kirkwall because the AA defences had not been completed at that time.

Once inside the hideaway, Prien brazenly cruised three or four miles across the calm surface of the Flow looking for targets and was about to give up when he spotted *Royal Oak* looming out of the murk and darkness. The First World War battleship had been modernised, along with others of the *Revenge* class, but was still a fine capital ship and on this occasion had taken on a new crew, including 120 boy sailors, in June 1939 and had sailed north to join the fleet at Scapa. Now, just before 1 a.m. on 13 October, Prien had the ship in his sights and manoeuvred his boat towards his quarry and gave the order to prepare to fire three torpedoes from the bow. All three slammed into her starboard side, 2,400 pounds of TNT exploding in a massive cascade of water and black smoke. Prien recalled later: 'Flames shot skyward, blue ... yellow ... red, like huge birds, black shadows soared through the flames, fell hissing and splashing into the water ... huge fragments of the mast and funnels.'

Royal Oak had been hit in an aft magazine and blazing cordite seared through her vents. 'It was like looking into the muzzle of a blowlamp,' was the description of one Marine amid the carnage of screaming, horribly burned men. Howard Instance, aboard the stricken ship, would remember the experience vividly, almost minute by minute, for the rest of his life:

The flames went straight up through the battery and would have incinerated anybody up there. All I could do was to huddle in the corner and cover my eyes and head and then I could feel the skin bubbling up ... it went on for ten, fifteen seconds, something like that, maybe more. But all of a sudden it stopped and it was pitch dark. The ship was in complete darkness. I went unconscious for about five minutes and when I came round I tried to stand up and I couldn't. I crawled across from the port side to the starboard side ... and when I got to the door I started to pull myself up and I suddenly realised then that I hadn't been crawling on the deck in the last 20 yards or so but on the bulk- head because she was over by about 60 degrees ... I knew by then she was going down and somehow I had to get out, although I was badly burned. A young midshipman was next to me hanging on the guardrails. He still had his telescope under his arm. I don't know who he thought I was in the dark but he said: 'Do you think we should abandon ship?' Before I could answer him the guardrails went under the water and we floated off into the terribly cold water. I laid on my back and I looked up and to my horror I saw the muzzles of two 15-inch guns slowly coming down on top of me. As the ship went over, the locking bolts of the turrets, which weighed about 300 tons, had sheared. I turned round and I swam the quickest hundred yards I've swum in my life until I was exhausted. I turned and looked back and against the night sky I could see the whole of the bottom of the ship as she was going over. The noise . . . the noise was terrific. The only way I can describe it is to say it's like having a large biscuit tin full of nuts and bolts and you turn it upside down. One can only imagine what was happening inside the ship . . .

Howard Instance's story was one of many such experiences among his colleagues on *Royal Oak*, and there were many examples of great heroism. In all, 833 men lost their lives, and of the 396 survivors many suffered severe burns and injuries. Howard, like a number of his colleagues, went through months of agonising skin grafts and treatment.

While the becalmed state of the ground war in Europe continued throughout the remainder of the year, at sea U-boats were taking a hefty toll on British merchantmen, with 115 ships sunk by the year's end. Many of those were down to the raiding operations of two of Germany's three pocket battleships, *Admiral Graf Spee* and *Deutschland*, which slipped out of Wilhelmshaven two weeks before the war began and headed off for operations in the Indian Ocean and the South Atlantic. It will be recalled that that was exactly the route taken by German marauders in the First World War, culminating in the Battle of the Falklands in which the renowned Admiral von Graf Spee went down with his ship.

This time, the *Graf Spee* name, borne by the pocket battleship, would cause havoc again. That ship and *Deutschland* were given free range to attack. They were fast and heavily armed, and easily a match for British cruisers. *Graf Spee*, under Captain Hans Langsdorff, carried six 11-inch guns and a secondary armament of eight six-inch guns. In ten weeks of operations, Langsdorff had sunk 50,000 tons of British merchantmen without loss of life to their crews, who were all picked up and taken prisoner. This was an important statistic to all sailors and the mark of an honourable captain. *Deutschland* was less successful and was subsequently called back to her home port to be renamed, Hitler realising the potential for embarrassment should she fall foul of British warships.

The roaming activities of *Graf Spee* continued to cause the British deep concern, if for no other reason than two key RN units, G Force, which patrolled the South Atlantic, and H Force, operating out of Cape Town, were spending half their time searching for the ship. Finally, after another string of sinkings, Winston Churchill, now back in command at the Admiralty, gave the order that *Graf Spee* must be hunted down and sunk with all due haste. Langsdorff's movements were plotted from reports of ships he had attacked and passed to Commodore Henry Harwood, commanding G Force. On 2 December Langsdorff sank ss *Doric Star*, which managed to send out a distress call shortly before the crew evacuated, putting their position in the mid-South Atlantic. From that, Harwood surmised that the most likely route would at some point take the German ship to the River Plate, where on the northern flank stood the neutral port of Montevideo and on the southern side pro-German Buenos Aires.

He was right, and soon all the elements were in place for one of the most fascinating episodes in naval history: the Battle of the River Plate, a tale that went well beyond that of mighty ships hurling shells at each other. Harwood had four cruisers under his command, one of which, *Cumberland*, was at Port Stanley for a refit. The remaining three were *Exeter*, under Captain Frederick Bell, Harwood's flagship *Ajax*, under Captain C. H. L. Woodhouse, and the New Zealand cruiser *Achilles*, under Captain Edward Parry. *Exeter* was an eight-inch-gun cruiser and the other two six-inch, all substantially outgunned by *Graf Spee*. There was also a good deal more riding on this battle than the ability of the ships. The German people were deeply unsettled by Hitler's failure to open up peace negotiations with the British, and the Führer needed a strong morale booster. The same applied in Britain, for different reasons. There was deep apprehension among a nation ill-prepared for war, and the PR spin from some good news would be a great fillip. Thus, on 13 December *Graf Spee*, Hitler's pride that he proclaimed would demonstrate that Britannia no longer ruled the waves, came into contact with G Force off the coast of neutral Uruguay. Commodore Harwood directed *Exeter* to steam west, while the two light cruisers moved in the opposite direction for a pincer movement. John Napier was on *Exeter*:

I had had a full night of action stations and off shift I went to sleep. At around 6.15 the bugler sounded action stations at the double. As I dashed to my station I could see smoke [from *Graf Spee*] on the horizon dead ahead. We could feel the vibration of the engines as the ship picked up speed towards the enemy. I remember the fall of shot from the enemy on either side of us, and at the same time we had been ordered from the bridge to take cover. At that order, myself and a colleague took shelter under the bridge superstructure. We hadn't been there a few minutes before the Marines in B turret had been hit, and the shell must have continued on straight through the bridge, killing most of the personnel except the captain and the commander. At the same time I was standing near the ladder that went up to the commander's cabin and at that time a decapitated head came tumbling down the steps and we recognised the face. We were devastated by the sight, and it is something I have never spoken of. The experience of it coming towards me shook me so much that I didn't know what to do with myself. It was terrible. I was just turned 20 at the time, although some of the sailors were 17 years old.

Langsdorff directed his 11-inch guns at *Exeter* for a full 25 minutes while his six-inch secondary armoury were sent towards *Ajax* and *Achilles* as they moved to their stations to open with their six-inch guns, which in fact did little damage and were unable to penetrate the German ship's protective metal but at least their harrying distracted the full attention of Langsdorff's guns. *Ajax* took further bad hits and Marine Lieutenant Ian De'ath was awarded the DSO for dealing with a serious fire in his turret. The situation on *Exeter* was also dire, as John Napier recalled:

I had the experience of seeing an 11-inch shell tear through the port side of the ship and come aft into the four-inch magazine and burst just past the magazine. The draught and the force of the wind, and the pressure coming up through the hatch, was terrific and at the same time the chief torpedo gunner's mate was blown up through the hatch. One of the damage control people went in directly after the shell had passed through and recognised our blacksmith and went to help him, and as he did so he literally fell to pieces. He must have been burned to smithereens. We were now on fire from the paint shop for'ard right to the bridge. We had jettisoned both aircraft but there was still a lot of aviation fuel about. People were busy up above washing down. We'd set a smoke screen and turned away to get Y turret bearing. When there was only one gun firing it was decided by the commodore to pull us out of the action. During this period our decks were swimming with water. The hydrants had burst in places through the shrapnel damage. I heard someone calling for help in directing steering orders from the after control position to the after steering position, and this I did until the ship drew out of the action and headed for the Falklands.

Before pulling away, *Exeter* had managed to land a direct hit that left a six-foot hole in the bows of *Graf Spee* before her own last turret was put out of action by another shell from the enemy. Meanwhile, *Ajax* and *Achilles* drew the Germans' fire with a fresh barrage of their own, and their shells, though not powerful enough to penetrate the main armour, were causing casualties and damaging the super-structure.

Exeter finally pulled out of the battle and headed off to the Falklands, shipping water and listing badly and with 62 of her crew killed and another 29 injured. *Ajax* and *Achilles* kept up the pressure and Commodore Harwood ordered them to close on *Graf Spee*. Although hit by two shells, which put two of her turrets out of action, *Ajax* landed more shells on the battleship, which started a serious fire. *Achilles* followed up with four torpedoes, which were avoided, but *Graf Spee* was already on the run, badly damaged and with 39 of her crew dead and more than 60 wounded. Remarkably, 62 captured British merchant seamen were safe and sound down below.

Captain Langsdorff pulled away, apparently having decided to seek shelter and repairs, a move that surprised Harwood, especially as he could easily have finished off *Exeter*. With his two remaining cruisers running short of ammunition, Harwood adopted the classic shadowing role, 15 miles from his prey. *Graf Spee* set a course for Montevideo, where the neutral government granted the German's request for shelter but limited her stay to just three days – nowhere near sufficient to carry out the repairs.

The two remaining British cruisers took station at the mouth of the River Plate, should the pocket battleship attempt to make a run for it. Langsdorff cabled Berlin, explained his plight and cited the three options open to him: to remain in Montevideo and accept internment, to try to make a run for it through neutral waters and then try to fight his way to Buenos Aires or – the unthinkable – to scuttle the ship. Although supposedly neutral, Montevideo had a pro-British president and was well known as a centre of intelligence intrigue, with the British representation well to the fore. The Germans now believed it was more than a possibility that if the battleship were interned it would not be long before vital codes and other secrets found their way into hostile hands.

All these possibilities and permutations were being eagerly discussed in the international press, and finally Captain Langsdorff sought a decision from Berlin: should he accept internment or scuttle the ship? Hitler himself made the decision: scuttle, and ensure that all security equipment and materials were destroyed. On 17 December 1939 all but a skeleton crew were taken off *Graf Spee* and transferred to the German tanker *Tacoma*, and shortly after 6 p.m. crowds lined the dockside as she weighed anchor for her last journey, surrounded by small boats carrying news media, cameramen and radio reporters. Four miles out of the River Plate, Langsdorff gave the order: stop all engines, drop anchor. He and the skeleton crew were taken off by steamer and soon afterwards there were six explosions aboard. *Graf Spee* blew up in a spectacular morass of flame and smoke.

Later that day Langsdorff rejoined the rest of his crew in Buenos Aires on the other side of the River Plate estuary. Two days later, overcome by remorse, he wrote letters to his family and then shot himself in his hotel room. His body was found lying across the German naval flag, which did not carry the swastika, that he had carried from *Graf Spee*. His funeral in Buenos Aires was attended by Captain Pottinger of the British merchant vessel SS *Ashlea*, representing the British crews whose ships had been sunk by Langsdorff but whose personal safety he had ensured. These were the prisoners who were still on board the *Graf Spee* when she docked in Montevideo. Almost another 300 were unaccounted for, and were in fact aboard the battleship's supply vessel *Altmark*, which had sailed unnoticed from Montevideo and made a dash for Germany, having dismissed the opportunity to land her prisoners at a neutral port.

The alert went up and, in spite of the needle-in-a-haystack potential, the Royal Navy picked up *Altmark*'s trail and she was spotted in the nick of time, in neutral Norwegian waters, and intercepted by destroyers. Captain P. L. Vian of *Cossack* challenged the German skipper, who denied he had any British prisoners. Unconvinced, Captain Vian pulled alongside and sent a boarding party scrambling on to *Altmark*. After a brief but violent fight, the men reached the hatches to the unlit hold and their leader shouted: 'Any British down there?' They were greeted by a loud, roaring cheer from below and out clambered 299 officers and men of sunken British merchantmen, starving hungry but otherwise safe and sound. There was an interesting postscript to the story concerning the fate of *Exeter*, now a heroic ship in the eyes of the entire British public. John Napier:

On the journey down to the Falklands [for repairs], there was a deathly quiet about the ship. We stopped twice during the journey to hold burial services. In Port Stanley, many of the wounded were taken ashore and put up in residents' homes because the ship was so badly damaged. We lost several other men from their wounds and they were buried locally. It was a remarkable effort. The hulk of ss *Great Britain* was lying there at the time, and we utilised some of the steel plates to make us watertight, and we worked for weeks cleaning up and making her habitable again, given all that had happened. That she was made good to get back to Britain under her own steam was nothing short of a miracle.

On the journey back, *Renown* and *Ark Royal* met us at Freetown and escorted us back to the western approaches, where we were met by eight or nine destroyers. At the same time as we were met by them, one of the Blue Star liners passed quite close to us and the men on board had waved and shouted to us as we passed. But, lo and behold, just as she got over the horizon we heard a thump and then a terrific bang. She'd been torpedoed. A lot of U-boats had been waiting for us and they'd missed *Exeter* and hit the liner instead.

Winston Churchill was waiting with a massive cheering crowd at the docks. He went on board and the occasion was used to promote a great story of British heroism and good fortune. Later, the crew took part in parades in London and attended a dinner at the Guildhall at which medals were presented by George VI. Theirs was a great story, and Britain was in need of some good news.

CHAPTER EIGHT

Commandos, but not Marines

In the decade before the outbreak of the Second World War a number of diverse studies had been made into various forms of guerrilla- or Commando-style units in the wake of the Madden Report that mentioned the Marines as 'striking forces'. The army, the navy and the Marines all had officers studying the creation of such forces within their own areas of operation, but separately. None had apparently been conferring with the other to any positive extent. Consequently, definite proposals for either Commando formations or Combined Operations between the three services did not arise until the spring of 1940, when the Atlantic coast of France was locked up and the Germans were on the brink of invading Norway.

By then, the Royal Marines were already under pressure to maintain shipboard and shore-base defences of the Royal Navy, which had first call on their services, and, bolstered by 'hostilities-only' recruits, the remainder were quickly earmarked for other tasks in the defence of the realm. This in turn meant they would miss out when the first experiments with the Commando ethos began in the spring of 1940, although, as we will see, there were other considerations that initially prevented the Marines from forming Commando units. In fact, it would be another two years or more before the land-based Marines officially became Commandos, the remaining force having now been placed in defensive mode to man an expanded version of the Mobile Naval Base Defence Organisation (MNBDO), which was formed in September 1939 with an establishment of 78 officers and 2,150 other ranks, with the aim of doubling that number by the spring of 1940.

However, equipment and vehicles were in short supply, with all available supplies being commandeered for the British Expeditionary Force going to France. This had the dual effect of increasing the need for adequate home defence installations while at the same time placing great demands on all available regular servicemen trained and equipped to meet the oncoming storm. The shortage of equipment, and men, delayed training programmes of Hostilities Only recruits for the MNBDO, which had to supply units for anti-aircraft gun placements, searchlight crews, gunnery and wireless instructors and coastal batteries, and 'the Organisation' was not fully operational until March 1940. Their brief was extended further with the creation of a Provost Company, Survey Section, HQ Defence Platoon and administrative sections.

Next came the formation of a Landing and Maintenance Group, utilising officers and men with experience of bridge-building for the movement of stores and vehicles over open beaches. As recruits grew in number, numerous small units were created for various other defence tasks, which became a vital role during the invasion scare following the Germans' rout in France. The Marines also found themselves in a variety of one-off tasks, such as protection for the removal of royalty and government heads from Europe and guarding various shipments of gold bullion to safe havens.

Running parallel to the latter stages of these developments, the army had already begun its own programme of introducing new units to meet the requirements at home and any other emergencies, notably with the formation of ten Independent Companies, which were the forerunner of Commando units and were based on studies made by a department within Military Intelligence. These studies were originally made by Major J. C. F. Holland, who had worked with T. E. Lawrence at the time he led Arab levies in revolt against the Turks and in support of General Allenby's triumphal advance into Damascus in October 1918. Holland was himself later wounded in Ireland and was given the task of studying guerrilla tactics in the mid-1930s. He was seconded to a research unit in the War Office to lead an appraisal of Special Forces, including the Boer Commandos, T. E. Lawrence and his use of guerrillas and the formation of special groups in more localised wars since 1918, including Britain's campaigns on the North-West Frontier. He was to report to the director of operations at Military Intelligence to a department that became MI(R).

Holland was joined by Lieutenant-Colonel Colin Gubbins, RA, who had served with him in Ireland as well as in northern Russia in 1919. MI(R) published a series of papers on guerrilla warfare, while Gubbins himself was sent on intelligence-gathering trips to the Danube valley, Poland and the Baltic states. He was in Poland when war broke out and escaped through Bucharest. MI(R) immediately wanted to put their ideas to the test by suggesting the raising of a battalion trained in the use of skis to be sent to the aid of the Finns in the spring of 1939 before the operation was eventually aborted by the end of the Soviet-Finnish dispute.

The MI(R) unit continued its work on other ideas, notably in the formation of units for irregular warfare techniques in the early months of 1940. These units were to be based almost exactly on the Boer Commando model although, brave and keen though they were, the initial line-up did not look at all encouraging, given that the bulk of British forces were already committed. The hurried plan was to form the Independent Companies, each consisting of 21 officers and 268 other ranks, and because time was so short they were to be raised largely from volunteers from the second-line Territorial Army divisions still in the United Kingdom. Since the whole setup was totally new to the British military, it was very much a case of make do and mend. Sir Ronald Swayne, who joined No. 9 Independent Company forming at Ross-on-Wye in April 1940, recalled his own experiences in words that speak volumes as to the planning of the raids and the readiness of the volunteers for any scrap:

I was in the 38th Division, which was a Territorial Welsh Border division, and I was selected from my regiment, the Herefordshire Regiment, to take a section of Herefordshire boys, which I did, selecting lads who came really from round my home, actually. It was all very nice and friendly. I called at my home on the way, stayed the night and the following morning my father drove me to Ross. As we approached the place where we were collecting, we saw a figure with his service cap pulled over one eye, with a Royal Welch Fusilier flash, wearing breeches without any stockings, gym shoes and swinging a shillelagh. He was a major, and he had certainly a DCM and bar and, I think, an MM. My father after a few minutes recognised him as a chap named Siddons who'd been his galloper in the Curragh in 1912 ... He was a terrifying figure, totally eccentric, usually drunk, anyhow, after about lunchtime ... He used to lecture us on how to kill people ... with a fork, a table fork and other instruments in trenches, and that sort of thing. And I was talking to my soldiers afterwards about it, and a nice young farm labourer called Jenkins asked me what I thought of it. He said, 'I don't think it's right, do you, Mr Swayne?' I said, 'No. I can't see myself doing it, can you?' 'No,' he said. 'I think it's very unchristian.' Well, Major Siddons wasn't a very Christian sort of chap. He was the original model of Brigadier Richie Hook, the fictional character in the trilogy *Men at Arms* by novelist Evelyn Waugh, who was soon to join us in the Commandos ... We eventually had a lot of characters like that; we did rather collect them ... [and] I have to admit it was all rather amateurish in the beginning. I don't think, at that point, the Jerries would have been too scared of us.

*

By the end of April 1940 the ten Independent Companies had been formed largely from local TA and county regiments, from Somerset to East Anglia, the Midlands, the north and on into Scotland and Northern Ireland, each designated simply by the number in the order in which they were formed. They were little more than groups of young inexperienced men drawn from a cross-section of British life, but the army had made its own start into the world of 'guerrilla' units, such as they were, and they were very soon called into action. Prevented by bad weather and adverse intelligence reports, the German High Command delayed its invasion of the Low Countries and instead Hitler approved the invasion of Denmark and Norway on 7 April through eight ports from Narvik and on down around the western and southern coastline to Oslo and, for the first time ever, using airborne troops to secure inland sites.

Within 48 hours, seven divisions had landed and captured all the main ports, while the airborne troops secured their position in Oslo and major airports. The weather halted planned parachute drops at Oslo airport, and infantry troops were landed in a succession of Junker 52s. Five companies of parachute troops did drop at other key airports, and the Germans established a firm hold on the southern half of Norway.

The Norwegian government decided to make a stand and sent word inviting the British and French to dispatch troops immediately to their assistance. The British army, already heavily committed with the BEF in France, sent troops who included the Independent Companies backed up by a Royal Navy task force and RAF fighter force consisting of bombers and fighters, the latter to be included in Fleet Air Arm action involving both RAF and Royal Navy fliers, with the carriers *Ark Royal* and *Glorious* coming up behind in support. Allied troops were to land in three places on the Norwegian coast, led ashore by Royal Marines from the cruisers *Sheffield* and *Glasgow*.

The Marines were to secure roads and bridges immediately ahead of the landing areas before the arrival of General Carton de Wiart's scratch contingent, and he was to be joined by other allied troops already on their way. It quickly became apparent, however, that the vast and rugged Norwegian coastline was no place for ill-equipped British troops, who had no suitable clothing, boots or transport for such conditions and certainly had received little or no training ahead of the expedition. Most of de Wiart's men had hardly ever seen such terrain and most had only modest soldiering experience up to this point. Nor did they have the clothes for it. While the Germans were kitted out in white uniforms and were equipped with skis and other made-to-measure accoutrements to suit the conditions, the 'special clothes' provided for the British troops consisted of fur coats, thick knitted jumpers, heavy-duty socks and gardening boots that leaked. As the general opined later: 'If my troops had worn all of those things together, they would have been unable to move about and looked like paralysed bears.'

When they arrived, the Royal Navy moved in to harass the Germans in what became known as the First and Second Battles of Narvik, on 10 and 13 April respectively. The first battle involved the 2nd Destroyer Flotilla under Captain B. K. W. Warburton-Lee made up of five H-class destroyers, *Hardy*, the flagship *Havoc*, *Hostile*, *Hotspur* and *Hunter*. In blizzards and fog, they moved into Westfjord and then on through Ofotfjord to enter Narvik Bay, where a far superior German destroyer force awaited them, along with a number of supply ships. In a sharp battle, the British sank six supply ships, two large German destroyers and damaged five for the loss of two destroyers. Among the casualties was the task force leader, Captain Warburton-Lee, who was later posthumously awarded the Victoria Cross for his courageous administration of the attack.

On 12 April the RAF joined in. Bomber Command launched 80 aircraft to hit German positions around the Norwegian theatre in daylight raids. But with a network of anti-aircraft guns already in position, the Germans shot down nine precious bombers, and thereafter Bomber Command restricted the Norway raids to attacks on enemy airfields and minelaying operations. The following day the Second Battle of Narvik opened up when a larger Royal Navy force with the battleship *Warspite* steamed towards Narvik habour to attack eight German destroyers and seven supply ships. Marines on board *Warspite* joined the action with an incessant bombardment of the shore batteries, and anything else that came into view, with 15-inch shells that caused the Germans much grief.

These two attacks on the German ships at Narvik were a preamble to the allied invasion of ground troops, which was preceded by a number of smaller landings by British troops to the south, around Trondheim and Bergen, again covered by Marines. With German aircraft screaming overhead, they made little impact, in spite of cover from the Navy's C-class anti-aircraft ships, *Cairo*, *Curlew*, *Coventry* and *Calcutta*, heavily staffed by Marines who were to be extensively engaged around the whole of the western coastline during the Norwegian campaign from mid-April until early June.

They were to be joined on 22 April by regular British army units along with a massive bombardment by the Royal Navy's capital ships carrying all the Marines that could be mustered for the gunnery tasks that lay ahead, supported by RAF fighters – including Hurricanes – brought up by the carriers *Glorious* and *Ark Royal*. A combined force of 24,000 allied troops was now available to fight the Germans, including Norwegian and British units, French Foreign Legion, the French 27th Chasseurs Alpins and a small Polish contingent. Leading the task force, now, was the brilliant First World War battleship *Resolution*, which had just completed the 'gold run' – delivering shipments of gold from the British vaults into safekeeping in Canada. She was deployed north of Narvik, with Marines and naval gunners bombarding the shore to cover the landing of the Legionnaires while under constant attack from German bombers. Frederick Hutchison, on the ship, recalls a poignant moment when the Royal Marines' band was hit:

We watched the Legionnaires going ashore and charging up the beach to attack the Germans. We always had a good view, because there was never any darkness. On the other hand, we were also good targets and we were subjected to continuous and heavy bombing from German aircraft. It got so bad in the end that we ran out completely of four-inch anti-aircraft shells. The ship remained at anchor at all times during those raids because the fjords were so narrow you just had to lie there and take whatever came. We became very, very efficient with our gun drill. At times we were not allowed to leave the gun. Our food was brought up and we could only take snatches of sleep between raids. The captain was still trying to maintain a level of discipline and used to parade the Royal Marines' band for the colours at eight every morning. And one particular morning the band was marching up and down the deck ready for colours and a German aircraft came over, catching the band unawares. There was a cacophony of noise as the band disappeared down below.

The Marine bandsmen headed for their mess deck but unfortunately, in the next wave of attacks, a 250-pound armour-piercing bomb dropped by a Ju-88 penetrated three decks between X and Y turrets, exploding on the band's mess deck, killing two and injuring 27. Temporary repairs were made by the crew and the ship remained in Norway until June 1940, when the troops were evacuated. The *Resolution* gunners, meanwhile, continued the bombardment of the shore positions with 15-inch guns on Narvik and other ports along the coast, firing from a range of up to 15 miles away, liaising with the army ashore.

The ground invasion at Narvik was given added support from bombers and fighters. They included the RAF's No. 263 Squadron equipped with Gloster Gladiators, the last biplane fighter in British service and no match for German equipment. Two days after their arrival, ten of the Glosters were still on the ground at a makeshift airstrip when they were virtually wiped out by Ju-88s and Heinkel 111s. The allies now relied on the 18 precious Hurricanes flown by the RAF's 46 Squadron and the Fleet Air Arm's much-loved but totally ineffective squadron of Swordfish that looked like toys against the Germans' vastly superior airpower.

However, notwithstanding early setbacks under a hail of superior German ordnance, this first Combined Operation of the war began to swing effectively into action, and gradually, by sheer weight of numbers against a lesser ground force, pushed the Germans back to the Swedish border. Battle commanders were confidently expecting to register an historic success when news of the German invasion of France came through. The following day, signals came from London ordering a total withdrawal of the entire allied force immediately. The air force was to cover the evacuation of the troops from the various fjords by destroyers.

As soon as the Germans got wind of the British evacuation, they began a massive aerial bombardment and moved battleships, destroyers and U-boats to the North Sea to attack the departing British convoys. The results were to be catastrophic. At all points of evacuation the movement of the British flotillas into the open sea was carried out under heavy fire from the constant air attacks. The remaining RAF fighters, the last to leave, put up a brilliant effort but were hopelessly outclassed by wave after wave of the Luftwaffe's finest, and the allied ships steamed out under murderous swooping fire. Lieutenant John Mosse, RN, in the destroyer *Havelock*:

> We heard the scream of a dive bomber as it roared out of the sky and dropped two bombs just astern of *Southampton*. Arriving in formations of fifteen or twenty planes at a time, they bombed us incessantly for two hours. Everyone increased to full speed and manoeuvred independently within the narrow limits of the fjord which was only three miles wide. The valley reeked with the bitter stench of cordite fumes from the guns. Time and again the ships were hidden from one another by vast columns of water.

Charles Hutchinson, in the anti-aircraft cruiser *Carlisle*, covering the evacuation from Namos, saw five planes swoop down on the French destroyer *Bison* and a bomb burst on the forecastle. Soon she was a cloud of smoke:

> Three destroyers went to stand by her [to take off survivors]. *Afridi* was the last to leave her, when a fresh batch of planes came. I saw a huge explosion on *Afridi*, she heeled over, her bows dipped low into the water. We steamed slowly on, guarding the troopships. It wasn't long before *Afridi* went down. What a tragedy after picking up the survivors of the French destroyer.

Several ships in the convoys were sunk or seriously damaged before they managed to pull away into the open sea, but there in the vast expanse of water ahead lurked a greater danger that promised to represent a major task ahead for the Royal Marines and navy gunners. The infamous German battle cruisers *Scharnhorst* and *Gneisenau* were, unknown to the allies, out there somewhere with the cruiser *Hipper* and destroyers. On 8 June, as the allied convoy cleared Norwegian waters, the captain of aircraft carrier *Glorious* decided, against the advice of his Fleet Air Arm colleagues, to press on ahead of the allied ships in company with two destroyers to return to Scapa Flow. Later inquiries revealed that he was hurrying back to Scapa to instigate a court martial against an air commander with whom he had had a violent row over the deployment of aircraft earlier in the campaign.

Scharnhorst and *Gneisenau* were on his tail, 20 minutes before he realised it. When their smoke was eventually spotted on the horizon, the two accompanying destroyers, *Ardent* and *Acasta*, turned to take on the approaching battle cruisers. *Ardent* was sunk almost immediately. *Acasta*, however, managed to fire two torpedoes, which hit *Scharnhorst* and put two of her three engine rooms out of action, before she herself was sunk. *Glorious*, meanwhile, had taken severe hits from *Hipper*, shell after shell fired from ten miles away. With 1,474 of her own ship's company as well as the RAF pilots and their badly needed Hurricanes aboard, she was sinking fast. Sir Kenneth Cross, then commanding the RAF contingent, was among the last to leave the devastated ship and paid tribute to the work of the Marines in the drama that followed:

The captain piped 'Abandon ship' but then, for some reason, he belayed the order. We just didn't know what was going on. Then finally the pipe came again and by this time there was a big list. There were bodies all over the place. The planes were on fire in the hangars; everything was just chaotic. The Marines tried to get things organised. They were cutting the Carley life-floats free and throwing them into the water and then telling the number of men they would carry to jump in after them. But eventually they were completely overwhelmed and those of us who could make it were going to go over the side. *Glorious* was a big ship, well out of the water, and the lifeboats couldn't be lowered down. They had no alternative; you had to get away. She was burning furiously.

Being in the water was no guarantee of safety. There were insufficient rafts; there was not another ship in sight and the water was fatal:

The ship was 40 miles inside the Arctic Circle, miles from anywhere, and the sea was ice-cold. The Germans didn't hang about to pick us up; they just cleared off as our trio of ships went down; there were so many bodies and fellows in the water, people dying with the cold, hundreds shouting and crying and then dying. We just couldn't understand why no one was coming to search for us or rescue us. I saw this Carley float and I swam towards it. It was totally overloaded, about 60 men aboard, all standing up. I tried to get on, but some were shouting that it was full up. I shouted back, 'It's not a bloody bus service.' And I pushed myself on. The padre was on board and he tried to keep our spirits up. He got us all singing and so on, but it didn't last. A number of the men became delirious and even by the end of the first day a lot had died. As it went on day after day, our hope of being rescued was fading, and these chaps were dying by the hour so that on the fourth day there was only myself and another boy left. To begin with, we had to slide the bodies into the sea, but in the end we were too weak, and when we were finally rescued there were eight bodies in the bottom of the Carley, and we just sat on the side. We were picked up by a Norwegian trawlerman who was escaping from Norway to go to the Faeroes . . . pure luck. In fact, there were only 36 still alive out of all the floats – 36 men out of almost 3,000 men [in the three ships]. Why did we survive, and all the others didn't? It's something I will never know . . . the sea is a funny thing, mysterious . . .

The rest of the Narvik task force came back, damaged but unbowed, into a new world of military activity. The German blitzkrieg finally came to the Low Countries, and the British Expeditionary Force began its unhappy retreat to the coast. The British nation went into shock, not least among them the military analysts when, in the aftermath, they pieced together the elements of the German invasion strategy: the lightning speed of the Panzer divisions that totally overran defences, backed up by the fearsome accuracy of the airborne artillery provided by the Ju-87 Stukas and the devastating – and totally unexpected – arrival of airborne and parachuted troops.

By the end of May the British Expeditionary Force was being evacuated from France, forced into a narrow beachhead around Dunkirk and, famously, hundreds of small craft of all kinds joined the Royal Navy's sealift to rescue 338,226 men from the beaches. In all, 222 naval vessels and 665 other ships were involved in the evacuation. Many thousands were killed, wounded or taken into captivity, and a very large slice of Britain's entire stock of weaponry, tanks, guns, lorries and general stores lay wrecked by the departing troops and burning on the roads and in the fields on every approach to the

Dunkirk beaches and other exit points along the coast. The inventory of weapons and equipment lost was staggering: 475 tanks, 38,000 vehicles, 12,000 motorcycles, 8,000 telephones, 1,855 wireless sets, 7,000 tons of ammunition, 90,000 rifles, 1,000 heavy guns, 2,000 tractors, 8,000 Bren guns and 400 anti-tank guns. On 6 June 1940 the War Cabinet was informed that there were now fewer than 600,000 rifles and only 12,000 Bren guns left in the whole of the United Kingdom and the losses would take up to six months to replenish.

Winston Churchill became Prime Minister and said it was 'a miracle of deliverance' that so many had been brought home. It also put a new emphasis on how to fight the enemy across the water and, short of the all-out invasion that came in 1944, that could only mean raiding parties and what Churchill himself called 'butcher and bolt' tactics. Churchill well knew the tale of the Boer Commandos. He had resigned his cavalry commission in 1899 to become a war correspondent and had been captured by the Boers, escaping with a price on his head to return home a national hero. Within 24 hours of becoming Prime Minister on the day Hitler began his march into the Low Countries, Churchill was looking for proposals for the creation of Special Forces of a kind that did not exist in the British military – Commandos and paras to spearhead assaults on German positions.

Picking up on the studies already carried out by both army and navy on the formation of such forces, a definitive proposal was prepared by Lieutenant-Colonel Dudley Clarke, RA, as military assistant to General Sir John Dill, Chief of the Imperial General Staff. These proposals were in report form two days after the Dunkirk evacuation was completed and approved at a meeting between Dill and Churchill on 9 June, although given that such an outfit could become operative in overseas operations only by tapping the resources of all three services – including the Royal Air Force – they were to be administered under the general heading of Combined Operations.

As an adjunct to this agreement, Churchill insisted that the men should be robust and properly trained, clothed and armed with the latest equipment, given that Europe was for the time being an impossible destination for any form of conventional troop landings. That was not a description that could be applied to the ten Independent Companies formed by the army, and they were now to be disbanded. Neither would large numbers of the original recruits be eligible for inclusion, given the particular nature of the men the recruiters were seeking.

The invitation that went out to barracks across the country asked trained personnel to apply for 'special duties of a hazardous nature', with the stipulation that 'volunteers must be able to swim, be immune from sea and air sickness, possess courage, physical endurance, initiative and resource, marksmanship, self-reliance and an aggressive spirit towards the war. They must become expert in military use of scouting ... and to move across any type of country by day or night, silently and unseen and live off the country for considerable periods.'

The vision of clandestine operations was expanded further, of course, with a whole range of seaborne and airborne Special Forces, saboteurs, espionage agents and the like that eventually emerged under this ethos, such as the renowned Special Operations Executive, the Special Air Service, created from within the Commandos, and likewise the Special Boat Service. In fact, long before David Stirling formed the SAS in Egypt, No. 2 Commando had provided volunteers for the first-ever paratroops in Britain, known as 11 Special Air Service Battalion, formed in 1940 and trained at Ringway, Manchester, where the first parachute training centre was being built.

Some in the higher echelons of the military objected to the name Commandos and from the beginning wished to call them Special Service units, despite the similarity of the title to the despised German SS. At that point, another inexplicable curiosity arose – at least to internal observers who were aware of it: although the creation of the Commandos had been the responsibility of the army, the first Director of Combined Operations (DCO) was Sir Alan Bourne, the current Adjutant-General of the Royal Marines, who was already fully conversant with the many Commando-style activities of his organisation earlier in the century.

His appointment seemed to have the advantage that the Marines were ideal candidates for Commando action and it was widely anticipated that they would form the backbone of the new organisation. But, in fact, the age-old animosity between army and navy came into play, even at that critical time, and the Marines did not have the opportunity of volunteering. The Admiralty and senior officers were worried about the possible depletion of their Marines and the Marine bands from their ships, and from the other land-based units. They especially did not want their chaps in units effectively under army control, nor were they keen on the idea of losing their independence in operations planned by the Combined Operations executive. In any event, according to Lord Mountbatten's biographer Philip Ziegler, the Admiralty considered the whole idea to be somewhat dubious.

Consequently, General Bourne's tenure as DCO lasted exactly one month, when he asked to be returned to the Marines. Churchill replaced him with Sir Roger Keyes, hero of Zeebrugge, which further alienated the Marines from participating in the Commandos. Ziegler noted: 'Under Keyes, the Marines fought shy of losing their independence and remained in unhappy isolation [in their new base] in Wales, until Mountbatten vigorously tried to woo them. For some time, they resisted his blandishments; then [in 1942] Colonel Bruce Lumsden took his battalion over to Combined Operations. The rest followed.'

Some still believe it was the right move on the part of the Marines to stand back and wait to see how the scheme developed. Certainly there were many in all quarters who were deeply suspicious of the usefulness of these bands of brothers who attracted a fair few eccentrics and egotists. Not least among the latter was the head of Combined Ops himself, Roger Keyes, then 64, and, being an excitable sort of chap, he had many detractors. Equally, it has to be said, he kickstarted the concept of Combined Operations.

Yet, Keyes began his term as DCO with mistrust and little cooperation from the military top brass, who by then were more concerned with actually winning the Battle of Britain, in which, incidentally, the Royal Marines were already playing their part, in both defensive positions and embarked on warships. In the meantime, the Commandos, without the participation of the Marines, came into being and went into training ostensibly as coastal raiders, under the overall auspices of Combined Operations.

Keyes took over the Irregular Warfare School started at the country estate of one of their leading participants, Lord Lovat, at Inverailort in May 1940 by MI(R) for the Independent Companies. Initially, each Commando was responsible for its own training, supervised by specialists in armed combat, weaponry, demolitions and medics. But because of the wide variations in the way troop leaders believed their men should operate, training schedules were later standardised at a training depot at Achnacarry Castle in Lochaber, while Inverailort was taken over by the Special Operations Executive. The school was a great success, according to former Independent Company commander Ronald Swayne, by then with No. 1 Commando:

> The whole Commando world attracted some very strange characters to it. Some were extremely confident, useful people who were very successful later in the war. Several were just total eccentrics, and the training centre became a sort of home for some of them. Some of them added a lot of imagination to training and I think helped and developed the eventual character of the Commandos. Talk among returning officers was of great tests of physical endurance, a trial of strength in every respect.

Winston Churchill himself, meanwhile, kept up the pressure. In a memo to Anthony Eden of 25 August he wrote:

> If we are to have any campaign in 1941 it must be amphibious in its character and there certainly will be many opportunities for minor operations, all of which will depend on surprise landings of lightly equipped mobile forces accustomed to work like packs of hounds instead of being moved about in the ponderous

manner which is appropriate. These have become so elaborate, so complicated in their equipment, so vast in their transport that it is very difficult to use them in any operation in which time is vital. For every reason, therefore, we must develop the storm troop or Commando idea. I have asked for 5,000 parachutists and we must also have at least 10,000 of these small 'bands of brothers' who will be capable of lightning action. In this way alone will those positions be secured which afterwards will give the opportunity for highly trained regular troops to operate on a larger scale.

Even Churchill's description of amphibious soldiers seemed to fit the Royal Marines to a tee, but their time on the Commando trail would come much later and, some say, when it mattered. For the time being a second unit of the Mobile Naval Base Defence Organisation (MNBDO II) would be formed at the Royal Marine Barracks at Eastney before being transferred to North Wales for a year to begin their own training for future operations, with an air of mystery attached which later attracted rumours of secret operations and preparations for the invasion.

In any event, as is apparent from the foregoing, the Marines were never short of employment. From the very beginning, the Royal Navy was fully stretched in its various arenas of battle in several oceans, some of which we have already visited and discussed some of the early consequences, and the war was still in its first year. Marine detachments and Royal Marine bands would be embarked on a total of 20 capital ships, 101 cruisers and 65 carriers over the duration of the war, a figure that must be offset by overall losses of five capital ships, 34 cruisers and 10 carriers in the process. They thus suffered high casualties, killed, wounded and captured.

Royal Marines crews always manned a main armament turret and secondary armaments in every ship. They also manned a heavy anti-aircraft battery of two twin barbettes in most carriers. For those in the Royal Marines bands, which were embarked in every ship from small cruisers to capital ships, the provision of music often became their secondary role in times of war. They were accommodated deep in the bowels of the ship performing the crucial function of plotting the fire-control table in the transmitting station.

In addition to the MNBDO units, a Royal Marines division was formed consisting of three brigades: the 101st RM Brigade (3rd and 5th RM), the 102nd RM Brigade (1st and 2nd RM and 8th Argylls) and the 103rd RM Brigade (7th, 8th and 9th RM and, later, 10th RM). In the event, these brigades were grossly under-used, partly because they were constantly being earmarked for operations that never materialised or were cancelled, but mainly because the naval hierarchy, either at the Admiralty or the RM management or both, refused to allow the brigades to fall under army direction, as had happened with, as they saw it, some unfortunate consequences in the First World War.

The old animosities still persisted, and these had the unfortunate effect of keeping large numbers of Royal Marines out of any real action for months on end. Ironically, it was only when they became involved alongside or in conjunction with the army in the principal theatres of the land war or on Combined Operations that they began to flourish as a fighting force.

CHAPTER NINE

Disasters at Crete and Dieppe

While the Commandos were in Scotland training for future operations, and the diverse teams with the MNBDO were building strength utilising recruits from civilian trades for their various defensive undertakings around the coast and home defence batteries, the Battle of Britain was raging and the Royal Navy and the Marines at sea were under great pressure. There were obvious shortages for the newly formed or enhanced Marine units whose roles were generally applied to the defence of the nation. Weaponry was initially of 1920s vintage and supplies of everything were difficult to come by. G. K. Hewitt, with the MNBDO, remembered: 'We picked mushrooms to help with our rations and we had lectures on what MNBDO's war role was. When an enemy port was captured, we were to move in and consolidate. This never happened . . . it is best to draw a veil over this [period].'

Similar frustrations were experienced in the RM brigade, originally formed to perform 'certain amphibious tasks which did not require the full supporting weapons or the services of an army division'. This was a curious statement, given that at the time in Britain there was still no capability for offensive amphibious landings, as the Commandos had already discovered. The RM brigade was, up to the time of Dunkirk, among the very few fully trained units left in the country to meet any invasion threat. When the BEF returned, the countryside was awash with soldiers, and the brigade was earmarked for a number of these so-called amphibious tasks for which the brigade had been formed, but without exception they were either never started or were cancelled without a shot being fired. These included operations to destinations such as the Azores, Cape Verde and the Canaries, where they were either actually under way to their destinations or indeed had landed. But at least they travelled in style, in passenger liners still to be converted into troop carriers, with white-coated stewards still in attendance. It was an impossible dream, however, to expect them to be ready for battle under such circumstances, especially in that the only form of 'amphibious landing' they possessed was to pile the troops into the ship's lifeboats and tow them ashore by motorboat because there were simply no landing craft. It was clearly going to take some time to resolve these frustrations, and in retrospect it did appear to be taking an inordinately long time.

At sea the embarked Marines were still under pressure, and immediately ahead was a task that no one in Britain's warships relished, but in the end had to be undertaken: the sinking of the French fleet. While the French were signing an armistice with the Germans in Paris, secret meetings were arranged in Bordeaux between British and French diplomats inviting Admiral J. L. Darlan, Commander-in-Chief of the French Navy, to sail his entire fleet to the West Indies, where the ships could remain under Royal Navy protection. But the armistice agreement changed everything, and it became apparent that the commander and others in the French hierarchy claimed they were unable to do so because of the conditions laid down by Germany. Contact with Britain was ended, and Churchill's War Cabinet was faced with the decision of whether to accept the situation or to send the Royal Navy to sink those ships of the French fleet that it could reach: battleships, destroyers and submarines anchored off the North

African coast, at Casablanca, Oran, Dakar and Alexandria. Part of the problem could be immediately dealt with: two battleships, four light cruisers, five submarines, eight destroyers and a number of smaller craft were already lying in England, off Portsmouth and Plymouth.

These were impounded on the afternoon of 3 July, when negotiations with the French finally broke down. At the same time in Alexandria, Admiral Sir Andrew Cunningham, Commander of the Royal Navy's Mediterranean Fleet, swung the fleet's guns on its former allies in Force X, consisting of one battleship, four cruisers and some smaller ships, and achieved possession without firing a single shell. It was a different story in Oran, where the French ships harboured at Mers-el-Kebir represented the biggest threat to the Royal Navy if they were to fall under German or Italian control. They included the two finest battleships in the French fleet, *Dunkerque* and *Strasbourg*, two older capital ships, one carrier, two cruisers, nine destroyers, six submarines and many smaller craft.

At Algiers there were seven cruisers and an aircraft carrier, while at Dakar the brand-new *Richelieu* had been undergoing final preparations for action, along with several other French ships. The British War Cabinet had agreed that, if the French refused to cooperate, the French ships would be sunk. This decision was delivered to the French Admiral Gensoul in command at Oran by Flag Officer, North Atlantic, Admiral Sir Dudley North, travelling by fast destroyer. He was ceremoniously welcomed aboard the French admiral's flagship, *Dunkerque*, but the British emissary received not a hint of cooperation or agreement. He reported back to Vice-Admiral Sir James Somerville, commanding the Mediterranean-based Force H, which had just been supplemented with the arrival, fresh from the Norwegian campaign, of *Ark Royal* and *Resolution*. They were later joined by the battleship *Warspite* and a protective screen of two flotillas of destroyers. Somerville, in his flagship *Hood*, Britain's largest and most impressive battle cruiser, then delivered a final ultimatum from the British: that the French fleet could join the Royal Navy and fight the Axis forces or sail with reduced crews under British control to a port where they would be demilitarised, or be entrusted to the still-neutral United States. The alternatives were that the French would be allowed to scuttle their own ships within six hours or Somerville would immobilise (i.e. sink) the French fleet.

When it became clear that none of the options was acceptable to the French, the navy and Marine gunners of Force H demolished the main part of the French fleet, with the loss of 1,250 French sailors killed. Somerville now moved on to Dakar, where another group of hostile commanders awaited the arrival of the British. Donald Cameron Gibson, who had come from action in Norway with *Ark Royal*, recalled: 'The French were in a very bad temper that we were destroying their fleet. *Ark Royal* was being fired at by shore batteries as soon as we arrived in Dakar. It was a complete shambles. Our job was to protect our ships from French fighters, who came out and tried to attack us.' Theodore Joughlin, RN, on board *Resolution* provided testimony for the conditions under which the navy and Marines' gunners went into action:

Our prime target was *Richelieu*, the brand-new ship. We were stood well offshore waiting. It was incredibly hot . . . the chaps in the turret must have been losing pounds and pounds in sweat. We lost one lad who died through drinking cold water. He got stomach cramps, and they warned us not to drink cold water but to drink tea or something warm. This lad from Gateshead was in one of the turrets. We buried him later at sea. The battle-ship *Barham* was to be the one that fired at the *Richelieu* if the negotiations failed, which they did. On the third morning we went in at nine o'clock with the *Barham* ahead of us, and we noticed a buoy had been placed at a point where we turned into the bay. We realised – too late, I suppose – that it was a marker to line us up for being torpedoed. As we went in, one of the French submarines fired six torpedoes at us. One hit us full on . . . a powerful strike and we heeled over. I thought we were going to turn turtle. But we didn't, although we remained at an acute angle, and we were badly damaged. The submarine surfaced and put up a white flag, but one of our destroyers rammed it and sank it. *Barham* had hit the *Richelieu* with her 15-inch guns, striking her stern, and a number of other, smaller French ships were sunk. We were in a bad way, and it was panic stations. We couldn't use our engines and we just sat there and the French sent a plane out from Dakar to bomb us. I saw the bomb coming out of the sky, a massive thing, but fortunately it missed the ship completely and caused no damage. There were other aircraft about and battles with our own planes from the *Ark Royal*. We had to get away, but couldn't move until *Barham* took us in tow all the way to Freetown, where we were laid up for about four months.

The sinking of *Richelieu* was the final act in this unfortunate affair, which Admiral Cunningham described in a message to his officers as 'a difficult situation for us all, but one that has to be cleared up so that we can get on with the war with the Italians'. But it was only the beginning of tremendous activity in the Mediterranean, which became a lifeline in so many ways to those fighting to maintain Britain's control of North Africa and the Suez Canal. Never in history was the prize of Gibraltar, won by the Marines long ago, so utterly crucial in keeping the thoroughfare open. Without it, Malta, Alexandria and possibly the Suez Canal would have been lost.

For the next three years, massive and often desperate activity fell under Cunningham's command and all those who successively joined his battle, and that would very soon include 4,500 Royal Marines shipped out from the UK, followed later by other units. Initially, it was not the Germans who were his main foe but the well-equipped, if somewhat erratic, navy and air force of Benito Mussolini, who regarded the Mediterranean as *mare nostrum* ('our sea'). With Britain already committed to a life-or-death struggle in the Battle of Britain, Mussolini sent his troops into Egypt from Libya on 15 September

1940. Hugely outnumbered and short of tanks, the Western Desert Force under the command of General Sir Archibald Wavell began what was to become a marathon defence of British territory, which subsequently drew German support for the Italians in the form of the Afrika Korps and the beginning of an epic struggle between Rommel and Montgomery.

At sea, Cunningham's Alexandria force consisted of three battleships, *Warspite*, *Malaya* and *Royal Sovereign*, the carrier *Eagle*, five cruisers, 17 destroyers and just two submarines, the larger ships complete with Marines and their bands. This force was totally inadequate to meet the relentless action that began to unfold almost immediately, battles to protect merchant convoys, troopships and the huge areas of British influence at the eastern end of the Mediterranean. At the same time, the Battle of the Atlantic was starting as the Germans tried to starve Britain to death by attacking her supply lines. A new kind of sea warfare was emerging in which the interdependence of air power in cohesion with big surface guns and fast submarines of the opposing navies began to appear on a previously unimagined scale. Every permutation of maritime warfare, conjoined with air attacks where possible, engaged the complete range of naval hardware in which the Royal Marines at sea – and some in the air as pilots in the Fleet Air Arm – played a substantial part.

The Italian invasion of North Africa meant a massive increase in seaborne activity in the Mediterranean and, although somewhat timid in terms of coming out to fight, the Italian navy included some of the newest and fastest warships, a strong submarine fleet and a few other cunning innovations too, such as human torpedoes, magnetic anti-ship mines and exploding motorboats. At that time, British aircraft carriers did not carry fighters to help defend their fleet, only reconnaissance planes and torpedo bombers. The first important clash came a month after Italy's entry into the war, when a British submarine sighted a convoy bound for Libya, protected by two Italian battleships. Cunningham, with three battleships, an aircraft carrier, five cruisers and 17 destroyers, headed to intercept the convoy. The Italians saw them coming and launched a torpedo bombing attack, which damaged the British cruiser *Gloucester*, but *Warspite*'s gunners scared them off when they found a bearing on the battleship *Giulio Cesare* and hit her from a range of 15 miles, establishing a world record for long-range gunnery.

In November Cunningham, one of the great commanders of the war, took the fight to the Italians in what became the Battle of Taranto. He sailed from Egypt with four battleships, two cruisers and seven destroyers to attack the Italian fleet in its home base. He also had plans to experiment with his first major airborne attack, sending out 21 torpedo bombers in two waves from the carrier *Illustrious*, a force led by Royal Marines' pilot Captain Oliver Patch. The Fairey Swordfish biplanes arrived over the Italian fleet travelling at a 'loaded' top speed of around 140 miles an hour and, so the story goes, because they were so slow the Italian gunners couldn't get a range on them and were aiming too far in front. The Swordfish sank the battleship *Littorio* and damaged the rest of the ships in the harbour, with the loss of only two aircraft.

It was a victory well applauded at home, but pressure on the British Mediterranean Fleet returned when Mussolini ordered his land forces into Greece at the beginning of November, an unprovoked invasion that brought a swift response from Britain. Churchill promised support from Cunningham's warships and to send troops. For the moment, Wavell had his hands full planning a December onslaught to force the Italians out of Egypt. Even so, he was being pressed to send troops to Greece, and plans were already being made in London to form a reinforced British staging post on the island of Crete.

The site was the British naval base at Suda Bay, and Churchill said he wanted it to become a 'second Scapa', given the likelihood of Germany becoming involved. It was handed to the Marines' Mobile Naval Base Defence Organisation, and the job description was exactly that for which it had been formed – defending naval bases. At the time, the organisation was heavily committed around the UK and still in the process of completing the training of recent recruits of 'hostilities-only' troops when it received orders to prepare for operations overseas.

The specialist teams and regiments of the MNBDO were to travel with an army Commando force being hurriedly assembled under the charismatic leadership of Lieutenant-Colonel Bob Laycock. This party was classified as top secret and no word of its destination was to leak out. The force consisted of 100 officers and 1,500 other ranks from Nos. 7, 8 and 11 Commandos, A Troop from 3 Commando and Roger Courtney's Special Boat Service. They were to link up with two other Commando units, 50 and 52 Middle East Commandos, formed *in situ*.

The MNBDO would not arrive until the end of April, and by then the nature of their original assignment had been substantially upgraded into activities altogether more demanding. Since the MNBDO's departure from the UK, the Italians were in deep trouble both in North Africa and in Greece, where finally British and Commonwealth troops were arriving in Athens to complete Churchill's promised Treaty of Alliance, which was why Suda Bay was required as a halfway house. The troops bound for Greece included the 1st British Armoured Brigade and the New Zealand Division under the command of New Zealand's First World War hero and former RND brigade commander, Major-General Bernard Freyberg.

With Mussolini now losing the fight on two fronts, Hitler was forced to come to his aid, first by deploying Fliegercorps X to Sicily at the beginning of 1941 in what turned out to be the preparation for sending the Afrika Korps to Libya. To cover these troop movements, he insisted on aerial supremacy over the central and eastern Mediterranean and consequently more than 80 aircraft were made available for the task. The results were immediate and dramatic, with an attack on the carrier *Illustrious*, part of a convoy escort, along with the battleships *Warspite* and *Valiant* and a screen of five destroyers, bound for Malta and then onwards to Greece.

The carrier, which had a larger-than-normal complement of around 1,700 sailors, Marines and the air group, was subjected to a ruthless attack, first by two Italian SM79 torpedo bombers north-west of Malta which proved to be a feint. Just as the carrier's four Fulmar aircraft thought they'd sent the Italians packing – and run down their ammunition in the process – 40 Ju-87 Stuka dive-bombers and a smaller group of Ju-88s coming up behind appeared on radar at 12,000 feet. The attack was carefully coordinated: 30 aircraft in the lead group attacked the carrier, and the remaining ten hit the two battleships. *Illustrious* suffered severe damage and numerous casualties and on the following day, 11 January, survived another onslaught before the German planes were driven back by the arrival of British Hurricanes from Malta. The cruiser *Southampton* was sunk, but *Illustrious* managed to hobble away to Alexandria and then on to America for major repairs, which took her out of the war for 18 months. Short on air cover at all points of his theatre of operations, Cunningham was under further pressure with the deployment of British troops to Greece.

Germany instructed Italy to at least make some attempt to interrupt the British convoys, and the scene was set for the Battle of Matapan when Cunningham and the Italian fleet prepared to do business in the Ionian Sea between the Greek mainland and the island of Crete. Italy's Eastern Fleet were given two objectives: to intercept British troop transports and supply ships heading for Greece and to attack the British base at Suda Bay. Cunningham, reinforced with the carrier *Formidable* with her Albercore aircraft, was one step ahead with reconnaissance and sailed with his fleet from Alexandria to meet the Italians head on. The result was devastating for the Italians, who suffered more than 3,000 casualties. British ships rescued 1,168 Italian seamen and took them in as prisoners, then signalled the Italians to provide them with the location of the remaining survivors. The British lost two aircraft but not a single man aboard their warships.

It proved to be the last time the Italians brought out their fleet in such a manner, which was just as well, because Cunningham was now under great pressure to maintain coverage of all developments around him. Although Wavell led his Army on the Nile towards swift and decisive advances, capturing Tobruk and taking 100,000 Italian prisoners, the euphoria of the British successes was to be short-lived. In February 1941 Hitler sent General Erwin Rommel with the advance party of the mighty Afrika Korps, which subsequently began landing at Tripoli in the coming weeks. The object was to rescue Mussolini's army and force the British to divert more men and materials to North Africa. As this movement was going ahead, Hitler then launched a devastating blitzkrieg against Yugoslavia and quickly onwards to Greece with an invasion force of ground troops supported by around 1,250 aircraft, including Stukas and the deadly Messerschmitt 109s.

With Wavell's force totally overcommitted and underequipped, Greece was as good as lost and he ordered the withdrawal of all British troops as the Greek army surrendered on 23 April. A mini-Dunkirk operation in the evacuation of troops from Greece began and, as at Dunkirk, a massive inventory of equipment had to be abandoned, including more than 100 tanks, 40 anti-aircraft guns, 290 field guns, 1,800 machine guns and almost 8,000 vehicles, along with a number of damaged but repairable fighters and bombers. Even so, some 43,000 troops and civilians were successfully evacuated, many of them to the island of Crete, which London had deemed a 'must-hold situation'.

This process was already under way when the MNBDO, which had set off in January, had finally arrived in Egypt after a long journey around the Cape and through the Suez Canal, because the Mediterranean was considered unsafe for the passage of troops. Elements of the organisation were shipped out to Crete posthaste to join the defence of the island. They got in some nifty practice en route to the island, with 40 Lewis guns mounted on deck, and shot down several passing German aircraft. Major-General E. C. Weston, RM, who had gone on ahead, took command of what was now known as Creforce, until the end of April when Major-General Freyberg took over command on his evacuation from Greece. Just short of 2,000 Marines of MNBDO in their various roles were deployed immediately around Suda, Chania and later Heraklion. The rest of the unit were held back through lack of transport, and then their movement was cancelled because of increased threat from Stukas.

There was already an air of impending doom on the island. Enigma decrypts from Bletchley Park had revealed that the Germans were already planning a massive invasion of the strategically vital island, which at that particular moment in time had only 14 Hurricanes and seven RN aircraft to defend the enemy onslaught. Churchill ordered Wavell to send reinforcements. The commander wired back that he could spare only six tanks, 16 light tanks and 18 anti-aircraft guns, although the allied manpower on the island was bolstered after the fall of Greece to around 30,000 Australian, New Zealand and British troops. Churchill, having viewed the Germans' precise order of battle, courtesy of the Enigma decrypts, still had grave concerns that they had insufficient firepower to hold on.

His worst fears were realised on the morning of 20 May. Lieutenant J. C. Donaldson, with the ground forces, recalled:

Bombers and fighters appeared overhead early, and attacks were frequent during the morning. By noon, 54 planes had been monitored ... But [by mid-afternoon] the sky was full of planes bombing and machine-gunning the aerodrome area. For an hour and a half this terrific attack was maintained. It seemed as if the Germans were trying to flatten the defences by weight of metal alone. Then, around 5.15, the noise of the battle died down. The bombers had ceased to bomb, but enemy planes still swarmed above. Then from the north flew in two never-ending lines of the Ju-52s, and in a moment the air was full of parachutists blossoming forth. It was a beautiful, wonderful and thrilling sight. Our guns on the ground came to life. Bofors, light AA and Bren guns blazed skywards. Many parachutists were dead before they reached the ground. Others never left their planes alive, for some crashed in flames ... The Germans had failed to spot many of our positions, and the first parachutists were wiped out completely.

Wave after wave of aircraft attacks and landings followed, including Ju-52s towing huge DFS 230 gliders packed with troops, vehicles and guns, representing the greatest airborne invasion force ever mounted in the history of warfare. By late afternoon on the second day, almost 5,000 men had been dropped or landed on the island at a captured air base, and one of the most costly battles of the war to date was under way as more German paras and mountain troops were delivered to the island hour after hour, eventually totalling 22,040. They met spirited allied resistance whose strength had been hugely underestimated by German intelligence. Even so, it was a hopeless task for the allies, even with the supporting bombardment from the Royal Navy, given that the troops who had spent the past weeks fighting in Greece had gone through the turmoil of evacuation and were now doing it all over again.

The Germans had in fact assembled a force of 650 combat aircraft, 700 transports and 80 gliders in Greece, many coming in on the west side of the island where the Nazis had succeeded in capturing the airfield at Maleme, enabling them to fly in troops directly. Furious fighting ensued among the ground forces, with the Marines in hefty battles with German paras, while their specialist teams in the various gunnery roles were in intense round-the-clock action and their signals section was welcomed with open arms by the evacuated units, who had left most of their gear in Greece. The battle for Crete lasted almost to the end of May, by which time the remaining British fighters had been shot out of the sky until, devoid of air cover, the British fleet was exposed to grave danger, and thus supplies to troops would have to be curtailed. Hopelessness dawned again, and the evacuation of all allied troops was ordered.

On the basis of 'last in, last out' the MNBDO was selected to take the rearguard position, a role they should have shared with the Commando units of Layforce. But Bob Laycock did not bother with such formalities and got out early, on the grounds that they were Special Service units, likely as not to be tortured if identified as such in captivity. It was an action that caused considerable ill-will among

the troops in the departure area who had been through much more
than Layforce. The MNBDO S Battery, and others, which had, anyhow,
been the last to come down out of the hills overlooking the evacuation beaches at Sphakia after close fighting with the much better
armed Germans now got shot up from the air while covering the
retreat.

Battery commander Major R. W. Madoc, RM, struggled to maintain his position in the last hours:

> We just hoped we could hold off the Germans until the evacu-
> ation was complete, and then get off on the last boats. We had
> no mortars, only our rifles and Lewis guns. We were short of
> water and food. During the day the Germans had tried to outflank
> us. Suddenly, at 2030 we were told to withdraw immediately
> . . . to form a protective screen round General Weston's HQ for
> their evacuation.

Weston told him that only 100 MNBDO 'specialists' could get away
on the last boat. The rest of the Marines would have to stay behind.
Some of those left to their own devices found broken-down landing
craft and set about re-floating them. The last one left was under the
command of Major Ralph Garrett, who sent Madoc a message offering
him a place on this final opportunity of escape. Madoc refused: 'I
had to decide there and then either to go with him or stay with the
troops. I decided to stay, as there were well over 1,000 MNBDO
people altogether left behind.'

Consequently, Madoc spent the rest of the war in a German prison
camp along with the rest of his Marines. Meanwhile, the landing craft
that he had refused to climb aboard set off with 137 officers and men,
including Major Garrett and around 50 Marines. They carried only a
modest supply of rations and water, and they were soon in trouble.
The diesel engines kept breaking down and then gave up completely,
and the men had to make sails out of any available material. Progress
was slow and often entailed men physically getting into the water to

turn the craft into the wind. By the sixth day food and water had virtually run out, and on the eighth day two men died. It was night-fall the following day before they hit landfall, pushing the craft up the beach near Sidi Barrani, Egypt, where they managed to get word to the 1st RM Anti-Aircraft Regiment, MNBDO, who came with supplies and transport.

Admiral Cunningham, whose admiration for his own Marines at sea was well known, sent a dispatch to London in which he complained that it was 'particularly galling that a large part of the men left to surrender themselves consisted of Royal Marines who fought so gallant a rearguard action'. At sea, during this operation, Marines and RN personnel in the ships took heavy casualties under the onslaught from the German air attacks. Three cruisers and six destroyers were sunk and an aircraft carrier, six cruisers and eight destroyers were hit, with varying degrees of damage. The final toll showed the extent of the disaster: 4,600 allied troops killed, 2,000 wounded and 11,000 taken prisoner – the last including 1,200 Marines who had covered the rear of the evacuation. Bernard Freyberg made a full report of the Crete affair to Churchill, ending his report on the battle with these words:

> The story I have told is an epic, one that will be told in many ways and will be retold many times. There will be charges of disorganisation, shortages of equipment, stores, food and, at the last, water itself. It will be said that there was a lack of control and often no orders. These charges are admitted. Despite the difficulties that faced us, I would not for one moment attempt to prove that the order to hold Crete was a wrong one. It was right and we knew it.

The future for the remaining elements of MNBDO now took an unex-pected turn. What was left of the organisation was split and sent off in various directions, mainly to the east, although the HQ and some anti-aircraft units remained in Egypt until 16 June 1943, by which time North Africa was firmly back under British control. After being re-equipped and briefly rested, the MNBDO was ready for action, but General Weston's plea to retain the organisation as a complete unit fell on deaf ears. Some found themselves heading to Ceylon. Others were dispatched to run coastal and air defences on Diego Garcia, the strategically important island slap in the middle of the Indian Ocean which later housed a joint Anglo-American facility during the Cold War and a base for B52 bombers in the various US bombardments of Iraq in the 1990s and beyond. Some Marines coastal units were dispatched to the Seychelles and others to Addu Atoll, where a naval and air base had been established ahead of the anticipated arrival of the Japanese into the war. These diverse operations eventually brought all of the remaining MNBDO I Marines into the Far Eastern theatre, and there emerged many stories of particular courage and steadfastness.

Three days after the Japanese bombing of Pearl Harbor, Britain's fine ships *Repulse* and *Prince of Wales* were sunk. They had been on their way to strengthen Australia's counterforce against a possible Japanese invasion but had turned in a bid to save Singapore. That mission was already too late when the two magnificent ships were attacked by torpedo bombers, although the casualty rate was much lower than many of the earlier sinkings. Remarkably, 1,285 out of a ship's company of 1,618 on *Prince of Wales* and around half of the 1,306 on *Repulse* survived and were picked up by RN destroyers. Their rescuers delivered them to Singapore, and most of them were still there as Japanese forces bore down on the city.

A platoon from the Royal Marines detachment aboard *Prince of Wales* volunteered for jungle training, and in January the men combined with the 2nd Battalion, the Argyll and Sutherland Highlanders, under the command of Major Angus Rose to move behind enemy lines using boats, severing communications and generally making a nuisance of themselves 140 miles up the west coast of Malaya. It was a costly venture in terms of casualties, but they caused the enemy considerable disruption.

In February the 2nd Argylls were joined by another combined force of 210 Marines formed from the detachments of *Prince of Wales* and *Repulse* and they were among those fighting to the last in the bid to hold Singapore; 29 of the Marines were killed in the battle and most of the remainder went into captivity, where other fatalities occurred. The main force of the MNBDO's 1st RM Coastal Regiment was in Ceylon when the Japanese invaded Burma. It was from there that four officers and 103 Marines responded to an appeal sent to all units requesting volunteers for hazardous duties. The force was being put together to conduct operations in support of the Royal Navy's coastal patrols in the Gulf of Martaban, at the head of the Andaman Sea. They spent a couple of weeks training on the cruiser *Enterprise* bound for Rangoon, having formed up under the command of Major D. Johnston, RM, with Captain H. Alexander, RM, as his number two. But barely a week passed before the Japanese advance into Burma put paid to original plans and instead Johnston and his colleagues acquired a number of boats and formed a flotilla for river work, including a double-decker steamer named *Hastings* which served as their HQ. There was no shortage of suitable craft along the great waterway. The Irrawaddy Flotilla Company, founded in 1865, for example, claimed to be the 'greatest river fleet on earth', with over 600 vessels carrying some nine million passengers a year along the Irrawaddy River at its peak in the 1920s.

The enterprising young officers decided on the name Force Viper and, using a 35-foot diesel-engined river boat and a number of heavily armed motor launches, set about demonstrating their enthusiasm and ability to cause the Japanese and their supporters among the Burmese nationalists a good deal of grief. As one officer recorded, 'We made it up as we went along', giving assistance to a variety of British forces while at the same time running skirmishes against the Japanese. They did so by swashbuckling raiding tactics up and down the Irrawaddy while assisting the British forces in river crossings and transport during inevitable withdrawals and attacking Japanese forces in their own attempts to cross the river. The motorboats, manned entirely by

Marines, carried two Brens each, while each launch carried one Vickers, five Brens, and one two-inch mortar. The Marines, according to Johnston's reports, behaved like a 'pack of unruly hounds', chasing every opportunity to attack the Japanese.

During the evacuation of British troops from Burma, Force Viper was sent 120 miles up the Irrawaddy to Prome, where they operated in support of the 17th Indian Division as they made a fighting retreat. Then downriver again, as the last British were coming out of Rangoon, Force Viper assisted with the destruction of dock and oil installations, including one refinery containing 20 million gallons of aviation fuel. Finally, they took army demolition parties out from Rangoon to a seagoing vessel waiting to take them to India. As Force Viper motored upriver, they stopped to burn or smash any boats they passed to keep them out of Japanese hands, or sank them in the channels to bar the enemy's progress. They were involved in a ferocious battle on 17 March, when cooperating with a 30-strong force from Burma II Commando under Major Mike Calvert, RE, travelling 100 miles downriver to demolish oil rigs near Henzada before the Japanese got to them.

The unit ran into trouble, and was surrounded by enemy forces until one of the Force Viper boats arrived with five Brens and a dozen Tommy guns blazing. The Vickers gunner, Lance-Corporal Marriott, took out more than his fair share of the enemy's 100 casualties. They were, of course, high-risk operations, particularly as the Japanese became aware of their presence. One platoon was attacked by a strong Japanese force, killing five and carting six survivors to a prison camp east of Mandalay. They were discovered almost a year later when the camp was overrun by Chinese forces. Another, smaller force was captured at Padaung, and one escapee reported that several Marines had been strung up and bayoneted.

With early summer approaching, however, the work became increasingly difficult and even more dangerous for Viper Force as the Irrawaddy reached its lowest level and a number of the boats had a draught that made it impossible to manoeuvre them with speed and safety. The river launches were slow, vulnerable and restricted to the main channels, which were also the most visible. The side creeks were inaccessible to them, and in the final stages of their operations Johnston was forced into a defensive role.

Throughout their time on the river, the Marines had been running courageous missions, operating their Commando-style raids while at the same time covering troop movements and the withdrawal up the Irrawaddy. By the time they concluded operations, they had ferried hundreds of troops, bullocks and mules across the river and carried out extraordinary work until they finally called it a day, when the river was no longer viable for their kind of operations. Then they sank their boats to block the river and escaped over the mountains into India. Out of a total of 107 of all ranks in Force Viper, 58 got back to India, the rest killed or taken prisoner, and as such many were tortured and killed.

No other unit of the Royal Marines would come up against the Japanese on land again for almost two years although they did meet them at sea and in the air. Marines were among survivors of HMS *Exeter*, which was sunk in the Battle of the Java Sea on 28 February 1942, and along with the seamen spent the rest of the war in Japanese prison camps. Meanwhile, Marines and seamen who survived the sinking of the cruisers *Dorsetshire*, *Cornwall* and the carrier *Hermes*, all sunk in the Indian Ocean in April 1942 by Japanese carrier-borne aircraft, went ashore at Ceylon. There, some joined the Marines of the Air Defence Brigade in Ceylon, who operated a staunch defence of Colombo and Trincomalee during intensive bombing campaigns by the same Japanese carrier force.

What these ad hoc groups such as Force Viper had demonstrated above all was their enthusiasm and courage and that the Marines and army Commandos were capable of conducting raids and mini-invasions on enemy coastlines, although the success rate was variable. As Chief of Combined Operations, Mountbatten positively welcomed ideas from all and sundry. Major Harry Holden-White, one of the original team in Roger Courtney's SBS and who worked for Mountbatten on a number of projects, particularly later in the Far East, told the author:

> The more outrageous, the more he liked them. With the benefit of hindsight, some of his early Combined Ops projects were a bit bloody daft, carrying risks far beyond their worth. Certainly, the casualty figures were high, when set against the benefits achieved. But Mountbatten would say: 'Bugger that! Let them have a go. Let's face it, it's all we can bloody well do at the present.' And he was right. With the whole of the French Atlantic coast in German hands, it was a very inviting target for Combined Operations.

One of the most famous small raids by Marines of that era was that organised by Major H. G. 'Blondie' Hasler, and was turned into the film *The Cockleshell Heroes*. For security purposes, his group was given the title of RM Boom Patrol Detachment. He devised a scheme whereby 12 men and six canoes packed with limpet mines and explosive would be delivered to the mouth of the River Gironde. From there, the six teams would paddle the 90 miles upriver to the deep-water harbour where German supply ships were moored and unloaded. They would lay up by day and travel by night.

Hasler, a tall and hefty 28-year-old with a well-known passion for small boats, pushed his idea all the way to the top; after several revisions Mountbatten finally gave it the all clear. Hasler personally selected the men to join him and after weeks of training Operation Frankton was launched on 5 December 1942. Only ten men in five boats set off from the submarine *Tuna*, which carried them to the launch site, the sixth boat having been damaged getting it out of the submarine. Soon after the five canoes set off, the tidal river began to become rough, and sadly one of the canoes was lost. Two more went missing on the journey upriver, and in the end only two boats made it to the harbour.The two canoes weaved in and out of the moored ships planting their limpets on seven ships.

Of the ten who set out on the mission, only Hasler and his paddler, Marine Ned Sparks, survived to scuttle their canoe and make their escape through a prearranged link-up with the French Resistance, onward over the Pyrenees into Spain and finally back to England, a 1,400-mile journey. Of the remainder, two were drowned when their boat capsized and the six others were captured and shot by the Germans after being identified as 'Commandos'.

The first major operation of this kind in March 1942 was, according to Harry Holden-White, another case of 'great expectations', although the plan was inherited from the previous Combined Ops boss, Roger Keyes, and bore a number of similarities to the Zeebrugge raid at the end of the First World War, which he had planned. There was an intelligence belief that the Germans intended to establish a haven for *Tirpitz* on the Atlantic coastline of France. Five U-boat bases were already established there, several large enough to service German battleships and destroyers attacking the Atlantic convoys.

The port targeted by Combined Ops was St-Nazaire, at the mouth of the River Loire. It had been suggested that the place should be put out of action by creating a very large explosion, and Operation Chariot was born. It did look, on the face of it, to be an outrageous idea, but slowly it developed into a firm proposal that was to be staffed by a joint force recruited from the army Commando units and the Royal Navy. They would sail a ship packed with explosives and crash it into the hugely fortified dock at St-Nazaire. Commandos would follow on behind the ship in a flotilla of 16 motor launches, dodging the flak and defensive gunfire, then scramble ashore and set a dozen other massive explosive charges. Their task was to ensure that the dry dock at St-Nazaire was blown apart by the ship, and that various installations such as the pump-house, used to empty the dry dock, the power station and fuel supply lines were damaged beyond repair. Additionally, two torpedoes with delayed timing mechanisms would be fired from two of the boats into the locks and set to explode at around the same time as the ship to ensure maximum damage.

That was the plan, and Mountbatten thought it was wonderful. The hunt was now on for a ship to be used as the exploding Trojan horse: Mountbatten called for suggestions from the Royal Navy and was presented with an old destroyer, *Campbeltown*, formerly an American vessel known as the USS *Buchanan*. Its funnels were cut down to disguise it as a German torpedo boat. The joint force would be made up of 240 Commandos and a similar number of RN personnel to sail the exploding ship and the 16 Fairmile motor launches, known as Eurekas, which would carry the troops into the attack. The flotilla of MLs, along with one motor gunboat and one motor torpedo boat under the overall naval command of Commander R. E. D. Ryder, RN, were to follow in a particular formation in front of and behind *Campbeltown*, which was under the command of Lieutenant-Commander S. H. Beattie, RN. The ship carried six tons of explosives, which had been cemented into her bows with timers set to allow the raiders plenty of time to escape. Two groups of the assault force and five demolition parties also travelled in the destroyer and would jump over her bows or clamber down scaling ladders on to the dock at St-Nazaire after she had rammed it. The rest of the assault and demolition teams in the motor launches would come ashore at given locations.

The night of 27 March was very calm, and the convoy had a remarkably uneventful journey across the English Channel into the Bay of Biscay. The flotilla travelled four miles along the Loire when, suddenly, from the St-Nazaire bank, searchlights panned the river followed by a short burst of fire. *Campbeltown*'s German-speakers managed to convince the guards that this was a German special force returning from operations and needed to land the wounded in the motor launches. She was allowed to pass but further upstream they were discovered and a massive fire fight developed. Mayhem broke out, with motor launches carrying additional fuel tanks exploding, and the ship took two direct hits on her bows, one of which blew off her 12-inch gun, killing the crew. But she sailed on to reach the dock.

Fighting went on for an hour or more while the Commandos placed explosives in other preselected installations, and by the time they were ready to make their exit the original force had been decimated and those who managed to get to their motor launches were well on the way out of the Loire as the minutes ticked by for the big event.

Campbeltown was well and truly lodged in the gates to the dry dock. That morning, the Germans, unaware of its lethal six-ton cargo of dynamite hidden in her bows, were crowding around the dry dock wondering what to do when fuses activated and the ship blew apart with an almighty explosion that rocked the port, completely demolishing the dock and killing 400 people, including many officials who had just come to look. In mid-afternoon there were two more explosions – from the delayed-action torpedoes fired by the first MLs and which had lain silently embedded beneath the surface in the harbour structure. The damage was greater than even the planners had anticipated, and the dock remained out of action for almost ten years.

For that reason, the raid was considered a great success. The human cost, however, was high. Of the 242 Commandos engaged in the operation, 59 were killed and 112 captured, many badly wounded. The Royal Navy suffered even worse casualties among the motor launch crews and those aboard *Campbeltown*. They lost 85 killed or missing, 106 captured and, again, a large number wounded.

And then there was Dieppe, the most spectacular, costly and controversial of all Mountbatten's Combined Operations projects, otherwise known as Operation Jubilee, which utilised a large number of Canadian forces for whom Churchill was anxious to find employment. This raid would also include elements of the first-ever Royal Marines Commando unit (see Chapter Ten) who originally had been earmarked for a lesser role but ended up among the heroes of the day.

The attack on the French port was launched in the early hours of 19 August 1942. It was described as 'not a raid, nor an invasion'. It was intended to seize and hold a major port for a short period, to prove it was possible and to gather intelligence from prisoners and assess German responses. The operation was also intended to use airpower to draw the Luftwaffe into a large, planned encounter; the information gleaned would be utilised for the eventual allied invasion of Europe. The surprise attack was to be firmly struck, followed by an equally swift withdrawal. The operation involved 6,100 troops, of whom almost 5,000 were Canadians, along with army and Royal Marine Commandos and 50 American Rangers. The troop carriers were screened by eight British destroyers, which also provided gunnery support at the point of attack, and their arrival was timed to coincide with air operations involving 74 RAF squadrons and 12 from the Royal Canadian Air Force. The plan called for assaults on five different points on a front of roughly 12 miles of firmly held coastline, but at almost every stage the raiding troops hit problems that either had not been anticipated or forewarned by intelligence.

In parts, the beaches were extremely narrow and overlooked by lofty cliffs where German artillery were well dug in, at some points with guns on rails, sited in caves, which they rolled out to the cliff's edge at a suitable point in time. Success depended on surprise and darkness and neither of those vital aspects was maintained. Fierce defensive activity was ready and waiting, and in the growing light the raiders met violent machine-gun and heavy artillery fire, cutting down the soldiers as they landed. On each of the designated assault areas, attempts to breach the German defences were beaten back, and even the British tanks were halted, bogged down on the shingle beaches. The raid was aborted soon after lunchtime, when the survivors retreated to their landing craft for the getaway, leaving behind a huge number of casualties. Of the 4,963 Canadians who embarked on this adventure, 907 were killed and 1,946 made prisoners of war.

Overall, it was a far greater toll when the statistics from other groups involved – fielding around 3,000 support personnel – were added. The Royal Navy crews manning the ships, motor launches, boats and landing craft suffered heavily. In their very first operation the Royal Marines Commandos lost almost a third of their men, killed or wounded, as did the army Commandos. The extent of the air battle over Dieppe was also evident from the disastrous losses suffered by the allies: 106 planes shot down, with only 30 pilots surviving, against Luftwaffe losses of 96 aircraft. Other hardware lost by the allies included 300 landing craft and launches, 28 tanks destroyed or abandoned and one destroyer gutted.

The recriminations began on the homeward journey, but the PR machine in London was already spinning a tale of success. Mountbatten's communiqué spoke of great lessons learned for the future and accentuated the positive by pointing out that two-thirds of the attacking force had returned home. But there was universal criticism among military leaders and outrage in some quarters. Royal Marines Major-General Leslie Hollis, who was secretary to the Chiefs of Staff, complained directly to Churchill that the whole exercise had been an abject failure, with many lives lost for no purpose or gain. For the more senior Marines, the reports of Dieppe brought back memories of Gallipoli – although on a vastly smaller scale. No account seemed to have been taken of that experience, and the lessons were now having to be relearned. The debate would go on for years, with particular bitterness aroused in Canada, quite naturally, whenever the topic of Dieppe arose.

CHAPTER TEN

Commandos at Last

That the army Commandos had had something of a baptism of fire while demonstrating energy and enthusiasm – not to mention more than a touch of arrogance – in their work, regardless of the level of success or failure, contributed to a growing wonderment as to the whereabouts of the Royal Marines. The war was three years old and it was an indisputable fact that more than half the total complement of the corps had seen little or no action. Even within the corps there was a total imbalance of experience in hostilities between those who were at sea and those fighting on land. The former, as we have seen, were at the forefront of every great naval event from day one of the war, suffering heavy casualties in the process. Their achievements and sacrifices, along with the rest of the Royal Navy, were of considerable historical note and importance.

By comparison, Marines in two of the three land formations had become very much a supporting cast, but in 1943 a total reorganisation of the whole structure of the Royal Marines was at last under way. Oddly enough, Lieutenant-Colonel Bob Laycock, commander of the Commandos' Special Service Brigade, was a catalyst to these developments. He and his men had come through a rough, tough initiation into this brave new world of Combined Operations, not least himself – the man who walked across the North African desert for 41 days after his own Commando unit was decimated behind enemy lines during an unsuccessful attempt to assassinate Rommel. Based on these experiences, which provided ample material for the process of self-examination, he had produced a paper in 1943 that set out the changes he felt were necessary to put the Commandos on a firm and lasting footing. He surmised that the days of small-party raiding were coming to an end as the land war intensified. Now it was the turn of heavy metal. There were still opportunities for such raids, but Laycock foresaw a much wider brief and an expanded role for Commandos, and it had as much to do with survival rates among his men as anything. Instead of being used as raiders, both the paras and the Commandos were increasingly being called on to fight in prolonged situations after they had already led the attack and had, as he put it, 'kicked the door down'.

Army commanders kept them *in situ* for long and arduous battles for which they were not equipped either in firepower or support. They still travelled light, had no base, often had no artillery backup and carried everything they possessed on their backs. Commandos travelled in cramped ships in dire conditions, with no facilities for off-loading any heavy equipment, and went ashore in a variety of landing craft and small boats that quite often were barely serviceable. Lately, as in North Africa, Sicily and Italy, their losses were high, and this highlighted another problem: there were no trained reinforcements immediately available overseas, and a Commando unit which may have lost more than half its men could be topped up only by drafts sent out from England or calling for untrained volunteers from the line.

Laycock maintained that this represented an unacceptable danger to existing personnel and to the incomers. There was, he said, really no substitute for the heavy-duty training at Achnacarry and elsewhere that instilled not only the methods of storming a target but basic lifesavers, such as endurance swimming, route marching with a 45-kilo-gram load strapped to their backs, fast reaction to a given event, silent approaches (surprise attacks) or loud approaches (screaming and shouting to scare the living daylights out of the enemy), understanding and recognising all types of explosives, survival techniques if stranded behind enemy lines and the craft of listening for sounds unrelated to the countryside which may spell danger of another sort.

These elements demanded weeks of training, and once a raid or target had been identified the work-up for the job would be precise and carefully timed. Basic rules of deployment, incidentally, became the handed-down tablets of wisdom that are still applicable in modern Commando operations. The intensity of the training was the reason why there had always been so many rejects – and, again, still is today. Men who did not make the grade for one reason or another were not only a danger to themselves but could put the whole unit at risk. The esprit de corps of the Commandos who had undergone collective training was a vital ingredient to their success. Laycock analysed these problems, and in his paper for Mountbatten he went as far as to state that unless there was an overhaul on the lines he suggested it would be better disbanding the Commandos altogether.

He submitted that the better course would be to upgrade the Commandos completely, give them a level of independence, with their own base, stores and with a substantial enlargement of their overall numbers, a holding station for trained reinforcements, and at the same time an upgrade of their firepower. Support for his theories on the development of the Commandos came from the respected body of Anglo-American Joint Staffs under General Frederick Morgan, and the use of the Commandos on the lines suggested by Laycock was included in their proposals for the eventual invasion of mainland Europe.

A draft plan was flown to Churchill while he was taking a break in Marrakech, where he was joined by both Montgomery and Eisenhower. When the two generals were shown a copy, Montgomery said he needed more initial punch by way of a spearhead force of paras and Commandos. It had already been the subject of some debate and now it was time for action. Sir Alan Brooke, Chief of the Imperial General Staff, called for nine army Commandos to be operational by late September 1943 and double that number by the time of the projected launch of Operation Overlord for the invasion of France. From a training perspective, that was a challenging target. Marshalling suitable manpower would be virtually impossible until Mountbatten suggested that the Royal Marines could provide all the additional units. In fact, he went further – that the Marines should in due course take over the whole Commando organisation.

That suited the Marines at corps level, but the old prejudices still pervaded the Admiralty and the army. Mountbatten insisted that there was no earthly reason why, with adequate training, the Marines should not become the predominant Commando force. He did not actually pass this thought on to the army at the time, although in due course he would get a barrage of abuse from the generals for having the audacity to make such a move. And so in the summer of 1943 it became a *fait accompli*. Two Royal Marines Commando, 40 and 41 RM Commando, were already in training and the go-ahead was signalled for the formation of six more, 42 to 47 RM Commando. A ninth, 48 RM Commando, would be added in the spring of 1944 in the build-up to the invasion of France.

In real terms this was a coup for Mountbatten. In one fell swoop he had achieved what many had long believed was the true destiny of Royal Marines: that of raiders-cum-soldiers aligned to amphibious operations – in other words, truly *per mare, per terram*. It was the beginning of a complete and badly needed reorganisation that would have ramifications down the century and on to the present day. The army Commandos were naturally not at all pleased, and there was much dissension over what many of the pioneers of the movement considered was an unwarranted and unwelcome incursion. The Commandos, they insisted, were shock troops, soldiers *par excellence*, and untried and untrained Marines simply would not do. The Marines countered that they had been preparing for such a move since

1664, and no Johnny-come-lately organisation could match their unique and proud lineage, while conversely the army Commandos had a short history that was not at all above criticism. These arguments, at the time, could easily be demolished by the Commandos with a simple question: what are you doing now? The level of animosity was recalled by Brigadier Lord Lovat, one of the founders of the army Commandos:

> I attended a conference to meet the Marines in the summer of 1943 and gave our views on the amalgamations. It was not a very tactful discussion. Some (Major Jumbo Leicester, Lieutenant-Colonel David Fellowes and their commander, Major-General Robert Sturges) became good friends, but the Royal Marine colonels, collectively, were not so amiable. Their outlook was, understandably, stiffer and more hidebound by the traditions that lay behind them. We had none. They could drill and countermarch better than most of the regular army ... but few of these Marines [currently available] had manned gun turrets or seen action in capital ships. None had Commando battle experience or knew what close fighting was about. I personally found the patronising 'old pro' attitude to us 'upstarts' very hard to swallow.

But swallow he had to, and as news filtered down the line men in the Commandos' ranks were spitting with rage that they, all volunteers and proud of it, were now to be joined by a force which included large numbers of untrained conscripts. One of the pioneers of the army Commandos, John Durnford-Slater, summed up the feeling of many of his officers and men: 'We were dead against the idea. I was proud of what we stood for. In spite of Mountbatten, whose idea this was, I felt convinced that units of conscripted Marines could not be expected to maintain the high standard of shock troops.'

Later, however, observing 45 RM Commando in training with 4 and 6 Army Commandos, he somewhat grudgingly acknowledged that they would probably make the grade 'in such good company'. There was merit on both sides of the argument, and it was the Marines' commander, Major-General Sturges, who, seeing that the animosity might get out of hand, suggested that the two groups should be moulded together in new brigades rather than kept apart, so that each could work with the other. This had already proved effective as the first RM Commandos joined the army units in Italy.

Even so, the resentment was not completely eradicated and continued among the veterans after the war, when, as will be seen, it was the army Commandos who got the axe while the units of Royal Marines stayed in business to carry the banner forward to the future. For the time being, however, they were to be as one, with the army and Marines Commandos combined to form four Special Service Brigades, although the command structure and their groupings would pass through a series of confusing changes as demands on their services developed with the progression of the war across all the theatres from Italy, Western Europe, the Balkans, South-East Asia and finally Germany itself.

One final appointment did help calm the anger of the army Commando chiefs in that Bob Laycock was to be brought back to London to succeed Mountbatten who, at the age of 43, had been promoted Supreme Commander of Allied Forces in South-East Asia. It was an appointment pushed through by Churchill, accompanied by the same murmurings of top brass dissent that accompanied his selection as Chief of Combined Operations. But it was also something of a poisoned chalice in that his priority task was to recapture Burma from the Japanese, lost after the humiliating retreat of the allied forces into India a year earlier at a cost of 13,463 casualties.

Laycock recognised immediately the quite remarkable speed at which the Royal Marines Commandos had buckled down to the job, as Durnford-Slater conceded. They had undergone training at the Commando Training Centre at Achnacarry, but in truth the short time available was hardly sufficient to prepare the men for the journey ahead. Even so, corners were not cut in the selection process, nor were men simply waved through to fill the numerical requirements. Generally speaking, only two-thirds of the candidates passed the course, and the rest went into the ships or reverted to defensive positions maintained by the Marines.

The arrival of the Marines Commando formations in the main theatre of war came as Montgomery and Eisenhower booted the last German units out of North Africa by the pincer that began with the Battle of El Alamein and carried on along the coast to meet up with the Torch landings in Oran. That task complete, a massive armada of allied ships, landing craft, aircraft and soldiers was assembled off Tunisia along with a vast stock of heavy-duty gliders for the first-ever major air landing of troops into enemy-held territory. Three British parachute brigades and the new glider-borne 1st Air Landing Brigade would lead the invasion while Commandos were earmarked for what became their traditional place with invasion forces, dashing in ahead of the herd to cover the landings and thereafter attacking the artillery outposts that could cause the main force much damage. It was in this role that the first new Royal Marines Commandos found themselves in July 1943.

The capture of Sicily was planned as a rapid pincer movement. With Eisenhower in overall command, the US 7th Army under General Patton would land on the south-west coast while Montgomery's 8th Army would come in on the south-east. They would be followed in on the west side by the 1st Canadian Division and the 51st Highland Division, while the British 5th and 50th Divisions landed south of Syracuse. A number of coastal batteries was identified from aerial reconnaissance, particularly overlooking the beaches assigned to the Canadians and 5th Division.

The allied movement began on 19 July, when the two Royal Marines Commandos were the first seaborne troops ashore in Sicily after an uncomfortable journey over unusually choppy seas whipped up by strong gusting winds that resulted in a good deal of seasickness among the newer recruits for whom this was a first-time experience. It was a fate that was suffered by the entire allied invasion force as the Royal

Marines landing craft flotillas made their debut. Among them were separate Marine units manning the LCFs (Landing Craft Flak) protecting the troop carriers and ships against potentially murderous attacks from waves of Ju-88s.

The Sicilian invasion also saw another highly praised element of the Royal Marines' establishment in operations, that of specialist amphibious units originally trained and honed by MNBDO II, which carried signals, medical supplies and other essential services, and it was the Marines, too, who handled much of the unloading of rations, ammunition and fuel. These operations alone were remarkable in their proficiency under fire and made a significant contribution to the Sicilian landings, as indeed they would elsewhere in the fightback to reclaim Europe from the Nazis.

As for the Special Service units, 40 and 41 achieved an exemplary advance from their landing positions and the Commandos moved rapidly towards their target areas with less opposition than had been anticipated. There remained pockets of substantial resistance, against which 41 RM Commando suffered most, with nine killed and 18 wounded. Ironically, their most serious setback in terms of losses came not during their encounters with the Germans in the field but when they were on board ship. They joined Paddy Mayne's Special Raiding Squadron (a temporary renaming of the SAS, its founder David Stirling having unfortunately been transferred to a German prison camp) for the assault into enemy-held territory; the group was going forward to Catania.

The advance was aborted at the last minute when intelligence reports confirmed that the Germans were heavily reinforcing the area. During the night, however, the RM Commandos' ship was hit during an air bombardment, killing 16 men and wounding another 63. Despite this setback, the Commando units achieved all their objectives swiftly and without great loss, and as the allies made swift progress through Sicily Montgomery decided that the Commando units should be retired into reserve to train for their landing on the Italian mainland, where immediate action would again greet their arrival.

The allies had reached the Strait of Messina soon after dawn on 17 August after battling a tough rearguard action by the Germans as they made their escape to the Italian mainland at Reggio. Two main invasion areas lay ahead: at Reggio itself and Salerno. Marines on the ships with their navy gunnery colleagues were now as heavily engaged as British and American warships. In total, 586 allied naval units were directly engaged in the landings, which included troopships, landing craft, supply vessels and a strong naval force and carrier support group, Admiral Cunningham's Force H, which included the battleships *Nelson*, *Rodney*, *Warspite* and *Valiant* and the carriers *Formidable* and *Illustrious* with Marines and bands aboard.

The warships covered the landings at Messina, where 2 Special Service Brigade, comprising 3 Commando, 40 RM Commando and 1 SRS, was to operate ahead of the British XIII crossing into Italy while 2 Commando and 41 RM Commando would spearhead the British X Corps assault on Salerno to join the American 5th Army under Lieutenant-General Mark Clark.

On the southern tip of Italy, the landings looked relatively straight-forward, given that on the day the allies headed for Reggio di Calabria the Italians surrendered, although the announcement was delayed until 8 September to coincide with the assault on Salerno. The unopposed arrival of the 2SSB, however, soon descended into a swift fire fight when the beach flared into action with an attack from two nests of German 88-millimetre guns in which 40 RM Commando took 36 casualties as they moved to silence the gunners. Thirty-six hours of hard fighting followed before the breakthrough, at which point the two Commandos were pulled back into reserve as the main body of Montgomery's force began the battle northwards to link up with the American 5th Army south of Naples.

With the landing in the south complete, the warships were redeployed to cover the convoy travelling north for the second phase of the invasion at Salerno. There was every reason to expect that the allied landings would be as quick and successful as they had been at Reggio. But in fact this first full-scale invasion of Continental Europe in the Second World War hit trouble from the beginning and floundered into a confusing and very costly battle lasting a dozen days. General Clark, it later transpired, had made many numerous last-minute revisions of battle plans that the British were not fully aware of. What they *did* know – and could barely believe – was that the general had insisted the attack would greatly benefit from the element of surprise and had given orders forbidding any bombardment of the coast before the troops were landed.

In doing so, he overruled protests from Admiral Cunningham. It is said that Cunningham had pointed out that the Germans would hardly fail to notice the convoy of around 680 assorted ships and landing craft heading north along the coast of Italy or the fact that British minesweepers were trawling around Salerno Bay before their arrival. And, of course, they did. German spotter planes did their job and reported the presence of the oncoming armada, allowing Field Marshal Albert Kesselring to bring in troops to replace the Italians in the hills ringing the beach. The Luftwaffe also had a welcoming group in the air; the attacks were initially countered by Royal Navy Seafires torpedo bombers and AA gunfire from the leading ships, but worse was to come.

The British contingent was designated to land in the northern sector of the invasion beaches and began turning towards the coast at a point level with the island of Capri, while the American troops took the southern approaches. As the invasion forces began leaping ashore, the flak boats and AA guns of the covering fleet were soon in action. By the end of the first day, British x Corps had landed 27,000 troops, 80 tanks, 325 guns and more than 2,000 vehicles over a seven-mile front. They had been given the objectives of securing the town of Salerno, an airfield at Montecorvino, some rough terrain leading to the Naples Plain and the towns of Battipaglia and Eboli, while the Americans were looping in an arc around the bay. In fact, it took nine days to gain the objectives that had been earmarked for the first 24 hours.

Allied troops faced murderous fire from the outset, and the onslaught increased as they fought inland. There was also confusion among the allied forces, in that some maps were out of date and several major troop landings had been put ashore at the wrong place. The British found themselves at least eight miles from the nearest Americans to the south, and the Germans soon filled the gap. It is said that the phrase 'we've got them just where they want us' came into being on that day.

Eventually, the big naval guns were brought over to range on the German emplacements and soon found themselves under attack, this time with a completely new type of German bomb loaded specially for the occasion. Intelligence officers intercepted and decoded radio messages from Berlin instructing its pilots which ships to attack the following day. A total of 58 bombers were sent to Salerno to meet the allied maritime force, which was locked up and with the Marines and navy gunners at action stations well in time for the attack. In the middle of the aerial battle, the crew of the American cruiser *Savannah* spotted an incoming Dornier aircraft at about 18,700 feet, out of gunnery range and then what the gun crews thought was a second aircraft diving very fast, making a severe correction about 400 feet above the starboard side of the main deck before it slammed into the ship at the number-three gun turret. In fact, *Savannah* had become the first allied ship to be hit by Germany's secret weapon – a primitive guided missile based on the early technology that produced the V-1 and V-2 rockets that were soon to hit London. Two types were identified: the HS293, the low-level glider-bomb, and the HX90, a high-level guided dive-bomb.

The missile hit with such force that it pierced 36 inches of steel at the base of a gun turret before exploding, killing 218 men. The British flagship *Warspite* and the cruiser *Uganda* were also hit and severely damaged. In the case of *Uganda*, the missile penetrated seven decks and exploded underneath the ship. Both ships had to be taken under tow to Malta for repairs. This development caused great concern for the safety of the allied ships against such attacks, and the shipboard Marines were called on to assist in setting up an experiment using a landing craft contraption to try to divert the guided bombs.

Captain Roger Lewis, a Royal Navy mine and bomb disposal specialist, explained:

> They collected seven LSTs – Landing Ships (Tanks) – that were damaged and were not fully fit for service. We drove on board lorry-borne RAF radar sets, through the bow doors, hoisted them on to the upper deck, and anchored these seven LSTs as an outer ring of radar cover for the anchorage, and a whole lot of scientists from London, who were researching the V-weapons problem, came out for the Anzio landing and listened in and did all sorts of funny things. I think they were trying to find out the frequencies used for the guidance systems. The fleet signal officer and I got hold of a very high-speed dental drill from a dentist in Bizerta and converted that to jam the signals. It worked quite well. Even so, these weapons were used, and they hit the brand-new cruiser *Spartan* and several other targets. And some of my former RN mine and bomb disposal team from the UK were sent over to Sardinia, where a specimen of the HS293 had crashed, and collected it for analysis, before subsequently developing countermeasures. The US Naval Command placed an army fighter direction team aboard two ships to monitor all Luftwaffe radio frequencies and intercept and jam any radio signals sent from a bomber to a guided missile.

One welcome statistic emerged from this high-tech interlude. Although 45 men were killed and 42 wounded in the attack, the cruiser *Spartan* was thankfully the last major loss in surface ships suffered by the Royal Navy in the Mediterranean. The land war, however, continued with ever-increasing ferocity. The Germans had pulled back to establish staunch defensive positions, and it took the landing force more than ten days to reach the objectives they had hoped to achieve within the first 48 hours. The Commandos were, as was now the norm, among the first ashore, probing the ring of German positions. The Salerno SSB force, made up of 2 Commando under Lieutenant-Colonel Jack

Churchill, and 41 RM Commando, under Lieutenant-Colonel J. C. 'Pops' Manners, landed unopposed and swept inland on a northerly route towards Naples planned for the British force, disposing of some outposts of German artillery on the way. But this initial swiftness of step was soon curtailed. The SSB was working ahead of the British 46th Division, which had been unavoidably detained by the 16th Panzer Division outside Salerno. The Commandos were now out on their own, facing a battle with other elements of the Panzers ahead, notably the 3rd Panzagrenadier Division, while unable to receive reinforcements from behind. Nine days of heavy and costly fighting ensued before the two Commando units were pulled out to reorganise, having lost almost half their men, while at the same time recording in the annals of Salerno history the fact that they were the only troops to reach and take their objectives on time, although at some considerable cost: 49 killed and 153 wounded. The casualty rate among officers was even higher: 21 out of 27 killed or wounded.

Montgomery's 8th Army made its rendezvous with the Salerno force 24 hours after the Commandos were pulled out. Naples was secured just over a week later. Although devastating in terms of casualties to the Special Service Brigade, the price of victory in turning the Germans out at Salerno was 7,811 allied casualties. Perhaps more important, the experience put fresh fight into the Germans and encouraged Hitler to send in thousands more troops, thus ending the allies' hopes of a steady march north. Instead, it became a tortuous slog that would cost 350,000 allied lives before it was done.

Across country, while the Battle of Salerno was unfolding, 2 Special Service Brigade, under the command of Lieutenant-Colonel Durnford-Slater and made up of 3 and 40 RM Commandos and Paddy Mayne's SRS, went back into the fray after Reggio, landing at the port of Termoli on the east coast of Italy. They were to establish forward positions in advance of the arrival of the 8th Army in spite of the brigade's dire shortage of manpower: 3 Commando had received no reinforcements since the casualties taken during its landing on the mainland and was down to fewer than 200 men, while 40 RM under the much-respected Lieutenant-Colonel Manners, RM, could muster fewer than 400. No. 3 came ashore at Termoli safe and dry, but the Marines hit a sandbank in heavy seas and had to wade ashore at a depth of five feet, which drowned their radios. No. 3, meanwhile, had already begun the task of forming a bridgehead a mile west of Termoli, while 40 and the SRS carried on through to capture the town and the main road out, which led cross-country to Naples. They were to take and hold these forward positions about 15 miles in front of the 8th Army and remain there until the main force came through.

The scrap at Termoli came at dawn the day after they moved into position. Fighter-bombers swooped low and gave them a pounding before the German ground forces made their counterattack, soon to be backed up by the unexpected arrival of the 26th Panzer Division, which had been resting after the action in Salerno. The Panzers had driven from west to east and now rolled up with infantry and tanks and started blasting the allied positions. The fighting developed into a close encounter, with both sides near enough to hurl grenades at each other. The battle all around the Commando positions continued throughout the next 24 hours, and there was still no sign of the 8th Army, which was supposed to be just seven hours behind the Commandos when they landed. It turned out that their forward troops had been delayed by blown bridges, and the situation was getting desperate.

The SSB was heavily outgunned by the enemy, as usual, but the men hung on until word reached them that the 78th Division was coming up as the recce force. Their arrival allowed 40 RM to take a break, but they had barely withdrawn from their positions when they were called back into line. The Germans resumed the attack with such force that the Commandos witnessed the unfortunate sight of allied soldiers running away from the action, leaving their guns unmanned. Colonel Manners pulled out his revolver and threatened to shoot them if they did not get back to the line. What they had hoped would be a brief encounter ended up being a ten-day engagement for the

Commandos, and at the end of the period both No. 3 and 41 were so depleted in numbers that they had to put out a call for volunteers from the 8th Army and landing craft crews.

Clearly, however, this could not go on. Like their comrades around Salerno, the SSB was shattered physically and mentally, and in mid-October both Commandos were withdrawn and sent home to Britain to re-equip and to get new recruits into training. The newly formed, newly trained 43 RM Commando, which included men of the old 7th RM Battalion, was dispatched to Italy to join 2 and 9 Commandos and 40 RM, along with a contingent of Belgian and Polish soldiers who formed No. 10 (Inter-Allied) Commando, the elements that now formed the No. 2 Special Service Brigade under Lieutenant-Colonel Tom Churchill.

No. 43 arrived just after Christmas 1943 and marched straight into something of a maelstrom in Italy and the Adriatic that would engage elements of the Commandos for the remainder of the war. Although slowly being pushed north by the 5th and 8th Armies, the Germans had been running in a constant flow of reinforcements and were stubbornly refusing to budge. They gave as good as they received, often better, in some of the most ferocious fighting the war had seen. Famous battle names of Anzio, Cassino and Lake Comacchio would take their place in allied military history amid appalling carnage during six months of relentless attrition. And so it was in the last months of the Italian campaign: attack after attack, with screaming shells and mangled bodies, scenes unmatched by any action since the First World War. The campaign was faced with great courage on both sides, it must be said, and for which numerous battle honours and a number of Victoria Crosses were to be won by soldiers of the various allied units engaged. Commandos were constantly being called on in support of the allies' long and difficult way forward. Matters really came to a head when the 5th and 8th Armies reached the Gustav line, which ran from the mouth of the River Garigliano on the west coast to a point 30 miles above Termoli on the east coast.

It was the defensive line beyond which the German army

commanders had been instructed by Berlin they should not retreat. There, they had to fight to the death. They had 130,000 men strung out along their defensive positions. Cassino became the focal point of a six-month-long stalemate in which thousands of casualties were suffered by allied troops from American, British, Indian, Gurkha and New Zealand forces. Battles of a previously unmatched ferocity raged day and night and only ended in May to allow the allies to revive their march north after the massive and controversial allied air bombardment of the Benedictine monastery at Monte Cassino, part of the fortress around which the advance north had been stalled at a cost of 6,000 men killed, wounded or captured.

Surprise allied landings at Anzio on 22 January 1944, for which the war planners had great hopes, represented an early attempt to break the deadlock. By midnight, 36,000 men and 3,000 vehicles had been put ashore ahead of the Gustav line, just 30 miles south of Rome. The British and American force included three battalions of American Rangers, the US equivalent of the British Commandos, the latter represented by 9 and 43 RM Commandos, who were landed from HMS *Derbyshire*. Although the news reports back in London claimed that the landings were a total success, virtually unopposed, the euphoria was short lived. The Germans rushed to form a semi-circle of defensive positions, and hellish battles were soon being fought.

Nor was this the only vital front engaging the Commandos. At the same time, a large force was being assembled on the Yugoslav island of Vis, with 2,000 Partisan guerrillas under their own leaders, while the Commando strength was bolstered further by the re-emergence of 40 RM in early May. Intelligence reports suggested that the Germans were about to attack Tito's headquarters in Bosnia, and liaison officers forming a top-secret British mission were arriving to meet Tito to discuss plans for joint action between the Partisans and the allies.

The Germans launched their attack on that very day, and Tito and the British liaison officers, who included Churchill's son Randolph, escaped into the mountains. The Commandos on Vis, under the overall command of Lieutenant-Colonel Jack Churchill (no relation), were ordered to mount a major assault on one of the key German-held islands, hopefully to draw forces from the mainland and thus give Tito the chance to escape. These schemes of drawing enemy fire had always been dubious in the past, and this one was no exception. For one thing, the island chosen for the raid was Brac, which had a substantial contingent of Germans in residence, although the landscape was horrendous. Jack Churchill put together a motley army for the raid, consisting of around 1,500 Partisans plus the whole of 43 RM Commando, one troop from 40 and an artillery battery from the 3rd Field Regiment under the supervision of an expert Royal Artillery fire-control officer, Major Turner, a veteran of El Alamein. The men had heavy loads to carry, including their three-inch mortar bombs and Bangalore torpedoes to blow beach defences and other obstructions. They pulled off a remarkable surprise landing that was unopposed and discovered that the Germans were secreted in a pair of eyries in high hillside positions for which Major Turner's big gun was pretty useless. Jack Churchill went to Plan B: flank attacks using the Partisans on one side and the Commandos on the other. The going was tough, however, and by the time they arrived at the starting line the Partisans decided that it was getting rather late and put it off to the following day, ignoring the swirling sounds of Jack Churchill's bagpipes that were already wafting across the hills, signalling his men into battle.

He was temporarily silenced by the arrival of a clutch of Spitfires that strafed his chaps instead of the enemy. As they recovered from the duck-and-dive positions a runner brought the message that the Partisans would not after all be turning out today. The Commandos pulled back quickly and were once again strafed by the Spitfires. Overnight, Churchill called for reinforcements in the shape of Lieutenant-Colonel Manners with three more troops of 40 RM Commando from Vis, and the attack began on what were now well-prepared German defences. The upshot was that the front-line attack of the British force, consisting of C and D Troops of 43 RM, took very heavy machine-gun fire, and because of radio failure in the mountains the men became isolated. Every one of the officers fell in the first attack along with many other ranks. Sergeants Gallon and Picketing, themselves both wounded, continued the assault until they were ordered to withdraw.

There were many heroes on that day, and many of them never came back: 43 RM lost six officers and 60 other ranks killed, wounded or missing. A second attack was led by Jack Churchill himself, again using his bagpipes as the signal for the attack by Y Troop of 40 RM. He took them into battle while calling for backup from the rest of 40 RM and for 43 RM to follow in behind. 'Y Troop of 40 was magnificent,' Churchill said. 'All in line, shouting, firing, just like on the assault course at Achnacarry.'

Radio contact was still poor, and only one troop from 43 RM had managed to get up in support. The Partisans, meanwhile, paid no heed whatsoever to the carefully negotiated order of battle and, according to Churchill, 'had buggered off to God knows where . . . and I never saw them again'. A brief respite merely meant that the Germans were regrouping, and when they realised that Churchill's force was more or less out on its own they put in a strong counter-attack. Now it was the turn of 40 RM to be hit by flanked counter-attacks, taking heavy casualties. Among them was Lieutenant-Colonel 'Pops' Manners, one of the great stalwarts of the Royal Marines, who was so severely wounded he had to be left for the German medical orderlies to pick him up. Jack Churchill himself was then captured, complete with claymore and bagpipes. In that one event, the Commandos were robbed of two of their finest leaders. Overall, the British units suffered more than 81 casualties, killed, wounded or captured in the attacks, and retreated back to Vis. German medical units immediately came out for the wounded of both sides. Colonel Manners died under treatment and word was later sent out that the German medics had done all they possibly could to save him. The British prisoners were allowed to dig a mass grave to bury their dead.

They all stood around in silent prayer as Jack Churchill played a lament on his pipes: 'Flowers of the Forest'.

Knocker White, of Y Troop, 40 RM, was not among those in the mass grave, although all his mates in the troop believed he had been killed. Knocker took a bullet wound to the neck, and one of his closest pals later reported that he was dead; and wrote to his wife to say 'Knocker died in my arms'. But, in fact, he was not dead; although he'd lost a lot of blood, he came round after his unit had left to discover a couple of Germans prodding him with their bayonets. He said a few choice words to them before he was taken to the medical wagon. Knocker was duly saved, and months later his wife received the good news, bad news letter from the War Office: 'Your husband's alive and would you now please return the widow's pension we have been paying you for the last six months.' Mrs White apparently responded in true Commando style.

Though the whole operation went badly awry, largely through the failure of communications and the unreliable nature of the temperamental Partisans, it was successful inasmuch as it had the required result. Tito was rescued from Bosnia and brought to the safe haven of Vis, where he had a number of visitors in that month of June. Among them was the overall commander of the Commando group, Major-General R. G. Sturges, who brought news of the D-Day landings and the part that the Commandos had played in it, and everybody on Vis was wishing they were there. All of the above provided proof enough that Mountbatten was right when he campaigned to switch the Royal Marines into Commando operations. His insistence on seeing this through caused great upheaval, retraining and planning within the corps and – as we have seen – was criticised to the point of ridicule by many across the whole spectrum of British military and naval life. The detractors could not have been more wrong, and if further proof was needed it would be provided in abundance over the coming months.

CHAPTER ELEVEN

D-Day

The invasion of Europe under Operation Overlord was the largest airborne and seaborne landing of troops in history and remains so today, ultimately involving almost three million troops. As will be seen from the order of battle (below), the Commandos were in the front row of the ground forces on each of the main British assault areas and were crucial in the plans for the break-out of troops from the British landing areas, a task that stretched them to the limit. Originally, the invasion plans called for ten Commandos to follow on from the spearhead landings of the parachute and air-landed troops. This was proved impossible because they were already heavily committed elsewhere. By the turn of 1944 there were four Special Service Brigades now consisting of 16 Commandos, but 2 SSB was still operating in Italy and Yugoslavia, 3 SSB was en route to the Far East in support of Mountbatten's South-East Asia Command. This left 1 and 4 Special Service Brigades available for D-Day: eight Commandos in all, three army and five Royal Marine. The Marines also provided one of the two brigade headquarters.

Of the RM units, only No. 41 had seen action under the SSB

banner, and many of the troops in the remaining groups had just come through a crash course in 'How to Be a Commando'. Henry Cosgrove was with 45 RM Commando; at the end of May, after training in Scotland, the men were moved south into a secure compound near Southampton. Once inside, no one was allowed out:

In one big marquee there were lots of big boards with over-lapping aerial photographs of the French coast. Didn't tell you where exactly. You virtually had a whole area in pictures. People were continually going in to look at them. This is some place where you're going to go, but nobody's going to tell you where. More and more photographs were added. And then things started to happen. We were issued with special 24-hour rations; we weren't allowed to touch them. There was ... a tin, like a sardine tin. It was a solid block of chocolate. It was as hard as iron. The only way you could break it up was to get at it with your bayonet. The rations were in a small box about eight inches by five by two deep. In it were cubes, little white cubes about the size of an Oxo cube with black specks. That was tea, sugar and milk. One of them would make a pint of tea. There were cubes, slightly larger, which were chicken soup. You had little cookers with cubes of solidified methylated spirits. They were round, about four inches high, with a floor in the middle where you put your billycan on the top and whatever you were going to make – tea or soup – in it. They were landing rations. Everyone had a clean pair of socks, a clean pair of underpants, a vest to match and a clean shirt. That was your clothing. Then ... your rucksack: in the bottom I had four two-inch mortar bombs, explosives and 200 rounds for the Tommy gun. I also had two smoke bombs. They were dangerous. They'd got phos-phorus in them. I was worried about getting a bullet anywhere near them. That was a tidy weight – about 80 pounds – in the rucksack. Then every man in the unit, including the colonel, carried 200 rounds of rifle ammunition in a bandoleer.

Everybody's boots were checked, and we had another look at
the aerial photographs . . . and we were moved to Hamble and
embarked in five lots.

Marines and Commandos were involved in virtually every aspect
of D-Day and beyond, and every theatre of the war, and it is worth
reminding ourselves of the full extent of their overall commitment
in 1944. They began the war with 12,000 men in 1939, and this
had risen to more than 75,000 in total by the end of it. After the
lacklustre start in terms of the deployment of the land-based body
of Marines in the early stages of the war, they quickly made up
for lost time and eventually fulfilled demanding deployments in
the major campaigns of the fightback. These gathered momentum
until the Royal Marines achieved their largest single commitment
in history with approximately 17,500 men involved in the D-Day
landings.

Apart from the Commando formations, the massive covering of
warships had expanded Marines detachments, with, as ever, the Royal
Marines bands in their hostilities role. The Marines also supplied two-
thirds of the crews for the landing craft as well as mechanics and
engineers for breakdowns, of which there were many, underwater
clearance operations, and various other tasks in which they joined
the Royal Navy teams in ensuring the uninterrupted movement of
4,000 landing craft and 1,600 merchant ships exiting ports all around
the south coast of England. They also provided an armoured support
and protection group consisting of 80 Centaur tanks, as well as anti-
aircraft units, provosts, signallers and radar operators.

The Royal Marines were therefore involved in the management of
this logistical nightmare of manoeuvring the landing craft and ships
as well as thousands of tons of assorted military hardware, millions
of rounds of ammunition and the 156,000 troops who would be placed
on the coast of France in the first 24 hours, a feat that was repeated
daily to achieve the landing of almost 400,000 troops by D+5. The
order of battle for the British landings was approximately as follows,

east to west, demonstrating the immediate involvement of the Special Service Brigades:

British 6th Airborne Division, comprising 8th and 9th Parachute Battalions of the 3rd Parachute Brigade and the 1st Canadian Parachute Battalion, airlifted by gliders and parachute east of the River Orne. 1 Special Service Brigade (under the command of Brigadier Lord Lovat), comprising 3, 4, 6 Army Commandos and 45 RM Commando, to land on Sword Beach at Ouistreham, the far-left Queen Red sector; 4 Commando was augmented with two French troops of 10 (Inter-Allied) Commando.

4 Special Service Brigade under Brigadier B. W. 'Jumbo' Leicester, RM, was split, with 41 RM and 46 RM Commandos to land on the far right of Sword Beach with the British 3rd Infantry Division and the 27th Armoured Brigade from Ouistreham to Lion-sur-Mer. (In the event, 46 RM Commando, earmarked to scale the cliffs on the left side of the Orne estuary and destroy enemy battery remained at sea in reserve until the following day because the battery proved not to be a threat.) 47 RM Commando was to land on the west flank of Gold Beach with the British 50th Division and the 8th Armoured Brigade from La Rivière to Arromanches, and specifically to capture Port-en-Bessin and link up with US forces at Omaha Beach; 48 RM Commando to land with the Canadian 3rd Infantry Division and the 2nd Armoured Brigade on Juno Beach, from St-Aubin to La Rivière-St-Sauveur.

From midnight on 5–6 June, paratroops and glider-borne units began landing at key points. Throughout the night, 230 RAF bombers began pounding German positions, and at daybreak 1,300 heavy bombers of the US 8th Air Force took over the air attack with escorts from Mustangs, Lightnings and Thunderbolts. Shortly before dawn, thousands of ships and landing craft assembled around the southern ports of Britain, packed to the gunwales with fighting troops, transport and equipment, set sail. As Cornelius Ryan wrote in *The Longest Day*:

They came, rank after relentless rank, ten lanes wide, 20 miles across, 5,000 ships of every description. There were fast new attack transports, slow rust-scarred freighters, small ocean liners, Channel steamers, hospital ships, weather-beaten tankers, coasters and swarms of fussing tugs. There were endless columns of shallow-draft landing ships – great wallowing vessels, some of them almost 350 feet long ... Ahead of the convoys were processions of minesweepers, Coast Guard cutters, buoy-layers and motor launches. Barrage balloons flew above the ships. Squadrons of fighter-planes weaved below the clouds. And surrounding this fantastic cavalcade of ships packed with men, guns, tanks, motor vehicles and supplies ... was a formidable array of 702 warships.

The Marines had the advantage over the infantry in that they were now well used to the transport that lay before them in terms of travelling by the various types of landing craft, but even they were badly affected by dire conditions. Most of those in the massive convoy would remember the crossing in rough weather for the pervading smell, a combination of diesel fumes and vomit. It was an appalling journey, buffeted by the sea and the rollers created by the sheer mass of ships. Thousands of men, packed like sardines into their craft, were violently seasick, which merely added to the overall discomfort and fear. Henry Cosgrove was among the early departees with 45 RM:

> It was an amazing sight. It appeared that the navy had made a roadway going across the Channel. You seemed to be travelling through a line of ships each side of you, as if going along a marked-out road. Once we left the shore and were on our way, we were told what was going to happen. We were told our job was to get to the Orne bridges as quickly as we could to relieve the paratroopers. But then, we knew it was going to be a hard slog.

Veteran of Commando operations, William Spearman, agreed:

> ... the enormity of everything began to become apparent. No matter which way you looked there were ships of all shapes and sizes as far as the eye could see. And as we neared the French coast, on our left, not too far away from us, we saw one ship explode into the air and sink, all in a few minutes. Some of the boats as they went in were blown out of the water long before they reached the beach. The mother ships got blown up, the transporters got blown up. The noise was just indescribable. We were led by minesweepers, but it was very hard for them to remove every mine. So a number of ships were sunk by mines before they even got there. Meanwhile, our bombers were going over all the time, to do the softening up. But when we landed you'd never believe there'd been any softening up. Troops that landed in front of us, the 3rd Brigade, East Lancashire Regiment, I think, and Canadians, were in severe trouble. As we came ashore there were bodies everywhere.

The airborne and parachute troops were to spearhead the invasion with Commandos providing assaults on gun batteries and key German positions to minimise the attacks on the great advancing force about which there had been great worries in terms of German attacks simply mowing down vast numbers before they could get off the beaches. But the key operation for 1 SSB was to support the new British airborne division, the 6th, under the command of Major-General Richard Gale, one of the pioneers of the parachute brigades, which were just as new as the Commandos themselves. Brigadier James Hill's 3rd Parachute Brigade was to be joined by the 5th Parachute Brigade, the 6th Air-Landing Brigade and a Canadian parachute battalion. The 6th Airborne Division was to go in ahead of the invasion force, dropping around Ranville, north-east of Caen, to cover the landings of the British 2nd Army on their designated beaches. The US 82nd and 101st Airborne Divisions were to perform similar operations for the US 1st Army, landing at their beaches of Omaha and Utah.

The area to be taken by the British 6th included high ground on the eastern sector around the River Orne and the Caen Canal. Priority targets for the paras and airborne forces on the British side of the invasion plans therefore included the infamous Merville battery, which was itself capable of knocking out thousands of troops as they landed, the high ground overlooking the route forward for the advancing British troops and the bridges across the canal and river to halt an immediate counterattack by enemy forces while the beach landings were proceeding.

Lord Lovat's 1 SSB came ashore on Sword Beach beside the River Orne, on the left flank of the allied armies, with 146 officers and 2,456 men. They had orders to capture Ouistreham and then push inland to support the Airborne Division in their mission to seize and hold the crucial Pegasus Bridge over the Caen Canal, famed as one of the Parachute Regiment's battle honours. Spearman recalled:

We had strict instructions of what we had to do. We were on the east flank of the whole of the landing. Our first job was to knock out a gun battery at Ouistreham, which was right on the east side of the landing. And then, after that, we were to take up positions in the Hauger area a few miles inland and defend that against all-comers. If our boat had sunk, I really don't know who would have taken over that job, because there were no reserves for us. It was a very thin green line. Luck was with us and we landed on the beach, struggling forward under the tremendous weight on our backs: a half-hundredweight or more. We carried our own weapons, flame-throwers, shells ... The idea was we had to have enough to support ourselves in case we didn't get replenished. And once you go down with that pack on your back, you can't get up again. We dashed ashore and we were all shocked by the number of bodies, dead bodies, living bodies, and all the blood in the water giving the appearance they were drowning in their own blood for the want of moving. The whole place was littered [with bodies]. There were great, monstrous fortifications on the beach, like tremendous cubes of crisscrossed steel girders to stop gliders landing, to stop ships coming in. There were girders and poles penetrating into the beach, sticking up to stop boats coming in. The whole beach area was covered by flame-throwers, and dominating the whole landing areas were these huge pillboxes. You just couldn't get out of range of them. The fortifications were excellent. For our chaps coming ashore it was a desperate situation. And it wasn't our job to stop and put them out of action. We had to get to the gun battery.

We had one object in mind: to get off the bloody beach. It was terrifying, and having seen all the bodies on the beach doubled our determination. No matter what happened, we had to get off the beach. Once you get off the beach, you're out of the fire, as it were. But it's a very hard lesson to learn, and people bloody won't learn it. Why did they put so many untrained troops on the beach first? Any one of us could tell you they wouldn't get off. They'd be so transfixed with fright they couldn't get off. We, of course, were transfixed with fright, but we had the certain knowledge that you either stopped and died or you made a dash for it. Some of our chaps did try to put some of the things out of action on the way. Lieutenant Carr deliberately went up to one pillbox and threw a couple of grenades in, and I thought it was a brave deed, just to hesitate in order to do that.

Lord Lovat's brigade left the beach areas under a hail of fire, and the men padded off in search of the designated targets. They had to rely on their maps and their memory of the reconnaissance photographs that they had viewed before setting off. It was really a case of establishing a general direction and following the noise. Henry Cosgrove of 45 RM:

On these aerial photographs there was a piece of slightly higher ground with a wood. That was our assembly area, which was about two miles inland. [From there] we set off for the Orne. These [airborne] lads had set up on one end of the bridge. When we got to the bridge there were a lot of dead Germans around and some of our paratroopers. There were snipers around, firing at us, but nothing serious. And then the brigadier set off over the bridge as if he was out for a stroll on his country estate, with bloody bagpipes in front. It was Lord Lovat [with Piper Bill Millin, who led a number of Lovat's attacks]. We followed him over the bridge and then the problems really started. We were to hold the high ground up round . . . [but] the Germans were in great strength all around there, and we started losing a lot of men. Then, to crown it all, we lost our radios. The first signaller was shot and then we lost the second signaller, wounded. Both sets were out of action, and we couldn't make contact with brigade headquarters. Fortunately, we managed to reach an artillery officer at a forward OP who was laying down fire for us from the ships if we needed it, and we managed to relay our position via him, to the ship and back to brigade headquarters.

They told us to come out at night – but that was a long time away and we were running out of ammunition . . . We had to try to break out and get back to brigade headquarters at Le Plein. We didn't do too badly for about a mile, and then two-inch mortars were becoming very accurate; we were mortaring very well with what we'd got then and managed to get through, although we lost a few men in the process. When we rejoined the brigade, we'd been out 36 hours without sleep.

One company of 4 Commando was late in arriving into the action because the men did not get ashore until after 7 p.m. Their landing craft were damaged as they were coming in and were left floundering off the coast for hours until the activity died down and they were able to get a tow. By then, the beach was an incredible sight of beached and half-sunk landing craft, tanks that had become bogged down in the sands, wounded men and the bodies of the dead. Once ashore, the company headed for the action and ran straight into serious trouble, as Bernard Davies recalled:

When we arrived, the 6th Airborne Division were in a very dodgy situation. Our object was to grab the high ground east of the landing strips which, if they'd got some guns along the top, could have commanded seven miles of beach. They were almost overrun. My unit, C Company, suffered heavily as we took up our positions. We suffered 80 per cent casualties, lost all of our officers and the sergeant-major, Peter King, was promoted to lieutenant to take over; he was awarded the DCM. The Germans had thrown everything at us, and we were armed with those blasted Bren guns which only fired about 400 rounds a minute. The Germans had one that fired 1,500 rounds a minute – 25 rounds a second.

We were, as usual, very inadequately armed. It was close fighting, 30 or 40 yards. We took heavy casualties but we held our ground until we were pulled out when a Marines Commando came up and we were able to take a rest until they moved us up to Breville, in the front line, still surrounded. The Germans held most of the ground all the way into Caen. We were to stay there for two weeks, battling away and eventually moving forward. We took quite a few casualties from night snipers. I was amazed at some of the things the Germans did. In the country lanes, there were high banks at the side of the road which had walkways cut through, except they were cut at 45-degree angles instead of straight, so you could never see them coming until it was too late. They had machine gunners in the hedgerows during the day; they fired down the hedgerows from positions where it was impossible to get sight of them, and then at night they pulled them out and put them into the fields so

our night patrols were sitting ducks. They could hear us coming
and cut us up. The RAF often saved the day for us against forces
that were far better armed. We had the men and the organisation – the 6th Airborne Division with Commandos stuck in the
middle of them – could not be bettered anywhere. We were
badly let down on firepower.

After four days of heavy fighting, Brigadier Lovat called in his
commanding officers at his HQ when he learned that the brigade had
already lost 270 men, killed or wounded. He stormed in, demanding:

Where the hell are the reinforcements to cope with this wholesale destruction? They're supposed to have a depot and a training
centre full of soldiers and they supply fuck all. Twenty-five lucky
lads as replacements for four days' fighting – less than half of
one troop – committed piecemeal to the battle the moment they
arrived. Killed or missing, poor devils, without knowing what
hit them. Fifty new men were needed before we cleared the
beach. We lost more than this handful, sunk at sea. Who is responsible for this balls-up? If the Germans repeat the same performance tomorrow, General Dempsey can expect a butcher's bill that
spells curtains for the brigade, and the high ground will fall.

But there was a further point to all of this. The Commandos, by the
very nature of their operations, were supposed to run short, sharp
campaigns and then pull back to replenish and train. There was already
every indication that they were to be pinned down for far longer than
they had imagined. Two days after the meeting, the divisional
commander issued orders for the capture of a strongly held area of
Breville Wood, where the Black Watch had taken serious casualties
the previous afternoon, even though he knew the brigade was short
of manpower. Henry Cosgrove's unit was among those who went in,
though still short of men. For a while it went quieter. Then, said
Cosgrove, as they prepared for the Breville assault, General Gale, of

the 6th Airborne, sent out probing patrols before the Airborne Division went in for the frontal attack, with the Commandos going in for a flanking attack to capture a German headquarters:

Casualties were very heavy. The Airborne lads were very badly hit and then they started belting us. They had mobile guns and were mortaring very accurately. We were taking quite a lot of casualties and getting short of men, some killed, some wounded and others missing. By now we'd lost over a quarter of our strength, and these casualties kept on coming through. Bloody hell! We were getting plastered by the mortars. One of the doctors arranged a convoy of Jeeps to shift the wounded. The Jeeps were flying to and fro, and there was mortaring going on the whole time: bloody brave men, they were, sitting up there. It's not so bad when you've got a hole in the ground and you've got a bit of cover, but out in the open, moving the wounded . . . It was quite a night, I can tell you.

Lieutenant-Colonel Derek Mills-Roberts, commanding No. 6, was temporarily out of action, receiving treatment for a leg wound. He was given an intra-muscular injection and ordered to remain in a prostrate position for some hours at the farm they were using as a base. His unit headed off into the Breville attack and he was left lying down, drowsy from the drugs he had been given. A few hours later, he was woken by a corporal bearing a message from Breville. Lord Lovat had been wounded in a violent German counteroffensive, and he was to get over there immediately. Mills-Roberts, still drowsy and in pain from his wound, managed to revive himself and get over to Lovat, who, he discovered, had been removed to some old stables:

It was almost dark and the ghastly scene was lit up by the farm buildings, which were on fire. Lovat was a frightful mess; a large shell fragment had cut deeply into his back and side. Peter Tasker, No. 6 Commando's medical officer, was giving him a blood transfusion. The brigadier was very calm. 'Take over the brigade,' he said, 'and whatever happens – not a foot back.' He repeated this several times. And then, 'Get me a priest,' he said. The parachute battalion making the attack on Breville had been badly hit by mortars and Nebelwerfers – petrol bombs from this last insidious weapon had burst, causing desperate injuries and burns among the parachutists. Their colonel was mortally wounded. Other wounded men were on fire, and we put out the flames by rolling blankets round them. Further out lay more wounded. The RAMC were doing magnificent work, while Sergeant-Major Woodcock found every available Jeep to get stretcher cases to safety.

I no longer commanded 6 Commando, and, as acting brigadier, had to get on with the wider battle, which was reaching round the whole area. I went back into the farmyard, where every available foot of space was covered with stretcher cases, but the Jeeps were making a good clearance. If more shells had fallen into the crowded farmyard, the slaughter would have been terrible. Lord Lovat was among those who were eventually carried back to field hospitals, and he survived his very severe wounds.

Elsewhere, the news was only slightly more encouraging. Brigadier 'Jumbo' Leicester's 4 SSB had, from the beginning, been sent off in various directions and suffered as a result. Most had the same kind of Beach landing experiences described above, and a good many of the troops of Leicester's RM Commandos never made it inland. 48 RM Commando had landed on Juno Beach with the initial objective of an assault on St-Aubin, following in behind the Canadian North Shore Regiment. But the men had a bad landing. The Commando was formed only three months before D-Day, and any veteran of Commando raids would put his hand on his heart to say that was simply not enough time to get a man fully fit and trained for present situations in which the risks to the men would be unacceptably high.

No. 48 discovered some of them immediately they came ashore bearing the huge burden of their backpacks. The wet landing experienced by many meant the weight they were carrying virtually doubled; at the very least it would be increased to not much short of a hundredweight. This, coupled with the inexperience of the Canadian units, made it a doubly dubious situation. But in fairness to No. 48, most of the problems were by no means the fault of the men. They were in totally different landing craft from those in which they had been trained; they literally had to manhandle gangplanks over the bow of the craft, and they were all getting shot doing so. The spot they landed on was also wrong; it was right under the noses of Germans inside a heavily fortified concrete strongpoint who let loose immediately.

The Canadians hadn't secured the beach, and chaos was developing rapidly. Men were dropping as they ran forward amid the tanks and other vehicles struggling to get off the beaches. One of 48's officers actually ran back to try to stop a Canadian tank that was attempting to get moving, seemingly oblivious to the fact that it was running over wounded men in the process. He banged on the turret and when the tank still didn't stop he disabled it by throwing an anti-tank grenade into the mechanism. What was left of 48 were assembled under the harbour wall and made off towards their target, passing through the Canadians to St-Aubin and on to another big scrap a couple of miles east along the coast. For all their losses, the men put up a spirited fight and eventually captured the strongpoint there and saved a number of lives among those coming through.

No. 46 RM Commando had arrived after special training for a clifftop assault on a German battery, but in the event it was cancelled and they were given a substitute objective: joining a French-Canadian unit in clearing enemy positions along the tidal River Mue. It turned out to be a far more onerous project than the one for which they'd been trained. The enemy troops were holed up in the villages of La Hamel and Rots and, unbeknown to the Commandos, they were Waffen SS of the 12th Panzer Division, dedicated young troops who rose out of the Hitler Youth. It was a bitter struggle, with street fighting and close-quarter combat. In the process, No. 46 lost more than 60 men, killed, wounded or missing. But they put the Germans to flight and captured 47 prisoners.

Because of their more diverse operations, the men of Leicester's brigade found themselves facing longer battles in which Commando tactics simply did not apply, and it soon became clear that they, too, would be fighting in the line for weeks. This was a particularly galling possibility for the officers, given that 41 RM Commando, it will be recalled, was the only one in the brigade to have seen action so far in the war as a Commando. Nonetheless, three of Leicester's Commandos had been assigned to progressive tasks, completing each one before moving on to the next with a sort of planned domino effect. No. 41, for example, was first designated to attack German positions at Lion-sur-Mer from their landing on Sword Beach, but the troops were put ashore in the wrong place, almost a quarter of a mile from their given landing area. They had to dash across the beaches under a torrent of shells and mortar fire, at a point already strewn with the debris of bad landings: blazing vehicles, bodies and stuck-firm tanks.

Once on the move, No. 41 formed itself into two, one group to attack a German strongpoint on the approach to Lion, the other to attack a stoutly defended château used as a German planning base. Both tasks resulted in an unexpectedly strong response from the Germans in residence and were not completed for almost 24 hours.

The Commando came back together to continue on to its next objective, which proved to hold even greater opposition: 41 and 48 were to combine to raid the vital Douvres radar station, surrounded by strong fortifications and minefields and which the Germans believed was impregnable. After more than a week of trying to break through, the Commandos sent for flail tanks to clear mines before launching a full-scale assault with a troop of tanks and naval bombardment. This time, the Germans gave up. They then moved on to Sallenelles, across the Orne, where General Gale put them to work in the highly dangerous business of patrolling.

And so it went on, with the advance moving ever outward, with the Commandos and the paras being committed to fighting in static situations far longer than they had anticipated. Some were still there in October, and No. 47, among the first ashore on D-Day morning, was still there 12 months later, caught up in the front line of the advance, having told their wives that they expected to be home well before Christmas. Many did not make it at all.

Both 1 SSB and 4 SSB suffered a similar number of casualties in the D-Day campaign: 39 officers and 371 other ranks were killed, 114 officers and 1,324 other ranks wounded, and seven officers and 162 other ranks missing. This represented slightly less than half the overall establishment of the two brigades and was a devastating total for them, far higher than the running average of the overall allied losses of 5,500 killed, 22,000 wounded and missing in 15 days since the D-Day landings.

Those who were disengaged and sent home to regroup were in a poor state, as Henry Cosgrove, with 45 RM, recalls:

> They took us to a rest camp on the coast and then we were homeward bound. To be honest, I'm not sure whether it was Portsmouth or Southampton, but there was a band there. We came down the gangway and we were filthy, and I mean filthy. We'd been away three months . . . our uniforms were rags, most of us had fleas, some had lice. We were in a bad way. We'd washed in puddles when we had a chance and that was it. As we fell in on a railway station on the jetty by this train, some silly blighter let off a firework. One minute there were all these men standing there; the next minute there wasn't a soul in sight, they were under the train. We were literally bomb-happy then; nerves were ragged. We'd been bombed and shelled sometimes for days on end. We went to Petworth camp, where we were ordered to strip off and all our clothing was burned and our personal belongings fumigated. Then there were showers, a medical inspection, many heads were shaved and painted with

gentian violet. When that was finished, we came to a big marquee, and as you walked in you got a pair of underpants, vest, a pair of trousers, jacket, socks and boots to get some semblance of a uniform before going home on leave.

It was a brief respite. Before long, they would be back in the fray.

CHAPTER TWELVE

To the Very Last

As the allies began to progress through the German lines and on into north-eastern France and the Low Countries, the supply lines to the great meandering columns of men and machines became a pressing problem. Without a free flow of the massive inventory of materials needed to keep up the impetus of D-Day, the whole project could have been jeopardised or, in a worst-case scenario, halted completely. Motor fuel was in huge demand, but the issue of maintaining a reliable source had been resolved in advance, at least in terms of getting supplies to the French coast. Undersea pipelines had been suggested by Lord Mountbatten during his time as Chief of Combined Operations when it was pointed out that conventional tankers and ship-to-shore pipelines would be at the mercy of the Luftwaffe, and there would be a huge risk of the thousands of vehicles and tanks simply running out of fuel. Many laughed at the prospect and some joked sarcastically, 'Why not dig a tunnel?' Mountbatten would not let the matter drop. Churchill was intrigued and in 1942, under conditions of great secrecy, Siemens Brothers of Woolwich were commissioned to design PLUTO (Pipeline Under the Ocean). Subsequently, 11 undersea pipelines were laid between Dungeness and Boulogne, each of 32 nautical miles, and two pipelines laid between Shanklin and Cherbourg, each of 70 nautical miles, capable of supplying a million gallons of fuel a day. The pipelines, connected to coastal pumping stations disguised as seaside ice-cream parlours, sweet shops and bungalows, were laid as soon as the allies had cleared the Germans from the French coast, and over the coming months 172 million gallons of fuel were pumped through them. The project was protected throughout by an equally top-secret force that included Marines.

The whole point of this fuel-supply operation was to ensure that the road tankers continued unhindered, supplying the thousands of thirsty vehicles and tanks storming across Europe. It also enabled the allies to forge ahead at such speed that the need quickly arose to free more Channel ports of France and the Low Countries to bring in the thousands of tons of supplies, ammunition, vehicles, armour and so on to keep the juggernaut rolling. It was hoped this could be eased by freedom of movement into the port of Antwerp, which had been reached by the 2nd British Army by early September. But to reach the harbour itself, shipping had to negotiate an 18-mile journey along the River Scheldt, the mouth of which remained heavily mined by the Germans, with the additional threat of enemy air raids and ground attacks ever present.

This was especially true of the protruding island of Walcheren, which dominated the mouth of the river. The Germans had already taken the precaution of sending a massive influx of defending troops and artillery and had flooded and staked large areas to deter airborne landings. Eventually, the allies decided that the only way to open up the port was through forced amphibious landings around the Walcheren coastline supported by a heavy bombardment of German defences. Churchill objected on humanitarian grounds, because of the risk to civilian populations around the town of Flushing, a prime target, but under pressure from Eisenhower he eventually agreed if bombing the town itself would be avoided. This meant greater reliance on a speedy amphibious landing of Commando troops going in ahead of infantry and tanks, a role for which 4 SSB – still on the Continent – was chosen, to attack all the German batteries that could bring fire down on the invading troops.

In fact, 46 RM Commando, by then down to fewer than 200 men, was sent home to recuperate and retrain and was replaced for the operation by 4 Commando. The brigade was further bolstered by contingents of Belgian and Norwegian Commandos, to make two forced landings using landing craft now equipped with rocket launchers and anti-tank guns. While troops of the Canadian II Corps attacked from the east, 4 Commando was to make a forced night landing at Flushing in LCAs (Landing Craft Assault). They would be followed in by the 155 Infantry Brigade along with elements of the 7th Armoured Division, while the remaining troops of 4 SSB were to come ashore at Westkapelle soon after dawn, covered by considerable artillery support from Naval Force T in 25 landing craft. Additionally, the RAF would embark on a limited bombing of the island and Spitfires would strafe enemy positions – and there were plenty of targets.

By the time the operation was ready to be mounted on the night of 31 October 1944, the Germans had assembled a formidable force as well as their now-familiar strong points constructed from reinforced concrete. Landing areas were also hazardous, heavily mined, booby-trapped and staked, while the sand-dunes had been ploughed. The Germans had also flooded vast areas of the flat landscape. They were also helped by the weather, when dense cloud appeared over the whole area, restricting the amount of air support the RAF could provide. Advance recce parties went in first to establish the landing sites and to guide the main body of Commandos forward. This was achieved with few casualties, and in fact a number of prisoners were taken. But the arrival of strafing Spitfires stirred the Germans into further action, and very soon their big guns were blazing even before the landings at both sites were complete. Some of the parties coming ashore took bad hits and landing craft were sunk.

The arrival of the first landings of the 155 Brigade was covered by 4 Commando, which had cleared fortified houses and strong points overlooking the landing areas, and by mid-afternoon most of the first-day objectives were met. But it took a further three days of hard fighting by 4 Commando and the infantry battalions before the area was totally safe. They then moved along to assist the three remaining Commandos of 4 SSB, 41 RM, 47 RM and 48 RM, landing slightly later and confronted with an even worse run-in, with six landing craft hit. Once they were ashore, the German guns opened up with terrifying might, yet the Commandos managed to create the beachheads that would allow the flow of troops ashore.

The battle was again hard fought. The Germans' carefully pre-registered firepower was deadly accurate, although it was soon matched by the allies' own naval and air bombardment. On the ground, indescribable noise, flames and explosions erupted as the artillery and gunners pounded away. The troops themselves faced six solid days of hard fighting that eventually came down to house-to-house battles ebbing and flowing in the midst of a civilian population who basically had nowhere to hide. One night, two British soldiers cut off from the rest of their troop were given refuge by a local family. The Germans, coming up later, discovered this and herded the whole family of five outside and shot them at point-blank range.

In spite of their defences, the Germans were on the run by the fifth day. On the eighth day they were waving the white flag; Walcheren and the vital approaches to Antwerp were secure. The surrounding areas, however, took longer to clear and it was the end of November before the Commandos were able to disengage from this commitment. The results proved to be greater than the mere possession of Antwerp and the surrounding territory. It was estimated that this one action affected the fortunes of 40,000 German troops strung out in the remaining battlefields of the Low Countries and on into Germany itself. By the end of the month, after the minefields had been cleared, the port was alive with allied activity, bringing in men, equipment and supplies for the onward march.

It was undoubtedly a remarkable achievement and, for 4 Special Service Brigade under the command of the brilliant 'Jumbo' Leicester, the Walcheren operation was a major success story that was highly applauded, especially among the senior ranks of the forces he had worked with. The cost was heavy. Already depleted after its assignments for the D-Day landings, the force suffered a further hefty slice of its manpower at Walcheren: 103 killed, 325 wounded and 68 missing during just eight days of fighting. The brigade temporarily pulled out to re-equip and to take in reinforcements, but half the force went back to Walcheren in case of an attempted German return. The remainder, plus 47 RM Commando and three troops from 48 RM, went straight away to join the British 1 Corps as backup against the short-lived Ardennes break-out attempt by the Germans in December and then came under the command of the 1st Canadian Army, tasked with clearing northern Holland. There remained a long, hard road ahead in the remaining months to the end of hostilities: the brigade carried out no fewer than 28 fighting patrols and 14 reconnaissance missions.

In December 1944 the four Special Service Brigades were renamed Commando Brigades to dispose of the SS connotation, given the reputation of the Nazi troops using the same prefix, and their operations were diverse and demanding across the whole spectrum of the war: 1 Commando Brigade remained in Europe, as did 4 Commando; 3 Commando Brigade was still fighting around the Adriatic, while 2 Commando Brigade was dispatched to the Far East to join Mountbatten's bid to reclaim Burma.

In fact, 1 Commando Brigade under Lord Lovat's successor, Derek Mills-Roberts, was originally destined for the Far East after being reinforced following its return to the shores of England in September 'stinking and filthy', as Henry Cosgrove described it. But even as the men were preparing for departure, the brigade, soon to be rejoined by 46 RM Commando back from loan duties elsewhere, was sent instead to Western Europe to begin what became one more remarkable episode to add to the wartime exploits of the Royal Marines Commandos: a long haul, mostly on foot and fighting all the way, from the heart of Holland to the Baltic.

The variety of tasks that befell 1 Commando Brigade ranged from strengthening defences at Antwerp against possible countermeasures, then onwards to join the line at Maas, marching across Holland and spearheading the break-in to Germany, featuring in four major opposed river crossings, including the Rhine and the Elbe, and ending up taking the surrender of Field Marshal Erhard Milch at Neustadt, a man whose arrogance earned him a swipe over the head from Mills-Roberts's baton. Henry Cosgrove was still there, slogging away with 45 RM Commando, having left Tilbury docks in a derelict old ferry-boat that was once used for crossing to the Isle of Man. They landed at Ostend, went on by train to Helmond in Holland with the 15th Scottish Assault Division before marching onwards to clear out the Germans from Massbracht and Brachterbeck, which were captured with few casualties:

We hit trouble further on, on the banks of the Maas, and a fair old fight developed. The Jerries had got us pinned down out in the open, and we were getting heavily shot up. One of the Army Medical Corps lads by the name of Harden was a real hero, wonderful fellow liked by everybody. He was dodging about getting the wounded in, then he was shot himself. They gave him a VC.* As the Jerries retreated, they had marvellous ways of setting up points to hold up the advancing army, and we fell for it. We got pinned down and we lost quite a few men there. Eventually, the lads behind us laid down a couple of smoke screens for us to get out of it, but as soon as the smoke screens

* Lance-Corporal H. E. Harden of the Royal Army Medical Corps ran forward to attend a wounded officer and two Marines, dragging them back to safety. In spite of orders not to risk his life any further, he twice went back with stretcher-bearers to help evacuate the wounded, and on the third occasion was shot through the head. He was awarded a posthumous VC for his actions.

came down the Germans opened up with everything they had. They knew the range, so we couldn't move. Eventually, darkness came and we were shifted out of it. By then, we were up in the front of the 2nd Army with the intention of carrying on through Holland and up to cross the Rhine [at Wesel]. It was freezing cold, snow on the ground, and we used to burrow into it at nights to keep warm.

The brigade's involvement came with the launch of Montgomery's Operation Plunder and the crossing of the Rhine by the 21st Army. The Commandos were to take Wesel after a massive bombardment by the RAF. It was, as Henry Cosgrove pointed out, a very noisy place to be in as 78 Lancaster bombers dropped around 450 tons of bombs in a first-wave attack on 23 March, followed by a second wave of 200 bombers dropping over 1,000 tons of heavy explosives and an artillery bombardment. This was to be followed by a landing of airborne troops from the US 18th Airborne Corps and the British 6th Airborne Division, arriving in 1,200 Dakotas, and the hard-pressed troops on the ground were overjoyed to see them:

We were in a bad way by then, and the message had gone out to get our wounded together, and we were going to get them back across the river. Then, fortunately, Dakotas were coming over dropping parachutists . . . Americans first. They were dropping from a tidy height, and they were ending up in the river and everywhere else bar where they should be. They were followed in by the British, who came in low – our old friends from the 6th Airborne. Anyway, they reinforced us. It was only later that we discovered that our one brigade of Commandos had been facing a whole division of Germans. It was no wonder we couldn't hold them. They'd got every support, mobile artillery, the lot. Here we were with light weapons. Once the bridges had been established, and the army came over, we had artillery and tanks courtesy of the Desert Rats, 7th Armoured Division. We set off again and took a ride on the tanks. We sat round the turret. That was fine for a while until we started getting up near the Black Forest, then you had to move off pretty sharpish.

The next battle for 1 Commando Brigade was Osnabrück, home to a large German garrison. But their resistance was fairly mild compared with what had been expected, and the town was captured in short order, allowing the Commandos to press on ahead of the main force coming up behind, hardly stopping for breath, towards another major hurdle at Lauenburg for the crossing of the Elbe. The brigade fought off the opposition dug in around a steep bank on the opposite side of the river and set up a bridgehead for the 6th Airborne Division and 7th Armoured Division to pass through. They then headed towards the Baltic, ending up at Neustadt. Henry Cosgrove:

There was a big concentration camp there. The smell was unbelievable. We just saw masses of people behind the fences, masses of them, all clinging on to the wire. All you could see were their hands, their faces and their eyes. They were all skeletal. They were mostly political prisoners: Belgians, French, every nationality you could think of. It was here that the brigadier, Mills-Roberts, hit Field Marshal Milch on the head with his baton over some remark or other. You could understand his feelings at the time. I was surprised when I heard he'd done it, actually. Although he was a wild man, the brigadier – oh, he was a wild man – he was also a damned good soldier. But none of us had any time for the Germans when we saw that place. There was a big pit full of bodies, and there were some still alive crawling around on top in the pit. There were dead everywhere, wherever you went. A lot of the survivors had got out and were roaming the countryside. You can imagine how they felt towards the Germans, and I'm afraid our unit wasn't too fussy about Germans then either after that lot. You can't believe that human beings could be like this, that they could do it to people.

By contrast, we were moved on again to Eutin, a most beautiful place, not very far from the Baltic Sea. It also possessed a huge barracks, and suddenly we found ourselves with thousands of German prisoners because peace had been declared. Anyway, we were supposed to be looking after these prisoners – God knows how many there were – when there was some kind of alert: 'The Germans haven't given up in Norway. We're going to Norway.' So we started getting down towards Hamburg. We were going to get aboard tank-landing ships and sail for Norway. But, thank God, we never went to Norway. We ended up in Tilbury. We'd come home.

The longest of all engagements for the Commandos fell to 2 Commando Brigade, by then under the command of Brigadier Ronnie Tod, veteran of 9 Commando, who had with him 2 and 9 Army Commandos and 40 and 43 RM Commandos. They had been working in Italy and around the Adriatic for more than 18 months, jointly or separately engaged in their raids with the Partisans on the coastlines of Yugoslavia and Albania and on the Adriatic islands, where on Vis, it will be recalled, they had provided a safe haven for Tito. German resistance remained heavy throughout, and severe fighting ensued, swinging back and forth in the battle for key positions. The brigade undertook numerous additional tasks, with units permanently on the move, including taking possession of the islands of Corfu and Solta, and in the latter a large number of prisoners were taken before they could escape to reinforce the fading German positions in Italy. By the late autumn of 1944 the Germans were on the retreat from the Balkans, and the Commandos were joined by the Partisans in ensuring an aggravated departure. Their tasks now included other aspects, such as helping to restore life's essentials to the locals.

However, with the Red Army advancing from the north-east, the British began to get the distinct feeling that their Partisan colleagues, who were of the Communist persuasion, would rather have the Russians alongside them than the British. Friction between the two groups emerged in spite of the camaraderie that had gone before in their joint efforts against German positions.

Life for the British troops became difficult at every turn as the Partisan commanders began to ignore the British and operate on their own account. They even stopped their men and civilians fraternising with the Commandos. Consequently, with the Germans retreating fast, Tod received orders to pull 43 RM Commando out of Yugoslavia in the third week of January 1945 to rejoin the brigade in Italy. They were followed by 40 RM Commando, which had remained active in the Adriatic, from their base on Vis, harassing remaining pockets of German resistance until early February. Now, Tod's 2 Commando Brigade was together again for what would go down in the Commando history as its last great battle of the war in Europe, at Lake Comacchio.

The brigade would receive the support of various 8th Army artillery units, including M Squadron of the Special Boat Squadron led by the Dane, Major Anders Lassen, hero of many major operations in the eastern Mediterranean at a time when the group was attached to the SAS. Comacchio was a combination of a natural lake and a huge flooded area, which was for the most part a shallow, smelly swamp with a base of deep, slimy mud with little more than 45 centimetres of water, although in recent dry conditions the level had dropped to around 15 centimetres in some places. For the most part it was not deep enough for any kind of landing craft. The so-called lake was in the epicentre of the final stage of the allies' advance north into the Po River valley and was surrounded by fortified German positions. This was, then, to be the object of 2 Commando Brigade's last major battle of the war, under the codename Operation Roast: to open the path for the troops coming up behind. The order was as follows: 2 and 9 Commandos would cross the lake to secure objectives on the north and east sides, deep behind enemy lines; 40 RM would hold their own line on the River Reno, flowing south out of the lake, and 43 RM would secure vital terrain between the lake and the Adriatic coast.

The first of the operations was launched at first light on 1 April

1945 when the troops clambered into a mixture of craft assembled for the crossing consisting largely of flat-bottomed storm boats each towing a string of Goatleys – ten-man collapsible canoes – all heavily laden, so progress was slow. A 5,000-metre smoke screen was laid to cover the landings, but it was insufficient to prevent heavy opposing fire as the Germans quickly mustered their response to the series of attacks now following on the targets set for the Commando units. The troops of 9 Commando met murderous fire for their landing, but they came ashore with the piper playing 'The Road to the Isles', and by the time darkness fell the men had secured their objective and captured 128 prisoners. Similar trouble faced 43 Commando as they approached their target area, and the leading troop was literally pinned down by machine-gun fire. Realising the desperate situation, Corporal Tom Hunter dashed out to an exposed position and began firing his Bren gun at five German gun positions lined up ahead of them. As he did so, a number of men who would surely have been cut down made their escape. Sadly, Hunter took a number of bullets to his body and fell fatally wounded. He was posthumously awarded the Victoria Cross. The remainder of his unit, meanwhile, held their position until they were relieved at first light the following day by the 24 Guards Brigade.

Not long afterwards, a further Victoria Cross would be awarded. In conjunction with the main objectives north and west of the lake, four small islands had to be taken. This task was handed to Anders Lassen and M Squadron of the SBS in conjunction with an Italian unit, the 28th Garibaldi Brigade. He was to lead a number of raiding operations over the coming nights, and in the early hours of 9 April he led a patrol to a causeway at the very northern tip of the lake, leading to Comacchio town. As the men headed towards the town they came under sporadic fire, which they silenced with a handful of grenades. A little further on, they came to a building from which six Germans emerged with their hands up, but as the men went forward to secure them they came under heavy machine-gun fire. Lassen himself was wounded instantly, and he ordered his troop to withdraw while he gave them covering fire. He kept it up until all his men were behind him and in their boats, but as he turned to join them Lassen was felled in a hail of fire. His gallantry was marked by the award of a posthumous VC to add to the three Military Crosses he had won during his exploits off the coast of France and with Jellicoe in the Mediterranean. Two more weeks of hard fighting lay ahead for the brigade before the German forces in northern Italy and Austria finally surrendered on 2 May 1945.

While the Commandos had been tested to the limit almost to the final gasp of the war in Europe, so, too, were the units of 3 Commando Brigade in South-East Asian theatres, where conditions were appalling and the enemy ruthless. No 'rules of war' were applicable here, and there was certainly no guarantees, for example, as to the fate of injured men left behind to be collected and cared for by the medics of the oncoming enemy, as happened with the Germans and the Italians and vice versa with the allies. Against the Nippon army, the troops were just as likely to be tortured, bayoneted or strung up to the nearest tree to be eaten by creatures of the forest. There were cases where severely wounded British troops who had little hope of survival were shot by their own officers rather than leaving them to the cruelty of the Japanese.

The Commandos followed Lord Mountbatten into the region on his appointment as Supreme Commander. They were among a number of 'must-have' units that he gathered for the task of recapturing Burma. He found conditions worse than he had ever imagined, with malaria endemic among the troops and morale at rock bottom. Memories of the dramatic British withdrawal from Rangoon and being chased out of Burma by the Japanese at a cost of 13,463 casualties still weighed heavily. Mountbatten's ambitions were undiminished by the mess he inherited. He had been warned what to expect prior to his departure from the UK, and he had especially been told not to take any nonsense from the expatriate communities and the colonial staffs of the British and French who had lived the life of Riley in the east oblivious to reality: it was all over, regardless of who won the war. The supreme irony was that the Supreme Commander who had come to sort out the appalling mess in the east was the one who would eventually manage to kick away the foundations of the Empire in India and beyond. But all that was in the future.

His job now was to get the British back into Rangoon. With all Britain's possessions in the region, with the exception of India and Ceylon, in enemy hands, this was an onerous task, given that he had inherited the most seriously neglected army in the entire British military establishment: the forgotten army, as Field Marshal William Slim described it when, perhaps understandably, all Britain's resources had been piled into Europe. Mountbatten was appalled to discover that 84 per cent of British troops under command were suffering from malaria, some very seriously ill; he toured the hospitals where British troops lay and found them 'disgusting and inadequate'. He immediately sent an urgent dispatch to London requesting 700 nurses and demanded that the Indian administration improve facilities for the soldiers. Next, he set about the generals, commanders and administrative staff, some of whom, he discovered, attempted to emasculate his orders from the beginning. He then got down to the business of reinvigorating the military effort, which was in a sorry state, and for that he would enliven the scenario with the Commando elements of which he was so fond.

Some had already been tried in the region, notably the Chindit patrols plotted and planned by the controversial Orde Wingate, the eccentric former intelligence officer in Palestine who had theories on long-range penetration into the jungles of columns of troops resupplied by air. The first expeditions of his jungle fighters ended unsatisfactorily, and he was already mounting a second sortie when Mountbatten arrived. The new chief initially gave his approval, which was not unexpected given his liking for larger-than-life ideas and Commando characters. As Wingate's demands became more aggressive, however, Mountbatten began to have second thoughts. Even so, by 10 March 1944 9,000 men and 1,100 animals of varying sizes were airlifted far behind Japanese lines under Operation Thursday. Then, Wingate was killed on 24 March 1944 in an air crash and was succeeded by former Gurkha officer Brigadier Joe Lentaigne. Many bitter battles were fought and won and a large number of medals awarded, including two Victoria Crosses. In the end, however, the Chindits fell victim to the pugnacious American general, Joe Stilwell, Mountbatten's Deputy Supreme Commander, whose misdirection and reorganisation shattered what hopes there were of success for the Chindits, and the survivors were pulled out, tired, shot to pieces and seriously sick but having at least given the Japs a few bloody noses.

Their operations were to run parallel to those of Mountbatten's former associates and units formed during his time at Combined Operations and, of course, these included the Commandos. The entire 3 Commando Brigade was destined for service under him for the remainder of the war, 5 and 44 Commandos arriving in March 1944 to join the Arakan campaign and 1 and 42 joining in January 1945 when the Japanese were already in retreat. Additionally, Mountbatten had replicated virtually all the smaller Special Operations groups that had come into being during his time at Combined Ops. He put them into what he termed his Small Operations Group – SOG, more commonly known as Soggy by those who were in it. It consisted of three troops from the SBS, along with Detachment 385 from the Royal Marines Commando assault troop, four parties from the Royal Navy's Combined Operations Pilotage Parties, two of the Royal Navy's own Commandos for beach landings and four Sea Reconnaissance Units (SRUs). The last was a relatively new organisation, originally formed to provide long-distance swimmers for specific reconnais-sance missions, and developed into Britain's first underwater swim-ming unit using fairly primitive oxygen breathing apparatus.

They were all to be involved in raids down the Arakan coast and out on the islands and then, in the grander scheme of things, were to regain Burma and then go on to Malaya and Singapore as the campaign picked up speed in the early summer of 1944. Mountbatten sent the creator of the Cockleshell Heroes, 'Blondie' Hasler, by then a lieutenant-colonel, and another redoubtable Royal Marine colonel, Humphrey Tollemache, to assist in fighting an enemy capable of every nasty trick in the book, in steaming jungle conditions, torrential rain, wading through swamps and rivers, battling killer insects, mosquitoes and subsequent disease that felled so many troops. SOG thus made a significant contribution to the allied effort in the Far East, in spite of a shortage of gear and leaky landing craft, and in the 13 months from formation to the end of the war the group was involved in more than 160 raids and operations, some under its own auspices and others as part of larger combined attacks during the final phase of the reoccupation of Burma.

The role of 3 Commando Brigade was in the classic mode of spearheading major troop formations being moved along the Arakan ahead of the new offensive into Burma planned for the later months of 1944. They were met with the news of a shortage of landing craft – virtually non-existent – and little air support. Mountbatten could only promise them the opportunity of jungle penetrations on similar lines to the Chindits. The advance party of the brigade, 5 and 44 Commandos, had also arrived at a point when the Supreme Commander was just about to change the rules of engagement. In fact, they had been sent out specifically to join Mountbatten's new routine. Until his reorganisation, the war had been virtually shut down during the monsoon period, from May to the end of September. The belief that it was virtually impossible to stage full-scale battles under such conditions was shared by both the British and the Japanese. Mountbatten, however, came armed with technical data gleaned from boffins in London who had worked out for him ways and means in which he could keep the armies of the east on the move during dire weather conditions. The Commandos were among the first to test these theories. The strategists had concluded that the dangers of fighting in the monsoon were more than made up for by the element of surprise, a theory which, incidentally, was supported by Field Marshal Slim, commander of the 14th Army, who wanted to get his men on the move. Based on the preliminary work done in the UK, Mountbatten also called on the services of scientists at South-East Asian Command headquarters for local calculations both in terms of weather and the condition of the ground, especially in landing zones. Their theories were not always on the mark, as the Commandos discovered landing on a muddy beach designated as 'firm mud' to discover that they sank up to their chests in mud topped with water. The MO of 44 RM Commando noted:

Officers and men were seen sprawling in the mud, which somehow seemed to remove boots and socks from some. Men formed scrums and managed to push towards the beach: some scrums collapsed wholesale and took some minutes to re-emerge from the sludge and re-form. The last man out was a subaltern who staggered back time and again to rescue men and equipment from the morass. It was only after he had washed in the water of a bomb crater that we discovered who he was.

It was also now that 5 and 44 RM Commandos, as the early arrivals, were to experience first hand the awfulness of fighting in the jungle in the torrential rain against an enemy the like of which no British fighting units had ever experienced. Archives of 3 Commando Brigade contain the men's reactions after only a few engagements:

Even in our short experience, we have had played against us all the tricks you read about in pamphlets: snipers tied to treetops, moving a wounded man into a field tempting you to come and get him, shouting in English, making a noise in one direction and coming in from another. Troops must be prepared for all this or they will be caught on the wrong foot . . . you are fighting a genuine fanatic who gives and expects no quarter.

As the various British amphibious raiders began probing the Japanese positions, the enemy commanders soon became wise. With the possibility of clandestine reconnaissance missions and the seaborne landings by the Commandos, the Japanese began inserting spiked bamboo stakes under water, 275 metres from the shore, which were virtually invisible at night but could – and often did – seriously injure the small-party raiders. And so it went on for the next year or more. From these frightening beginnings, 3 Commando Brigade hurled themselves into attack after attack, and leading in the greater troop formations behind them fought back the Japanese counterassaults. Gradually, the sheer weight of the allied assault pushed the Japanese further south and east to a point where some of the most bitter battles of the new offensive were fought.

Every one of the Commandos and all of Mountbatten's SOG units were involved at some point or other, every one suffered the harshness of the terrain, the terrible conditions, the monsoon and the sickness. The elements that were found to be most frightening when they first arrived remained so until the end. This is amply borne out by the missives back to HQ and to their base in England from the officers engaged. One of the Commandos wrote of the crucial Battle of Kangaw in January 1945: 'I've never been so bloody scared in all my life. It wasn't so much the fighting as the shelling . . . they had 20 guns firing at us all the time.'

It was one of the most hard-fought battles as the war edged closer to conclusion in 1945, and especially around the infamous feature known as Hill 170, which the Commando brigade had taken and had orders to hold. They defended it with their lives against a tremendous Japanese onslaught. In one section, just 24 men of 1 Commando defended their position against 300 Japanese. Led by Lieutenant G. A. Knowland, the survivors of a violent assault managed to hold on to their position for eight hours. Knowland himself, leading from the front, was seen firing mortar from the hip, killing six Japanese with his first bomb. When he ran out of bombs, he dashed back through enemy machine-gun fire to get more. As there weren't any, he snatched a Tommy gun from a wounded soldier and stood bolt upright spraying the enemy, who were by then just 30 feet away from him. Although badly wounded, Knowland killed a further ten before he fell back into a trench. For this action, and the inspiration to his men, he was awarded the Victoria Cross. Veteran of the Commando movement and Deputy Commander of 3 Commando Brigade, Lieutenant-Colonel Peter Young, wrote after they came off that hill and its surrounds:

> Japanese dead were interlocked with our own in a proportion of at least three to one. The back slopes of the hill were thick with victims . . . It was a real epic. I never saw dead so thick. The Boche could not have stood five hours of it. Several 1 Commando soldiers were found well forward, dead, in the middle of Japs, having pushed on in these counterattacks after their first section had finished. One RM officer killed four Japanese and got four wounds . . . all this in about two acres of ground . . . I'm convinced that no British troops ever fought better than ours on that day.

Only later did the enormity of what they had succeeded in doing become clear. If the Japanese had secured Hill 170, they would have cut off the supply routes to the British troops in this vital stage of the battle for the Arakan. There were congratulations all round and a large number of awards for the brigade, although the downside was a hefty casualty list of 45 killed in action and 96 wounded. Mountbatten was overjoyed with their success and made sure that the Commando operation received well-deserved publicity. He, too, was embarrassingly generous with his praise and said that if the Commandos had only completed that one single operation during the whole time they were under his command it would have been worth it. But they had been kept busy throughout and remained so to the point when Burma was won back. It was Malaya next stop. The Commandos were already in training for Operation Zipper, the invasion of Malaya, when the Japanese capitulated.

The irony of this was that the Royal Marines Commandos would be back there 'ere long, for a totally different kind of war.

CHAPTER THIRTEEN

Under Threat Again

There was an element of *déjà vu* as the corps of the Royal Marines prepared to disengage from the war. Almost identical introspection among the military hierarchies to that which occurred after the First World War was under way to discover whether or not the Marines should remain in existence, and for quite some time it appeared possible that they would not. These considerations were already in progress while the Commandos were still scattered around the theatres where they were last engaged because everyone knew that the issue of affordability would raise its head immediately the hostilities had ceased, and, of course, money was always a more demanding consideration than tradition or the servicemen, some of whom were still overseas long after the war had ended.

Elements of 3 Commando Brigade were to remain in the Far East until the autumn to assist the Royal Navy and to be on hand for the formal surrender of the Japanese and other necessary tasks where a show of strength might be necessary. Not least among the latter was the nervous eye the British were casting in the direction of Mao Zedong and his Communist army, which began its 'long march' to power in 1935 and was edging closer to victory over Chiang Kai-shek's nationalists, and that in turn ultimately represented a threat to the British colony of Hong Kong. In Europe, meanwhile, 1 and 4 Commando Brigades remained in Germany until the late summer, joining a vast deployment of allied military personnel engaged in the overwhelming multiplicity of problems left in the wake of the defeat of Germany, which included rounding up Nazi officials likely to stand trial for war crimes before they could escape to foreign climes. First home, though, was 2 Commando Brigade, which had remained in action to the last gasp of the war, returning to England in June 1945. By the end of the year, however, 3 Commando had been moved to Malta, and thousands of hostilities-only Marines throughout the corps had been released. The warships and landing craft were being parked up, and the detachments at sea were largely freed from duty. Of the 76,500 Royal Marines engaged during the war, only 13,000 were to remain in the service; that reduction was achieved within 18 months. Fewer than 2,000 were now to be deployed in the traditional roles at sea, and there were to be substantial cutbacks in the number of bandsmen. Even these reductions were insufficient in the eyes of some. The Harwell Committee, set up to carry out a post-war review of military requirements for peacetime, recommended the abolition of the Corps of Royal Marines altogether. However, the Admiralty stood its ground and insisted that the Marines should remain in business, although agreeing to a curtailment by suggesting that their strength should be reduced to approximately ten per cent of the Royal Navy's total manpower.

To achieve the required reduction, pressure was exerted on the Commandant-General to disband the Commando Brigades, but the Marines fought a strong rearguard action and managed to stay in business. Instead, the axe was to fall on the original British Commandos – the army units. They were to be disbanded immediately; the volunteers who manned them would be either demobilised or returned to their original regiments.

Great despondency fell over the army units as Brigadier Bob Laycock broke the news to his men:

I am today more moved in speaking to you than ever before, for my emotions are not now those which I felt when I spoke to you in the past, the inspiration of battle and the exhilaration of coming danger, but they are deeper and more poignant emotions and they are these. First, the emotions of unbounded gratitude which I feel for every one of you who has helped make the green beret of the Commandos a symbol of bravery and honour whenever it has been worn. Secondly, I am very conscious of the great privilege which I myself feel in having been associated with you. And lastly, and most poignant of all, the emotions of sadness . . . for who can say that there is a more splendid example of endeavour than that which the Commandos have set during the dark misery which the world has just been through – the high resolve to volunteer . . . the love of adventure, and the skill and loyalty, and bravery unsurpassed which sometimes ended so tragically in the supreme sacrifice of many of your comrades.

The disbandment order included the SAS that had originally emerged from the Commandos. They were demoted to a Territorial battalion, although of course the SAS would rise again, and soon, as the colonial wars began erupting across the declining British Empire in the late 1950s. Other Commando-linked units were also to be dissolved. These included groups such as the Royal Navy's Combined Operations Pilotage Parties, which had conducted beach reconnaissance for wartime landings, 'Blondie' Hasler's RM Boom Patrol Detachment and the Sea Reconnaissance Unit, although the skills and techniques invented by all of these specialisations during the war would be retained and incorporated into the Special Boat Section, which itself now was to operate as part of the Royal Marines, eventually to become the renowned Special

Boat Service.* The bands were also to be cut back and amalgamated to form the Royal Marines School of Music and the appointment of its first Principal Director of Music, Lieutenant-Colonel F. Vivian Dunn.

The Commando banner and the Green Beret would now be passed to the Royal Marines' 3 Commando Brigade, which went on to become one of the great fighting groups of the second half of the twentieth century. Wartime Commando numbering was picked up to maintain the links with those units that had served in the major battles, and thus the brigade was made up of 40, 42 and 45 Commando. The Royal Marines Forces Volunteer Reserve was also formed to provide a backup for special duties, and the reorganisation was completed with surprising speed. A new Commando school was established, first in Wales and then at Bickleigh, near Plymouth. Basic training for all Marines was at the Royal Marines Depot at Deal, Kent; an infantry training centre was set up at Lympstone, on the Exe estuary, and the new raiding squadrons were to be based at Eastney, in Portsmouth, and later at Poole, Dorset. New and tough training courses were designed for the Commando units, based largely on the techniques first introduced by the army Commando school at Achnacarry but updated after studies of the experiences of the war years. Also noticeable as this reformation began was a sudden sense of urgency that emerged at senior levels, and there was good reason. Although the new Labour government of Clement Attlee had made it clear that it wanted to disengage the cash-strapped nation from expensive military activity, across the Empire there was disarray and dissent. Even if anyone in government had felt the Harwell Committee's recommendations ought to be adopted, they would soon have been silenced by fresh demands of a new and dangerous arena that would call for strong counter-insurgency measures and confrontation with what amounted to uprisings by people's armies.

---

* See *SBS: The Inside Story of the Special Boat Service* by this author, published by Headline, the only officially approved history of the service.

The collapse of organised governments under the Axis boot left a void from which revolution and independence movements would emerge in many different forms, especially in India and the Far East. The domino effect, denied by some British politicians, would soon be evident with nationalistic and Communist uprisings across the Middle and Far East, notably in Malaya, Burma, Korea and Vietnam. As *Time* magazine noted in 1946:

> The world, struggling nervously with the problems of how to place in peaceable association even more diverse groups, finds the British Empire an embarrassment and an inspiration. Meanwhile, the Empire, a hodgepodge of real estate scattered all over the globe, is changing more rapidly than ever in its confused history. Most of the changes turn around the sincere efforts of the British government to satisfy (without exchanging anarchy for stability) colonial peoples' hopes of self-government.

It was the emergence of these new flashpoint situations immediately after the war that had much to do with the decision to maintain the Commando force, and indeed the Royal Marines as a whole. The first arose even as the units were undergoing the transformation into career-based entities, as opposed to the bulk inclusion of hostilities-only recruits who had been the main source of new manpower for the previous five years, and many new recruits fresh out of training found themselves thrust into action. The scene of their first post-war operations of a fire-brigade nature was the Middle East, where the Jews and Palestinian Arabs resumed their hostilities, which had been largely put on hold during the war.

Palestine, then, became the first real focus of the re-created 3 Commando Brigade. Its partner in so many past – and future – operations, the Parachute Regiment, was already *in situ*, having been among those sent at the end of 1945 as the trouble between the two sides flared into violent confrontation. This was, in fact, a leftover from the First World War, when the region was placed under British administration by the League of Nations, whose local advisers were convinced that Jew and Arab could peacefully co-exist. This judgement was made before the Nazis began their purge of Jews in Germany, leading eventually to the mass arrivals of immigrants of unexpected proportions into that area. They had every reason to expect that they would be allowed to settle, given that, in April 1937, the partition of Palestine between Arabs and Jews using the model of Ireland was recommended by a Royal Commission and accepted by the British government as 'the best and most hopeful solution of the deadlock'.

The results were a parallel of discontent and unrest that similarly emerged in Ireland. British officials in the region at the time were convinced that the two races could live together in harmony, which turned out to be a gross misjudgement. So began decades of bloodshed, exacerbated by the arrival of thousands of European refugees seeking a home in the Promised Land, which the Palestinian Arabs claimed had been promised to them long before the immigration of vast numbers of Jews from Europe, displaced, homeless and emotionally fired up by the fact that six million of their brethren had died in the Holocaust.

By the end of 1945 refugees, encouraged by Zionists and other powerful Jewish groups, were pouring into Palestine. The British government tried to limit the numbers, in spite of calls from the Americans to relent. With thousands of Jews sailing towards Palestine in ships from Europe and elsewhere, Britain's answer was to send troops and gunboats to keep them out, and to arrest those who tried to get in and place them in camps on Cyprus. Thousands of soldiers were moved in and immediately faced the wrath of Jewish armed extremists. Open warfare developed between the Arabs and Jews, and each separately with the British. It was into this maelstrom that 40 Commando was among the British force attempting to bring calm to this troubled land, later to be joined by 42 and 45 Commandos.

It was a dangerous place in which to be a British soldier. In July 1946 the British military headquarters at the King David Hotel, Jerusalem, was blown up by delayed-fuse explosives planted by Zionist terrorists, killing 94 and wounding 52. In November eight British soldiers were killed when their Jeep was blown up in Jerusalem. In January British families were evacuated from the region. In April British police barracks near Tel Aviv were blown up. Meanwhile, a ship called *Exodus* manned by an American volunteer crew left Baltimore and sailed to a small French port near Marseilles to pick up a cargo of 5,000 Jewish refugees. Intent on breaking the British immigration embargo and watched by media from around the world, the ship reached Haifa on 18 July 1947 and, amid chaotic scenes, was boarded by British troops, who engaged in hand-to-hand fighting. Eventually, the troops gained the upper hand and herded the refugees on to ships to join 20,000 other would-be immigrants already held in camps in North Africa and Cyprus, supposedly to be returned whence they came. In the terrorist reprisals that followed, two of the British troops, Sergeant Mervyn Pace, 43, and Sergeant Clifford Martin, 20, were kidnapped by Zionist extremists and were discovered hanging from two eucalyptus trees in a suburb of Haifa, with notes pinned to their shirts stating they had been executed as spies. Many other atrocities were committed before Britain decided to place the whole dispute before the United Nations. There, politicians bickered and stalled. Britain said it was pulling out anyway, with or without UN intervention. The UN Special Committee did not reach Palestine for its inspection tour until the early summer of 1947.

George Richards was still a teenager when he joined 42 Commando in 1946. He was among the intake of new recruits who went through the newly established training school, and he – and many like him – was soon to see action in the Middle East, having been placed on stand-by in Malta in 1947:

We embarked for Palestine on Landing Ships [Tank] *Striker* and *Dieppe* to sail across and ended up in Haifa at the alert. All guns were manned. It was a landing under arms because at this time the Jews had really got their act together. We took over an empty hotel and set up our guns on the roof. I had a wireless station up there. Our tasks were generally to put ourselves between the Jews and the Arabs, running security patrols searching for terrorists and weapons. It was while we were in Haifa that the Jewish vessels were trying to land their illegal immigrants, and threats were made to kill our CO, Lieutenant-Colonel Riches, after we stopped two or three vessels from landing. So he had to have a bodyguard everywhere he went. We stayed at Haifa for about a month, and then suddenly the whole brigade was ordered to move to Jerusalem, where we set up in different areas; 42 Commando was at a village settlement just outside the city, in an old nail factory.

The Commandos were thrust into the middle of the dispute. On one side of them were three Jewish settlements and on the opposite side there were three Arab settlements. The potential for trouble was evident from the beginning, and it came when a woman in one of the Jewish settlements came outside to hang out her clothes and the Arabs opened fire. Such events happened daily in tit-for-tat manner, using small-arms machine-gun fire. In one six-week period monitored by the UN, nearly 2,000 people were killed in Palestine: 1,069 Arabs, 769 Jews, 123 British and 23 others. In the end the UN resolved to oversee the formation of an independent Jewish state by the partition of Palestine. Britain was in the end pleased to accept the verdict and leave as quickly as possible, especially as the end of the British Raj in India had been presenting problems on a far greater scale.

Even so, a dramatic upsurge in the violence as each side jostled for position and territory occurred in the last weeks before the deadline for partition. In March British troops used their biggest 25-pounder guns to shell Arabs dug into a hillside position 20 miles west of Jerusalem, resulting in 100 casualties. But the withdrawal went ahead on 14 May. George Richards recalled the scenes in the period leading up to the deadline:

The Palestine police force, which was largely British, had been pulled out of Jerusalem and we were to go in to replace them and, it turned out, to destroy their barracks. We found that in Jerusalem at night it was just a case of everybody shooting at anybody. They were all on flat roofs, if you can imagine, firing at each other. You'd hear bullets ricocheting around our area. One particular night they made a terrific raid against us. We found out later they were [Jewish] Haganah people. The machine guns opened fire and there was quite a big fight that night. Next morning there were quite a lot of Haganah people with their blue and white sashes killed on the perimeter. A lot of them were girls. It was a tragic sight, just young girls . . .

Two days later the Commandos were ordered to destroy everything in the barracks that could not be carried. The evacuation was under way, and in its wake the mayhem left the Palestinians and the Israelis pitted in seemingly never-ending strife, with the Commandos glad to be out of it, and rewarded for their even-handed intervention with a clutch of medals.

Opening shots were already being fired in other troubles that would engage the British Commandos for the next five years. In July 1949 Communist China threatened the sovereignty of Hong Kong by massing troops on its border. British troops were sent to do no more than put on a token show of military presence, given the vast armies available to Mao Zedong. 3 Commando Brigade arrived aboard ss *Georgic*, with HQ, 40 and 42 Commandos embarking in Malta and picking up 45 Commando from Port Suez, where it had been guarding British facilities in the aftermath of the Palestinian crisis. For the next eight months the Commandos provided the internal security for Hong Kong and the hundreds of outlying islands. But gradually the situation grew dangerously menacing, with far greater implications for other British territories in the Far East, notably at that time Malaya.

The Chinese Communists, from bases deep in the jungle, began an onslaught of terrorising the locals with arson, murder and other

anti-colonial activities directed against the British-owned rubber plan-
tations. The Far East was already on a knife edge as Mao Zedong's
army continued its rout of the Chinese nationalists in spite of massive
American aid. In a knock-on effect Malayan leaders who had been
allies of Britain during the war turned their forces, trained with British
help and arms to fight with the Japanese in Malaya. On 22 June
British troops rounded up 800 known Communists following the
murder of a number of rubber planters and 3 Commando Brigade
was pulled in to the action.

The brigade was now tasked with counter-insurgency warfare in
support of the civil administration and police over vast areas of
the country. The Headquarters and 42 Commandos were first based
in Ipoh, while 40 Commando went to Taiping to patrol the Thailand
border areas of Grik and Kroh, and 45 Commando had an equally
vast area based at Tapah. The sheer scale and impossible terrain
of the territory to be covered was in itself a tribute to the Marines
in that they tackled their task over the coming months in many
gruelling patrols with a professionalism that drew praise from
Britain's foremost counter-insurgency authority, General Sir John
Harding.

This praise was all the more deserving, given that, not many months
before, quite a large number of the younger troops had been languishing
in the bosom of their home towns and had never even heard of the
places they were now at. Among them was Jim Green, who had been
a farm labourer in Ormskirk, Lancashire, when he signed on for 12
years' minimum service in the Royal Marines, reporting for duty at
Deal on 18 May 1948 at the age of seventeen and a half:

> We went to Portsmouth for gunnery training, then 14 weeks'
> infantry training, then to Bickleigh for six weeks' Commando
> training. I was about to begin a specialist training course when
> the panic in Hong Kong arose and we were told to prepare to
> go straight out. There was a huge draft, five or six squads, and
> we were to join brigade base at Malta and went on board the

liner requisitioned specially for it. We were dropped off at Malta while the ship went to the Middle East to pick up the other Commandos and then it came back to pick us up for our journey onwards to Hong Kong. I joined 42 Commando stationed at Whitfield Barracks at Kowloon and went straight into duty. We were on border patrols in the New Territories, guarding ammunition dumps and the governor's residence. The border patrols were to stop refugees getting across from China. There were quite a lot getting through. There were four rifle troops, A, B, X and Y, so named because they corresponded to the gun turrets on a cruiser. Then there was S Troop, support troops with heavy weapons – Vickers, mortars and so on – and then there was a headquarters which dealt with administration. It was a terrific posting for me. The furthest I'd ever been from home was Liverpool. It was wonderful, and as it happened there was very little trouble that we couldn't handle.

By December 1949 Mao Zedong's Communist army had taken Beijing, where the nationalist troops lost 600,000 men and the government shifted its capital to Taipei on the offshore island of Formosa (later Taiwan). North Korea then declared itself a Communist republic, and the French were facing increasing troubles in Indo-China, later to be known as Vietnam, having outlawed the Communist leader, Ho Chi Minh. In the same month, the British government ordered four regiments into Malaya in the biggest onslaught yet against the Communist terrorists operating in the dense jungles. The rebels were calling themselves the Malaya Races Liberation Army, run by Ching Peng, a Chinese Communist who had amassed a well-trained and disciplined army of 5,000 men. By March 1950 the Communist Terrorists (CTs) had taken a hefty toll: 863 civilians, 323 police officers and 154 soldiers. Their own casualties ran to 1,138 killed and 645 captured. Jim Green was with 42 Commando when it was shipped out of Hong Kong:

We moved to Malaya in early 1950. We went to Penang island first to get jungle training, learning ambush patrols, anti-ambush drills, setting ambushes and tracking. It was all very new to most of us. I learned how to become a scout, working well ahead of the main troop. It was a dangerous job but surprisingly quite popular with the men. You had to be very alert and you saw much more, like wild animals which would have dispersed by the time the main troop came up. You also had the possibility of running into the ambush first, but that merely kept up the adrenalin. There were two scouts, a leading scout and a second scouting, and in between them a Borneo tracker, very loyal little chaps. They were excellent trackers: a disturbed leaf, a footmark on a jungle floor – they'd see it and be able to tell us what it was. The Bren group, meanwhile, were bringing up the rear, so there'd be ten in a section on patrol – three in the Bren group, seven in the rifle group, of whom two would be scouts.

Their first billet was two wards of the Central Chinese Mental Hospital but, because it was close to an open sewer, most of the men fell ill and were moved to a tented camp in a rubber plantation:

Each troop was allocated quite a huge area to operate in. On normal patrols there would be two section patrols, or, depending on what the range was, the sergeant might be in charge. We were constantly out on patrol. We did one patrol lasting seven or eight weeks, passing through three states in Malaya, sometimes in uncharted territory. We'd set ambushes on bits of tracks we'd find. We'd hang grenade necklaces, but more often than not all we ever trapped in them was a wild pig. The necklaces consisted of 36 grenades with the pin of each one tied to a string attached to a tripwire; if something kicked the tripwire it pulled all 36 pins out and they all went off within seconds of each other – the idea being that the lead man of a terrorist group would hit the trip and the guys coming up behind him would be in the ambush zone. That was the hope of it.

Fresh food and clothes were supplied by airdrops to allow the men long stays inside their allotted territories. The Commandos spent much time with jungle police searching villages thought to be harbouring terrorists. Jim Green:

> You would take up positions all round the village and then a party would go in and rouse out all the inhabitants: males, females, separated in lines. The informer would be brought in under cover and he would go down the lines and point out anyone connected with the terrorists, and they would be arrested and taken to the local police station. Sometimes, to reach the villages by first light, we'd have to turn out at two or three in the morning ... wading across rivers. When a patrol ran into terrorists, we knew they would fight to the death, then we would go in and arrest any survivors. The routine for identifying those killed was that you didn't carry the whole body back; you cut the head off. None of our guys were rushing forward to do it. So the tracker from Borneo was asked.

As the campaign wore on, General Harding, Commander-in-Chief of Far East Land Forces, initiated a study of problems facing the troops in Malaya, headed by Mike Calvert, the former SAS and Chindits hero. With his armed group, Calvert made a 1,500-mile tour along routes infested with terrorists in 1950 and then prepared a report of his findings. which became the basis of the Briggs Plan, which called for the closure of 410 Malayan shanty villages that the terrorists used for supplies and shelter. The villagers were moved into fortified settlements, where they could live and farm without fear of being harassed by the CTs. Next, the troops would embark on ambitious operations to deny food supplies to the guerrillas in their jungle hideouts.

A newly created SAS-style force known as the Malayan Scouts, to be led by Calvert himself, would go into the jungle to gain the trust of indigenous people. Jim Green recalled that the results were soon evident to the Marines:

> They were classic hearts and minds operations intended to deny the terrorists food supplies. The process, as it developed through the country, gradually cut down the terrorist incidents substantially, and by the time I came back to Britain in November 1951 there were very few incidents; our patrols were finding nothing. The native population were quite happy because they didn't have to support the terrorists. In spite of everything, I thoroughly enjoyed my time in the jungle . . . it was a great adventure, slogging over the hills and mountains. The comradeship, everything, was great. We've often talked about it, friends in the service, in later years, and I think it's quite true that the older you get the more sensible you are. Because in those days, as youngsters, we did some damned silly things.

The Commandos remained in demand as the Malayan emergency continued intermittently for another four years until the country was granted independence. Across the distant horizon, however, more trouble was brewing.

The Korean War had the distinction of being the first conflict in which the United Nations had sponsored the use of military force against an aggressor, although it was largely driven by the Americans, who also supplied 90 per cent of the troops, hardware and equipment. The causes lay once again in the history of the nation. Japan had ruled Korea since 1910, but in 1945 Soviet troops occupied Korea north of the 38th parallel, while the Americans controlled the country south of this line. Two years later, the United Nations General Assembly declared that elections should be held throughout Korea to choose one government for the entire country. The Soviet Union refused to sanction elections in the north, but in 1948 the people of South Korea elected a national assembly. The north responded by forming the Democratic People's Republic of Korea. Both claimed the entire country, and the Communists made their move and invaded South Korea on 25 June 1950. When UN demands for withdrawal were ignored, member nations were asked to provide military aid to South Korea. Sixteen UN countries, including the United Kingdom, sent troops to help the South Koreans, and 41 countries sent military equipment, food and other supplies. The North Koreans had the backing of the Soviets for equipment and advisers and the Chinese for additional manpower, of which they had a vast reservoir.

The ground forces of the UN nations, along with the South Koreans, came under the command of the US 8th Army, led by General MacArthur. US troops were the first to land, followed soon afterwards by the British and Commonwealth ground forces, which included an initial draft of around 4,000 from the United Kingdom, departing in late July and early August. These included Commandos and a section from the SBS, raised under the banner of 41 Independent Commando, made up almost entirely of volunteers from the Royal Marines and hurriedly assembled in July under the command of Lieutenant-Colonel D. B. Drysdale, RM. The troops were dispatched to the US naval base at Yokosuka, Japan, and were soon involved in many operations with American and British army units.

Among them was NCO Gersham Maindonald, a native of Guernsey who as a young man had been locked into the island during the German occupation. He joined the Marines immediately after the war and had served with 40 Commando in Palestine:

It was put out that everyone in 41 Commando were volunteers but, because Commandos have certain specialities, not all were. In fact, my group was transferred out on a BOAC flight in civilian clothes so that neutral countries would allow us through. We flew to Hong Kong, where we picked up our Marine uniform, and then on to Japan, where we were fully equipped with American gear and weapons. We had to be introduced to the

251

workings of this equipment and then trained with their rubber boats for assault. We stayed there for a few weeks for training before we moved down to Sasebo, operating off USS *Horace Bass*, a fast destroyer-type craft. We were operating in very rough sea conditions, six- or eight-feet waves, which made it difficult to land the boats. Each craft carried explosives, which were going to be used in our first raid for blowing up a viaduct. My section was the first to land and called in the remainder of the force when we had established it was safe. The operation went through, the charges were laid, got back out to the *Bass* and as we pulled away we heard the explosion. The whole of the viaduct was destroyed.

Our second raid was from a submarine, again from rubber boats which were brought up on the casing and inflated by the US navy. This time it was to blow up a railway line and make large craters so that it could not be easily repaired. We were then ordered to join the US Marines and the 5th Cavalry that had reached the Manchurian border and were being driven back by the Chinese. The Americans had infiltrated Manchuria itself, which was the excuse by the Chinese to state that they had been invaded, and thus enter the war. The main camp of the US forces was at the Chosin reservoir, which had been cut off when the Chinese advanced south. They were isolated within a perimeter, and our task was to travel north from Wonsan to open up a corridor for the Americans to withdraw. It was a very hilly terrain on both sides of a river with only one roadway going north. We were therefore very vulnerable in a ravine valley as we progressed up this road, because the tanks that had been allocated to accompany us were reluctant to expose themselves in the conditions because they were [sitting ducks]. However, we did finally go forward and unfortunately we ran into a Chinese ambush. One of our chaps sitting on the cab of the three-ton lorry was shot through the head and toppled off the lorry, dead. Then a phosphorus bomb hit the ammunition lorry ahead of me, caught fire and was blazing away. The truck I was in contained all the Arctic clothing for the unit, and it was needed because it was cold in Korea, sometimes 40 degrees below zero, so it was imperative that we move before it caught fire, and I was detailed to move it forward, away from the blazing ammunition truck. We progressed on and with covering fire [during battle over a considerable time] managed to break through the ambush and continue on and save our clothing truck. I was awarded the Military Medal for that particular incident. But in reality it was a question of survival, not for winning any medals.

Anyway, we reached the American camp later that night. It was a fully established camp with wooden huts and a perimeter ringed with foxholes, which were constantly manned to fight off attacks by the enemy. When daylight came along, it was amazing and frightening to discover that there were Chinese dead within three or four yards of our foxholes. Although you had actually seen them in the night, we were firing at silhouettes without realising how close they were. The curious thing was that few of them had much ammunition – just a few rounds – but they came in hordes, literally hordes. You could relate it to a Western film, when the Indians would appear on the top of a hill. Here, they came forward when a bugle went, and because of the sheer weight of numbers in these attacks they obviously didn't need much ammunition.

Eventually, the camp was to be withdrawn, or, as the American general put it, to advance south. So we were all set up over a couple of days to break out of this camp and go back down the same route that we'd come up. The American 7th Division was the spearhead, and 41 Commando was designated to protect the American general in charge of the whole force, and his head-quarters. They travelled in Jeeps, and we lined both sides of his group for protection. Going back through the ravine valley, we once again had to dodge machine-gun fire until we got down into safe territory, where we were withdrawn on amphibian tank craft to the ships that were waiting for us to be returned to South

Korea. We were awarded an American citation for our work. We were returned to Japan and a few weeks later transferred to islands to work around the port of Wonsan, again beyond the 38th parallel.

After initial success by MacArthur's troops, the Chinese returned to the attack, this time fielding huge numbers of soldiers and heavy armoury, and in the bitter Korean winter they soon had the UN force in retreat. The Communists advanced back into the south, and it took a strong counterattack by the entire UN command, codenamed Operation Killer, on 21 February 1951 to hold them. Heavy fighting continued, month on month on the ground and in the air. The UN now had more than 300,000 troops in Korea in addition to the 340,000 of the South Korean army. The Communist forces were put at close on 900,000, which included two Chinese armoured divisions and one mechanised division with 520 tanks.

As casualties among the allies rose by the day, a large draft of reinforcement was sent out for 41 Commando. Among them was John Peskett, from Suffolk, who had joined the Royal Marines in 1947 at the age of 17 and after basic training had joined 45 Commando. Within a year he, too, was in Palestine in a rifle section, then Malaya and finally had a brief encounter with a Communist league of youth in Somalia, threatening an RAF station in Mogadishu. Now, in September 1950, he was in Korea, also operating from the Bay of Wonsan:

We began operations almost immediately with patrols about a hundred miles behind the lines. It was a listening patrol, landing by rubber boats. We would crawl up to the outskirts of a village, listening and noting all that we heard and saw, slide back to the boats and slip away to the island. These were followed by what were called tongue-snatching patrols, where we would go ashore, ambush a North Korean patrol, snatch the officer to bring back for interrogation and dispose of the rest. These patrols were essential; it was the only way we could get information and intelligence because the villagers were scared to death. They'd be slaughtered if they talked.

In June 1951 Peskett was seconded to a troop, staffed by men from 3 SBS who were on sabotage missions behind the North Korean lines. On one of these raids, a typhoon hit while some of the group were ashore; others had stayed with their landing craft, which they kept close to the beach. The next morning Peskett and a scratch crew were to relieve the Marines they'd left with the boat and sail her to the lee of the island. He set off with Quartermaster-Sergeant Day and Marines Aldridge, Hicks and Bamfield:

The storm was still going strong. The waves were high and the wind whipped the tops off; it was like sailing in a blanket of water. The engine stopped and it took some time to get it restarted. We couldn't see anything because of the wind-driven sea, and we struggled to keep afloat. We limped around for several hours before I noticed we were moving into shallower water. Then we saw a beach, with a ring of rocks with a lagoon visible beyond. There was a hole in the rocks that the landing craft would go through, but as luck would have it a huge wave took us right over the top of the rocks and we hit the lagoon. The boat was beached; we were safe and ashore. The sergeant-major detailed me and Marine Hicks to do a reconnaissance. We climbed to the top of the hill and saw in the valley below a lot of lights. It was now dark, and we decided to lay up for the night and get some sleep. At first light we went back to the top of that hill and saw that it was the encampment of a whole North Korean battalion. We had hit the jackpot.

There was only one way out – by sea. I went to inspect the landing craft and discovered that the sea had gone down considerably, and to my horror the landing craft was stuck 200 yards from the water's edge. And since it weighed 30 tons there was no way we would be able to move it. Marine Bamfield and I hauled the floor out and decided to see if we could build a raft. The sergeant-major agreed; he wasn't at all happy about the raft, as to whether it could do the job. It would mean two of us in the water all the time and two on top. One thing was certain, however: we couldn't stay where we were; there was nothing else we could do.

In fact, even before they managed to leave the beach, they were overwhelmed and taken prisoners by the North Koreans and marched to the town of Wonsan, which had suffered greatly from air raids. Oil containers had burst, and oil was running all over the streets. The five Brits were in danger of being attacked by the local populace, but the captain of their guard held them back. They marched on to a huge camp. The date was 29 August 1951, and they were kept in a hole for several days and received meagre rations of rice. They were then back on the road, now with transport, heading for the main prisoner-of-war interrogation centre at P'yongyang. En route, Peskett had developed serious dysentery and was left in a village with one guard, lodging with a family, two women and two children. 'They did everything they could to help me,' said Peskett. 'I stayed there for a couple of weeks. They were wonderful. They used to take me down to the river and let me sit in the water and clean up. I couldn't shave or have a haircut, of course.'

Eventually, he was taken to the interrogation centre to join the others, although first he was thrown into a hole. The prisoners were interrogated for weeks before they were on the move again, heading north to a permanent prison camp. There they were met by Captain Anthony Farrar-Hockley,[*] who had been tortured and beaten for escaping. Peskett recalled:

[*] A veteran of the Second World War, he was adjutant of the 1st Battalion, Gloucestershire Regiment; later General Sir Anthony Farrar-Hockley, Colonel-Commandant, the Parachute Regiment and of Land Forces in Northern Ireland. Author of two volumes of the official history of the Korean War, published by HMSO in 1990 and 1995.

I saw this dishevelled figure standing in the doorway. He straightened himself up and said in a very well-spoken voice: 'How many officers are there?' I knew I was in the presence of a real soldier. By then there was a real mixture of British army, United States Air Force, a couple of South Africans, a Dutchman, a Turk, a couple of Frenchmen, and we'd paired off. Our food consisted of two handfuls of meal that they fed chickens on. If it was a male soldier giving it out, we had a large handful; if it was a girl soldier, we had a small one. Sometimes we could steal some salt. This turned out to be a forming-up place for what we were about to embark on – a long march north. The weather by now had begun to get cold. There were flurries of snow the further north we went, and having been captured in the summertime we had no warm clothing. On the way, a Korean soldier pinched my boots, heavy climbing boots. He wore them for a day and then threw them over the side of a cliff because they gave him blisters. We eventually got to a village in a snowstorm. Captain Washbrook, Royal Artillery, and Captain Farrar-Hockley were laid low on an ox cart. We were all struggling. Several had already died on the way. Walking was far better than lying on a freezing cart, but they couldn't walk and had to be carried. I think if they'd been other ranks, they'd have been shot and left. When we got to this village it was snowing like mad. We took the two captains inside a hut and worked on them and worked on them. Unfortunately, Captain Washbrook had died. Captain Farrar-Hockley we did manage to get back.

No. 41 Commando was recalled to England at the end of 1951 and was disbanded the following February. They had lost 31 killed, including three RN medical staff, while 29 were taken prisoner, 10 of whom died in captivity; 18 officers and men were decorated and 13 received American medals and a Presidential Unit Citation. There were also mentions for Royal Marines detachments at sea that were involved in many bombardment actions and for a number of officers who saw action as Fleet Air Arm pilots.

Although there had been a cease-fire, there were long delays over freeing prisoners of war, and many died in the interim. Those who recovered physically, like John Peskett, were returned to their unit, but they were undoubtedly troubled by their haunting memories. Peskett remained in the Marines and later gave many lectures and talks on resistance to interrogation, and he and others had much to convey, since they had been subjected to psychological warfare on a scale never experienced by British troops. At the armistice in July 1953, the overall toll was: America, 157,530 casualties; deaths from all causes, including illness and PoWs, totalled 33,629, of which 23,300 occurred in combat. South Korea sustained 1,312,836 military casualties, including 415,004 dead. Casualties among other UN allies totalled 16,532, including 3,094 dead. Communist casualties were put at 1.9 million. An estimated two million civilians, north and south, were killed, and many million were made homeless.

CHAPTER FOURTEEN

End of Empire

'Internal security duties' had become a well-used phrase for the dispatch of British troops in the 1950s and 1960s, and 3 Commando Brigade had long assumed the role of a heavily armed police force. Most assignments were tense and dangerous deployments for the British troops, who were constantly under attack from terrorist groups while at the same time operating with one hand tied behind their backs to avoid totally alienating the local population. In 1955 the Commandos were shipped out to deal with the latest nagging thorn in the side of the British government: the activities of the EOKA organisation on the island of Cyprus. They were renewing their demands for the island's union with Greece, while the Turks were keeping an anxious watching brief in support of their own brethren, largely populating the north of the island. A further element of this troublesome area was that the British possessed a large base on Cyprus which was constantly under attack from the Greek Cypriots. In September 1955, at 48 hours' notice, 3 Commando HQ, along with 40 and 45 Commandos, were hastily embarked to join troops moving on to the island to combat serious outbreaks of renewed terrorist activity. EOKA leader Colonel Grivas had taken advantage of the drama around the Suez Canal (see below) to mount a fresh campaign against the British forces on his island. Jim Green, a veteran from the Malayan skirmishes, recalled:

Our time in patrolling Cyprus was very reminiscent of our Malaya days in that we were dropped by helicopter on hillsides and mountaintops looking for EOKA terrorists. The terrain was totally different, of course, but again it was a beautiful country. We were largely engaged on internal security, controlling riots, stop and search and so on. We would also go out into villages suspected of harbouring terrorists, turf them all out of their houses, line them up, and an informer would be sitting in a covered wagon with a little peephole. The villagers would be parading in front and we would pick out the terrorists. We took part in many searches and set up many observation posts. Quite often we would find ammunition and arms and arrest terrorist suspects. They would be identified by the informers, and we would cart them off to the police station. What happened to them after that was not our responsibility. It was a lovely country to be in, and for R and R we went swimming in Limasol. Again, we had to be careful of ambushes; several units took quite a few casualties there over a period of several months. But generally there were few close-quarter encounters.

Prime Minister Anthony Eden had already proposed a new constitution, putting Cyprus on the road to independence, but this was not enough for Grivas and the EOKA leaders. On 27 September four newly arrived soldiers were severely injured by a bomb in a toffee tin placed in a rest room. The result was that the Cyprus crisis continued to demand the intermittent presence of British troops, and elements of the brigade were still there when in the summer of 1956 the Suez crisis blew up. President Nasser announced that the Suez Canal Company, in which Egypt had sold its shares to the British in

1875, was being nationalised without compensation. The announcement came six weeks after the last British troops had left, in accordance with Nasser's earlier demands.

All units of the brigade were recalled to Malta to prepare for 'immediate action' and the scene was set for retaliatory action as Anthony Eden said he would not to allow 'a man with Nasser's record to have his thumb on our windpipe'. Both Britain and France were terrified that vital oil supplies from the Persian Gulf would be disrupted if Nasser took control of the canal; the French were also concerned that he was supporting the increasingly violent independence movement in Algeria. Without taking America into their confidence, Britain and France finally agreed a much-pawed-over plan of action to repossess the canal. In the meantime, the Israelis had arranged some significant side action with the French by amassing 30,000 troops along its 120-mile border with Egypt, ready for a swift and unhindered invasion.

The action began on 31 October when Britain bombed military airfields near Cairo and the Suez Canal, but a defiant Nasser refused to negotiate. His stance was supported by international condemnation of the bombing, which was ignored by Eden and the French, who promptly proceeded to the next phase of their plan to take back the canal. The key elements in the assault on Port Said were 3 Commando Brigade and Parachute Regiment, but the order of battle was to change when the force was already on its way to Suez, as Major-General R. W. Madoc, commanding 3 Commando Brigade, explained in a summary of events now lodged at the Royal Marines Museum:

The mission of the Commando brigade in the final operation orders was to land at Port Said and seize the town, the harbour and the area to the south of the city, firstly with the British seaborne assault on either side of the casino pier by two Commandos, Nos. 40 and 42. H-hour for the landing was to be 6.45 a.m. local time. It would be preceded by air strikes, and naval gunfire would destroy beach defences. The two Commandos would set up a beachhead to allow a squadron of Centurion tanks to land behind them. Ten minutes after the seaborne landing, the French seaborne assault on Port Said would begin. Thirty minutes after H-hour, a British parachute battalion was to drop on Gamil airfield, and French parachutists were to drop on Port Said. No. 45 Commando would land by helicopters north of the interior basin and take the bridges and causeway. Having achieved those objectives, the three Commandos would then dominate areas within the city while the parachute troops mopped up any resistance as they advanced forward.

The Commando brigade was aboard a convoy of 20 ships that had been assembled at Malta. These included the carriers *Ocean* and *Theseus*, which had both been adapted for the new addition of helicopter operations, the first of the kind. Two other carriers, *Bulwark* and *Eagle*, provided additional air support, while the navy's firepower included the cruisers *Newfoundland*, *Jamaica* and *Ceylon*, along with eight destroyers. Detachments of Marines were also aboard the carriers and cruisers. Even as they set off on their journey, changes to the operational orders were made. Madoc received a signal from the Allied Force Commander cancelling a planned helicopter assault by 45 Commando, keeping them back as a floating reserve, and allotting the task of seizing bridges to the French paras. 'This meant a completely fresh appraisal of the Commando tasks,' Madoc wrote, 'and the brigade was spread among the ships with the landing only a few days off. I decided 40 Commando would carry out its tasks as before, 42 would advance south to the southern end of the city and 45 would stay in reserve until, when ordered by myself, it would land by helicopters within the beachhead and support 40 and 42 as required.'

However, on 4 November, while still at sea and apparently having been monitored by an American submarine, fresh orders were received. The parachute troops, previously set to go in after the Commandos, would now land a day earlier, on 5 November, to launch a surprise attack ahead of the main assault, which the Egyptians were well aware was heading in their direction. The seaborne assault would go ahead as planned, except that a ban was placed on the use of naval guns whose calibre was larger than six inches, although if events indicated that an opposed landing was likely, ships giving close support could be ordered to give 'drenching fire' on the beaches with their 4.5-calibre guns. 'To put it mildly,' said Madoc, 'these orders were slightly confusing, and up to the last moment of the run-in a large number of individuals were not at all sure whether there was to be gunfire support or not. I was one of them.'

The same confusion was met by the commanders of the paras as they prepared to go in, and at the last minute two battalions had to divert to a seaborne landing. Originally, the entire 16th Parachute Brigade was to have dropped on strategic targets, but Britain did not possess enough aircraft to lift them in one go. The RAF could supply only enough Hastings and Valettas to carry 668 men, which was to be 3 Para, with just six Jeeps, only four trailers, six 106-millimetre anti-tank guns and around 170 supply containers. Thus, just one battalion, 3 Para, landed at Gamil 24 hours before the seaborne assault came in and were met by Egyptian self-propelled artillery pieces and a good deal of machine-gun fire. Several paras were shot as they came down. The biggest and most upsetting pieces were lorry-mounted batteries of rockets that came hurtling over during the landings, and there were many acts of bravery and heroism as the paras, as yet alone in the battle, began to make headway towards their objectives. As the convoy of ships appeared off the coast soon after first light, there were already clouds of thick black smoke over the city from burning oil tanks.

Madoc's seaborne assault went in shortly before dawn on 6 November, supported by almost an hour of naval bombardment, and the landing was carried out without much incident after the Fleet Air Arm Sea Hawks dived in to silence a pair of artillery gunners shelling the beaches. In fact, the ship-to-shore deployment was perfectly handled, and the initial landings were ashore within two hours of arrival, including C Squadron of the 6th Royal Tank Regiment, which joined 40 and 42 Commando in their advance to their specific objectives. Madoc's account of the proceedings is fascinating if for no other reason than he knew nothing of shenanigans being played out on the international political scene until he took a break after the first day's fighting and listened to the BBC World Service:

It was not until minutes before H-hour that I was informed for certain that I was going to get [naval] fire support for the run-in. On the morning of 6 November, first light was shortly after 5.30 local time, and at that time we could see Port Said in the distance, with a dense pall of black smoke over the city from blazing oil tanks in the south. There were no lights showing and no signs of life. 40 and 42 Commandos got in to their amphibians [LCTs – Landing Craft Tanks – a fast, versatile tracked vehicle] and LCAs [Landing Craft Assaults] and set off to the beach. 40 Commando landed at two minutes to H-hour, which was 6.45 local time. Their first task was to establish a small beachhead with 42 Commando on their right with the same assignment. During the run-in there was very little shooting, and the actual landing was carried out without incident. There were no mines on the beach, and it is very interesting that there were only two beaches at Port Said where the amphibious assault could land. The other one beside Gamil airfield was heavily mined with anti-tank and anti-personnel devices. At about 15 minutes after H-hour, the LCTs beached at the fishing harbour to the left of 40 Commandos, and anti-tank guns and a certain number of vehicles were landed from these craft. Some 20 minutes after H-hour the tanks of C Squadron, 6th Royal Tank Regiment, all landed successfully in the beachhead.

At 7.35 40 Commando was ready to move off and, supported by tanks, advanced down the Bund towards the basins, and the commercial basin was reached in 15 minutes. It was now realised that due to the number of block ships in the harbour, the importance of the primary task, which was to clear the basins, was now considerably minimised. At 9 a.m. the mortar officer of 40 Commando, who was searching the High Lighthouse near the Bund, captured 20 Egyptian soldiers, including an Egyptian brigadier who described himself as the garrison commander-in-charge of Port Said. He wished to stop the fighting, and he was taken to my brigade headquarters. 40 Commando subsequently advanced but on continuing the advance towards Arsenal Basin they came up against more severe opposition, and from then on fighting developed into house to house. Navy House was strongly held by the Egyptian navy and finally, in the late afternoon, an air strike was put on the building, which had been on fire since quite early afternoon. But it was not until the following morning, when we were preparing to launch another attack on Navy House that the survivors surrendered.

42 Commando, landing on the right of 40 Commando, had some more opposition on their right flank, which they cleared up fairly quickly, and soon after 40 Commando's break-out 42 Commando, supported by their tanks, were ready to carry out their advance down Shari Mohammed Ali [highway]. This, in the words of the commanding officer, was a short but extremely interesting ride, carried out under intense small-arms fire [with snipers in virtually every window en route] and with a good many grenades flying about. But the assault reached its objective south of the built-up area and after a battle captured the power station and cold storage depot, both of which were heavily held. We had asked for the amphibians in which this advance took place to be armoured; in the event they were not, and we were fortunate that we did not have more casualties, which may have been partly due to the fact that the Egyptians thought they were tanks. [However, a few soldiers were injured by bullets piercing the walls of the LCTs.]

For the rest of the day, 42 Commando had a considerable amount of fighting, mainly house to house, and by nightfall they were established in the south centre of the city. Meanwhile, the beachhead had been reorganised, and at about 90 minutes after H-hour the first elements of 45 Commando were landed by helicopter. [In fact, this first helicopter landing of troops from ship was a hair-raising experience for the young Marines. The helicopters, originally by the name of Experimental Landing Force, were small and had to carry 415 men, their packs and supplies. Consequently, arms and legs and bodies were dangling out of the open cockpit.]

As 45 Commando advanced down Shari Mohammed Ali, they were also involved in house-to-house fighting, which continued throughout the day. Shortly after 9 a.m. the Egyptian garrison commander was brought to my headquarters and asked if a cease-fire could take place. I told him I was not empowered to order a cease-fire and that in any case if a cease-fire was ordered it would be on the same conditions as had been refused the night before when Brigadier Butler of the Parachute Brigade was trying to arrange a cease-fire with the Egyptian authorities. After a short time he said he was prepared to accept these conditions, so I signalled headquarters ship HMS *Tyne* to this effect. I was then ordered to take the Egyptian to the house of the Italian consul, who was also trying to arrange a cease-fire. After some discussion, negotiations broke down. By the afternoon I had established my brigade headquarters in a block of flats on the seafront.

From every military perspective, this first major test of the new amphibian-heliborne landings had gone exceptionally well. Madoc stated: 'The amphibians proved their value from start to finish and, as regards helicopters, their value in amphibious operations was proved beyond doubt, as it is clear that their use can be greatly developed. Firstly, it was shown that fighting elements of a Commando unit can be put ashore rapidly in an acceptable military order and, secondly, it was shown that this method of landing had very great flexibility.'

Madoc was, however, critical of other aspects of the landings, especially singling out for mention the 'almost total lack of coordination and pooling of intelligence between the three services ... the intelligence organisation was without doubt the weakest link in the chain of planning ... and requires fundamental examination'.

He also spoke in similar vein of an appalling so-called 'friendly fire incident', when an 'uncontrolled British air strike' came in on 42 and 45 Commando, causing 18 casualties, including the commanding officer of 45, Lieutenant-Colonel Norman Tailyour, who was seriously injured. Yet when the commanding officer of 42 had called for air support, none came. Gordon Burt highlighted the chaotic state of British preparedness for this expedition:

> We faced the situation of being short of aircraft for striking. I only ever saw two Hunters, and they had to go back to Cyprus to refuel. When you called for an air strike, you had to wait ages for anything to happen. This manifested itself again when 45 Commandos went on. They called for an air strike, and it didn't come. They were left there for quite some time, an hour or so, and decided to move on themselves. They had just moved on the objective when the air strike came in, and so that was a sad occasion.

By 5.30 fighting had practically ceased, but contact with the paratroopers was not made until the next day. In the meantime, the Royal Navy was unloading the 16th Parachute Brigade. These were the last of the assault troops to be engaged. On the east bank of the canal, the French found no resistance at all. The landing force came ashore to widespread damage and almost total quiet. This quiet remained throughout the occupation, so thoroughly had any possibility for resistance been stamped out. The next day's operations were already being discussed, but they would never be put into practice.

Other things were happening that would negate these orders. The strength of the allies on the battlefield was unquestioned. On the international field, however, a situation beyond their control was forcing them to come to grips with their weaknesses. The Commandos had been fighting in Port Said for exactly 18 hours when they were ordered to call a halt: Cease-fire! Urgent meetings were called at the United Nations Security Council as soon as the landings became a fact. British troops who were within sight of securing the Suez Canal were confused and furious. Indignation and protests were flooding in from around the world, including Russia and America.

And now the whole episode began to unravel: political wrangling had intervened. There were threats of 'modern and terrible weapons' from the Russians, and word from America was that President Eisenhower was furious that he had not been kept informed – especially as the attack was launched on the eve of the US presidential elections. Eisenhower, running for a second term, didn't want to send the Americans to war – or even support his former allies in one – and certainly not on election day. In the event, he won and showed great hostility towards the British and the French for some time to come. The invasion caused a run on sterling in the world money markets, and the US would only intervene to help the British Treasury if it were given cast-iron guarantees that the British would pull out. They did, and so did Eden, resigning six weeks later. By 21 November a 6,000-strong UN force moved into the Canal Zone and Britain was out for good. All in all, it was a shoddy ending to a disastrous misadventure. 'Fiasco' was the word used worldwide by the media, but it was a political not a military fiasco. The Commando landings and subsequent actions had been impeccable, especially in that the troops had utilised ship-to-shore helicopters for the first time in any major British event, a trial run for what would become an integral part of Commando and Special Forces operations thereafter. Also lost in the international coverage of these events was the fact that the Chiefs of Staffs had positively advised against a forced bid to seize back the Suez Canal and send Nasser to a political graveyard. The result was the total reverse of everything that Eden had attempted, and the cost for this short, sharp operation was high – and it could have been so much worse. British losses were 24 killed and 98 injured, and the number of deaths would have been higher had it not been for helicopters ferrying wounded back to the ships for immediate medical attention. Of the Commandos, nine were killed and 60 wounded.

And so the Suez Canal was wrested from British possession and temporarily blocked by sunken ships. The last vestiges of the Empire were disappearing fast. The Malayan crisis ended in 1957, at least as far as Britain was concerned, with the country's independence. But trouble persisted in Cyprus, where the duel between Greek and Turkish patriots and the unwanted British presence, by way of a most important military base and its long-standing administration, meant that the Commandos were called back there immediately after Suez. Colonel Grivas was still giving the troops a run for their money, and in 1956 a £10,000 reward was offered for information leading to his capture, which he persistently avoided.

In the same year the British administration ruled that every person over the age of 12 should carry an identity card. None of this had the effect of bringing peace and order, or relief for the British troops from their role as target practice for EOKA soldiers, and in 1958 the British government finally agreed to seek United Nations mediation for independence. It would be another two years before a peace deal was hammered out and, much to the chagrin of the military commanders who had been on the ground there and whose troops had suffered, Archbishop Makarios, chief ally of Colonel Grivas, became president. In the intervening two years, the Commandos continued with other elements of the British military to police the island, with EOKA keeping the pressure on almost to the last, which in turn kept the troops engaged in endless patrols through the wild Cyprus countryside.

Even as the British troops were pulled out of Cyprus, fresh conflicts in both the Far and Middle East would split 3 Commando Brigade virtually for the next decade, first with 45 Commando assigned to the British colony of Aden, where it was to remain for the next seven long years on difficult and always dangerous counter-insurgency work, and secondly, from 1962, with 40 and 42 Commandos deployed in the jungles of Borneo to face more of the same but in a different climate and with severely restricted operational capabilities.

All units were in for yet another baptism of fire – a common phrase among the Marines at that time – for the newest recruits, for whom tough fights became an immediate and daily ingredient of their lives, often operating with either SAS or SBS detachments. Undoubtedly, however, the heroes of the 1960s were the men of 45 Commando – for two creditable records: they served in Aden for seven years without a break, the longest single tour of duty by any British military unit in the Middle East, and when eventually they returned to England in 1967 the men had been in continuous service overseas since 1946.

Although tensions in the Middle East and around the last of the foreign interests had long been volatile, President Nasser's self-proclaimed victory over the imperialist forces of the West stirred the pot even more, and the first in a series of troubling subversions inspired by his success occurred in another regularly erupting region, Iraq, Britain's major supplier of oil. There, a group of young military officers slaughtered the young King Faisal and his uncle, Crown Prince Abdullah, while the Prime Minister, Nuri el-Said, was kicked to death by a mob as he pleaded for calm. The coup immediately put pressure on Jordan, Iraq's partner in the Arab Union, and on 31 July 1958 2,000 British paratroopers landed at Amman while American Marines waded ashore at Beirut.

Unrest spread throughout the Middle East, with British political and economic influence over a string of sheikhdoms, sultanates, monarchies and protectorates becoming the focus of bitter reaction among Arab republicans. The one remaining vestige of colonial power in Aden, which Britain had ruled for 128 years, hung tenuously in the balance. The last strategic base there was a fortress at the mouth of the Red Sea through which southern access was gained to the Suez Canal. This piece of British-controlled turf sat uneasily among a string of tribal sheikhdoms spread around the southern Arabian coastline along the Gulf of Aden, which formed the South Arabian Federation. The vast and mountainous lands that stretched far into the distance towards Saudi Arabia became the location of a war between the Soviet-funded People's Republic of South Yemen and the Federation, which was backed by Britain.

By 1960 Aden was surrounded by hostility, and in a chain reaction of events 45 Commando found itself posted to the country, where, incidentally, they would be joined by the newly re-formed SAS. A detachment of the SBS was also sent, to be based at Bahrain. The Commandos arrived from Malta in March 1960 and took over what was known as the BP camp at Dhala, which became the home and base of the unit throughout its tour of service in South Arabia. Initially, half the unit remained in Dhala and half went to the remote and desolate Radfan region, where the men saw action for the first time since leaving Cyprus, against so-called Arab dissidents.

The Radfan was an almost waterless, baking, mountainous region 50 miles north of Aden. The area was sparsely populated by fierce tribes who ran a tollgate system for caravans passing through their territory on the traditional supply route along the Dhala road up to Yemen. The Commandos had their first taste of internal security duty in August when they were deployed to patrol the fetid alleys of Aden itself at a time when legislation was introduced making strikes illegal. Those first few difficult months set the pattern for the years that were to follow. They became ensnared in the sustained campaign of terrorism and bloody guerrilla warfare of the worst kind across this most inhospitable land. The unit found itself alternating between upcountry operations in the Radfan and internal security duties in Aden, while still committed to carrying out exercises to retain amphibious and limited war skills.

To add to the troops' woes, the newly created republican state of Iraq began eyeing up the oil-rich state of Kuwait over which it claimed ownership. Britain's ending of its protectorate arrangement with the tiny country spurred Iraq into action. In June 1961 intelligence sources reported that the Iraqi army was being mobilised for an invasion, just as Saddam Hussein did 30 years later. The Commando brigade was flown en masse to Kuwait in July, there to be joined by 42 Commando, who arrived by sea from Singapore, and 6 SBS, from Malta. The SBS detachment performed beach reconnaissance in case a major force landing becoming necessary. In the event, the arrival of 1,300 or so British Marines patrolling on the streets of Kuwait was enough to deter the Iraqis, and in due course 45 Commando returned to Dhala, where its patrols were intensified.

Skirmishes with guerrilla forces were becoming more frequent. The whole region seemed to be heading towards a total breakdown, and in November the troops marched the 80 miles back to Aden for another spell of internal security duties. While they were in the city, the military staged another show of force for the benefit of local dissidents with a major amphibious exercise involving HMS *Bulwark*, the new Commando ship, in the Gulf of Aden, in which 45 Commando played a major part. A few months later a second exercise was staged, bringing together 45, 42 and the Headquarters Company of 3 Commando Brigade, again centring around *Bulwark*. A third exercise in the Aden area was staged the following year, this time with 40 Commando, who came by sea from Singapore, and the recently re-formed 41 Commando, which sailed out from England.

Soon, however, exercises were overtaken by the sheer weight of patrols. In 1963 the Yemeni civil war reached the Radfan, and once again 45 Commando was called into the region, now to be joined by successive waves of parachute troops from 3 Para and the SAS. The Radfan campaign settled into a long-running affair in which several elements of the British army became embroiled, including the East Anglian Regiment and the 39 Brigade. It was during this period that 45 Commando began to pioneer the use of helicopters in tactical deployment, a development that was to have far-reaching effects in the future. Their use was highlighted in a report from Lieutenant-Colonel T. M. P. Stevens to the Commandant-General of the Royal Marines in May 1964 describing a recent action in which 12 dissidents were killed.

The narrative provides an insight into a number of issues that confronted the Commandos, ranging on the one hand from chasing shadows through challenging country, with little water, to out-and-out fire fights:

In late April we were warned that we would be needed for operations near Thumeir on the Dhala road, and B Company of 3rd Bn Parachute Regiment was brought from Bahrain and put under my command. At that time I was extremely worried about the outcome, as some extraordinary military doctrines were being laid down, bearing no relation to either the ground or the circumstances, particularly helicopter availability; and much of my time was spent arguing for a different approach. However, when Force HQ moved to Thumeir and the ground things began to sort themselves out I moved up to Thumeir for final planning, and on 29 April X, Y and Z Companies concentrated there, leaving B Coy to prepare for a parachute drop. The main dissident stronghold appears to be in the mountains of Radfan, but they gained much support from the Danaba Basin and the Wadi Taim. The plan was to hold the dissident attention on the Rabwa pass and outflank them through the hilly country to the left. 1st East Anglian, FEA and 4th Tanks secured the road and kept up pressure on the Rabwa, and SAS operated in small parties right among the dissidents south of the Rabwa pass. The plan was for B Coy to drop in the Wadi Taim and seize [their designated area] while X and Y Coys moved by night to secure a nasty line of hills. I insisted on taking Z Coy to secure hold at least some high ground to our rear.

On the afternoon of 30 April we moved in MT to an assembly area. As the light was fading, we set off along a difficult wadi bed through hilly country towards the Wadi Boran (our exit into the Danaba Basin) on a route that by day might have cost several days' fighting. Just as Z Coy was moving up, we were told that the para drop had been cancelled [two attempts to get SAS

Pathfinders in had failed], and we were ordered to go firm ahead. This was no joke, as [the designated attack zone] is a high and difficult hill, and we had not studied the approaches to it. However, we managed to get on to it before first light, mortars, machine guns and all – much credit to Mike Banks, who led the way. This was the end of Phase 1, and we now held an entrance to the Danaba Basin and a new approach towards the Rabwa. Pressure was kept up on the Rabwa to deceive the enemy into thinking we were still heading that way. The task given me [next was to take] a very difficult feature indeed, rising about 1,200 feet above the surrounding plains and almost sheer in places. There were only two practicable approaches, from the east and west, both narrow and easy to defend.

My plans were for 7 Coy to secure a rather easier feature to the west, so that we would hold at least some high ground at first light. Meanwhile, X would take the short approach to a precipitous final approach, and B Coy, who had not yet suffered from a long night march, would go right round to the south, with the longer route but slightly easier final approach. Thus we would have two bites at the coconut, in the hope that at least one would break in. X and Y were more tired than we thought; we were late getting down and did not start until an hour after we had hoped. However, Y Coy, leading the way, kept accurately to the chosen route and Y and Tac HQ got on to their feature (very, very tired) and X likewise before first light – no opposition, but signs that the dissidents, who seemed to live in the villages below by night, had begun to move up behind them.

B Company, who had been delayed by three exhaustion cases, minor losses of direction and lying up while dissidents (with lanterns) passed by, had seemed to be well on their way round. But at first light we heard firing. To cut a long story short, they ran into a village and a series of fortified houses containing 40 to 60 dissidents, attacked them very vigorously and effectively, killing 10 or 12 and dispersing them. They had won their battle quickly, and were just getting ready to move up the slopes when they quickly suffered several casualties from a few snipers who had escaped into the foothills. They had two killed and 10 wounded, but were perfectly secure in their buildings. I could not afford to release X Coy to relieve them (it is a very big feature indeed, and X Coy could not support B Coy from the top), so ordered them to lie up while Z Coy was flown in helicopters. Meanwhile, we brought in air strikes (we were out of artillery range) and in the early afternoon Z Coy moved down the slopes to prevent the snipers firing, the casualties were flown out by helicopter, and Z and B returned at last light. We went firm with Y [and] next day the Danaba Basin was proscribed and we searched the villages there and found them empty. On 9 May we were relieved by East Anglians and marched out. It was a successful operation, an exhausting time and a fascinating experience. We lived in the clothes we started in (our packs never caught up with us), had just enough water to drink and slept on bare rock. By the end we were getting used to it, and now know enough of the game to fight in that kind of country. The most remarkable lesson was the extreme power that a few well-concealed snipers on high ground can have. The dissidents site and conceal [their hideouts] very well indeed, although they were 20 yards long and with hidden communication lines. I walked past one three times without seeing it. It might have cost half a battalion to take it in daylight. Our occupation of the feature virtually finished this phase of the operation, and the dissidents left the Rabwa area to go back into the mountains. Some of the tribes have made overtures for peace, but I doubt if this is worth much. There is now likely to be a long pause while the captains and the kings debate.

Logistics is the snag and helicopter resupply almost the critical factor. By the end only one Belvedere was operating. The two Scouts of the Light Aircraft Squadron were great value. We were 'spearhead' throughout, and the East Anglians are justifiably sour at spending most of their time trailing round behind us. The operations of SAS were remarkable. They lay up in small parties right among the dissidents, bringing down artillery fire and air strikes whenever they saw a target. They must have inflicted 40 or more casualties. I have turned the Recce Troop complete over to the SAS; they are off upcountry today for their first operations. They are being given special kit as theatre stores.

Water: we carried three water bottles per man, and might survive 24 hours or more on this in static work in the shade. On long and tough night marches the heavily laden men – wireless operators and support weapons – drink the lot. We had several cases of heat exhaustion and a lot of exhaustion. The evenings, nights and mornings were pleasant, but the heat of the day on bare mountaintops very unpleasant indeed. We were proud of our beards in the mountains – necessity, not policy, through lack of water and packs never reaching us. These have now sadly vanished down the plugholes.

As the cycle of upcountry and Aden duties became more intense in the mid-1960s, the length of time 45 Commando spent on the mountains became progressively longer as the helicopter supply situation improved. In a seven-week period alone, 45 Commando conducted 305 night patrols and, in the early weeks of 1966, mounted eight major operations. During its last upcountry excursions that year, they logged 24 confirmed kills, and after those long treks into the Radfan became the first British troops to evacuate the area, leaving it mainly in the hands of the paras and 39 Brigade.

The departure of 45 Commando from this wild country did not, however, mean the men would enjoy a period of rest and relaxation – far from it. The British were finally on the way out. Under an agreement formulated by Harold Wilson's Labour government, Aden was being given independence. The deadline for complete withdrawal had been set for 1967, and 45 Commando now moved to Aden and took over internal security duties in the Ma'alla area, which in fact turned out to be one of the liveliest spots during a period of extreme civil unrest to send the British on their way. In one of their last major incidents in Aden, 45 Commando recorded 13 terrorists killed at a cost to themselves of one killed and two wounded. In the event, it was the last unit to leave Aden, covering the backs of the withdrawing troops being flown out in the final days of the British occupation of Aden. During its time there, 45 Commando collected numerous medals and awards, including three MBEs, two MCs, four MMs, six Mentions in Dispatches, three Queen's Commendations and 15 Commander-in-Chief's Commendations for operations. All this had been at the cost, to date, of only six killed and 62 wounded during seven years in action, which the company log recorded as 'a small number in relation to the time and effort spent on operations'.

While their colleagues in 45 Commando had been away in the awfulness of South Arabia, the rest of 3 Commando Brigade had been, for much of the time since 1962, engaged in another equally difficult and tedious campaign being fought in conditions very, very different from the heat of the mountains and deserts of the Radfan. This time, it was in the wet and impenetrable jungles of Borneo, where the war that wasn't – it was merely a 'confrontation' – flared when Doctor Sukarno, President of Indonesia, made advances towards British protectorates on the island of Borneo.

At the time Britain was responsible for the defence of the Sultanate of Brunei and the colonies of North Borneo (later Sabah) and Sarawak. Those states, it was hoped, would join the Federation of Malaya to form a powerful and stable alliance. Sukarno had other ideas and backed local Communist guerrillas in a flare-up in Brunei which rapidly gathered pace across the island. The three British protectorates shared borders with Kalimantan, the Indonesian region of Borneo which accounted for three-quarters of its land surface. Sukarno was intent on taking control of the remainder, to add 7.5 million inhabitants to the 100 million he already ruled. His further ambition, inspired apparently by the Japanese in the Second World War, was to take over the whole of the Malayan states and with them the plum target of Singapore. In 1961 he was poised to continue, and the British government approved a hurried, if limited, military response and sent in an initial force drawn from the Royal Marines Commandos, the Gurkhas and the Queen's Own Highlanders and, later, the Parachute Regiment.

Before long there would be 28,000 men deployed, topped up with Australians, New Zealanders and what proved to be a very active contingent of the Special Forces. The last consisted of the SBS and 22 SAS – one of whose squadrons was commanded by Major Peter de la Billière (later British commander in the 1991 Gulf War) – and elements of the Parachute Regiment who went in to join patrols devised by the SAS. They were under the overall command of General Sir Walter Walker, who apart from being the Gurkhas Brigade major-general was appointed director of military operations in Borneo, he being the foremost military expert on jungle warfare in the British army. On this occasion he was in something of a dilemma. British troops were governed by strict terms of engagements, specific and limiting. They were drawn up to comply with both UN requirements and the British government's fear of engaging its forces in a long and costly jungle war in a terrain that was naturally hostile and, in parts, still uncharted. The overall penetration depth allowed in cross-border attacks was just 5,000 yards, although this could be increased to 20,000 yards for specific operations authorised by Walker himself: 'It was a ridiculous situation when you think about it – how can you expect a patrol hacking its way through dense jungle to actually measure 5,000? They might be 9,000 yards . . . or even more.'

Walker was the architect of what would become a most successful campaign, with very low casualty figures and innovative in its use of the Commandos and the Special Forces in what were known as the Claret Operations. Other rules: the MoD insisted that absolutely no member of the British forces should be taken prisoner and absolutely no British casualties, dead or alive, should be left behind in case they might be photographed and produced as evidence to the world of British attacks. So, with lightness of foot and fingers on the triggers, 42 Commando sallied forth into an eventful and tragic opening of their account on 10 December 1962 in a campaign that would engage them for the next three and a half years.

The Commando's L Company went first by air to Brunei, where the British resident, his wife and seven others were being held hostage at Limbang, 12 miles south of Brunei town. It was estimated that 200 rebels were surrounding the resident's house. The company, with a machine-gun section, went in at 6.15 on the morning of 12 December and in a furious fire fight released the hostages unharmed, although five Commandos were killed and five wounded in the action. The enemy lost 35 killed and at least that many again wounded. Despite this setback, 42 went on to settle down to a very successful start to the campaign, and within a month had captured 421 enemy – the most rounded up by any unit in the time. The troops were hampered, however, by heavy rains in January which caused major floods across their patrol area, and Lieutenant A. D. M. Morris and his troop sailed away when the rising water level lifted the complete house they were resting in. That mishap apart, 42 set in motion an operation to find and capture one of the most senior enemy figures in their area, Yassin Effendi. Lieutenant Colonel George and Sergeant Smith formed a special team to track him, and eventually caught and arrested him in March.

The Commandos then settled into an ongoing succession of amphibious and jungle patrols in liaison with the rest of the British forces. The bulging report of the Claret Operations – each one meticulously written up and now in the National Archives – ranges through many skirmishes and ambushes and includes another first – the use of a hovercraft on river patrols. 40 Commando arrived on 14 December 1962, to remain in action in Borneo for almost four years. The initial deployment included Pugforce, for A Company, run by the redoubtable ex-SBS commander and Second World War Royal Marines veteran, Major 'Pug' Davis. They went straight into patrols and raids and then, in April 1965, the unit began the innovation of operating a curfew across a belt five miles wide from the Indonesian border while night ambushes were laid. The unit itself was spread over a front of 140 miles, manned by 32 radio stations in continuous contact.

Strong points were set up all along the front, and any one of them could be reinforced by helicopter within ten minutes. Later, 40 Commando was the only one to add its own airborne troop when it took responsibility for an area covering 140 square miles. For newcomers to the Commandos during this period, it was often an eye-opening experience, in more ways than one. Major-General A. M. Keeling recalled his Borneo story:

I found myself in 1963 as a troop commander in 42 Commando at the tender age of 19 with Brunei campaign veterans in the jungles of Sarawak. We didn't then realise that we were embarking on what was to develop into a protracted, large-scale operation; we did know that we were looking very hard for terrorists, armed and inspired by the Indonesians, and that they were probably looking for us. That part of Sarawak was still very primitive then and along the Indonesian border, deep in the jungle, there were very few signs of encroachment by the twentieth century. Our lot was to patrol the border by day and to ambush crossing points by night, and to do this we lived a very simple life alongside the Dyaks in their villages. In that sort of situation, where the privileges of rank almost completely disappear, you all get to know each other extremely well. This, of course, is part of the fascination of this type of soldiering. We also came to be almost totally assimilated into village life, for we shared all the privations of the Dyaks' meagre existence. We came to accept their habits and lifestyle as if we had grown up among them, although in many respects it was a far cry from our own previous experience. We even became quite blasé about the fact that the women dressed only in a sarong and that sarongs in Sarawak are tied at the waist. This, remember, was long before the days of topless bathing.

The 1960s were a busy but in many ways unsatisfactory time for the Marines given that the opportunities for amphibious work had diminished substantially, especially in the case of 45 Commando. They had suffered the continuous grind of attrition in Aden and the Radfan and managed to keep up their amphibian skills only by the deliberate action of training. The other two units did at least see water, and plenty of it. Nor was the decade of indifferent postings over. As the British government pursued its policy of withdrawing all troops from east of Suez, 3 Commando came back to their bases in England, there were other stirrings, closer to home, that would also very quickly involve them and, ultimately, virtually every military unit in the UK on a rotational basis. What became commonly known as 'The Troubles' erupted on the streets of Northern Ireland out of civil rights demonstrations in 1968. On the backs of those, the IRA returned to its traditions of bomb and bullet and, as history has well recorded, before long 20,000 British troops, like the Commandos, fresh from the colonial wars, would find themselves patrolling the streets of the province. 41 Commando was the first to be deployed there, in September 1969, and had the honour of being the first to be fired on while patrolling in Belfast. In that first tour, 41 took on patrolling the areas around the Shankill, the Falls and the Boyne Bridge – names that were to become all too familiar in the years ahead. Few could have predicted then that, 30 years later, troops would still be engaged on patrols in those self-same areas, engaged on the vagaries of complicated and dangerous Internal Security operations that saw so many casualties.

They were followed by 45 Commando, whose tours there began when they placed 400 of their men in between the opposing group of Catholics and Protestants in Ardoyne. In July 1972, when 22,000 British troops were involved in Operation Motorman in Ulster, the whole Commando Brigade, along with Royal Naval personnel, manned landing craft that took Royal Engineers bulldozers up the River Foyle and into the heart of Londonderry. This movement allowed security forces to clear the no-go areas, and the Ulster conflict entered a totally new phase. Thereafter, new recruits of a youthful age found themselves in the line, and not a year passed without 3 Commando being represented by one or occasionally two of its units in the province.

Between 1969 and 2002, 3 Commando Brigade collectively completed more than 40 separate tours of Northern Ireland, lasting four, six and occasionally 12 months, in which they suffered 25 killed by bomb or bullet and countless numbers wounded. This did not include attacks classed as 'out-of-theatre' events described elsewhere in these chapters. It was also during a year-long assignment to Londonderry by 40 Commando that the IRA chose to assassinate Earl Mountbatten, Admiral of the Fleet and a Colonel Commandant of the Royal Marines, on 27 August 1979, while holidaying with his family.

Nor were Internal Security operations confined to Northern Ireland. Throughout the 1970s and beyond, numerous events called for the attention of 3 Commando Brigade. They were back in Cyprus following the Turkish invasion of the island in 1974, not to intervene but to protect British interests and assist in a general calming down after a peace deal involving partition was signed. They also put detachments aboard numerous frigates during the dispute with Iceland over fishing groups and later went on an emergency deployment to Hong Kong to join the Gurkhas and other British forces in dealing with an unprecedented crisis in illegal immigration from the Chinese Republic. From a trickle in the early 1970s, the flow became a torrent, threatening to deluge the already overcrowded colony. It was soul-destroying work for British troops involved in this saga that dragged on for almost eight years, peaking in 1979 when in that year 90,000 illegal immigrants flooded across the border while thousands more had been successfully turned back by the troops and Royal Hong Kong Police.

The Marines introduced seaborne anti-immigration patrols using high-speed boats, and they were so successful that the Hong Kong government asked for the patrols to be maintained. Consequently, a new force, 3 Raiding Squadron, was set up exclusively to deal with the Hong Kong situation, using fast Avon Searider Rigid Inflatable Boats (RIBs) for the task. However, the immigration pirates and people smugglers very quickly responded, and the Marines found themselves being outrun by faster boats. In the early 1980s, therefore, they were re-equipped with FPCs (fast pursuit craft) and in the six months after they were introduced over a hundred speedboats were successfully intercepted.

The squadron remained operational until July 1988, long after the main immigration crisis in Hong Kong had subsided. By then, the troops had boarded no fewer than 4,200 boats and had arrested over 1,000 people involved in the immigration racket.

Patrols were also undertaken around the British coastline with the formation of the Comacchio Company – named after the Second World War battle fought by 42 Commando. This was set up to take on the responsibility for the security of various sensitive installations, such as coastal nuclear power stations and naval and military sites. The group also developed what became known as the Oilsafe programme for fast-action protection for Britain's offshore gas and oil industry which was initiated by L Company of 42 Commando. This rapidly expanding group also enjoyed the assistance and advice of the SBS on this programme of entirely new projects.

Additionally, the brigade also undertook a demanding new role in the Cold War, assuming responsibility for the Southern Flank of Europe and the Mediterranean area, and later 45 Commando took on the Arctic role in Norway to support the Northern Flank of Europe. By 1979 the whole of 3 Commando Brigade was committed to Arctic warfare and thus a whole new range of training manuals was introduced to cover a vastly expanded set of skills and disciplines for the Marines, new and old.

CHAPTER FIFTEEN

Spearhead Falklands

On 17 October 1981 the IRA next tried to assassinate General Sir Steuart Pringle, Commandant-General, Royal Marines, and lifelong career Marine, by placing a bomb under his car. It exploded seconds after he started the engine outside his home in Dulwich, London. He was severely injured and subsequently lost one leg and part of the other. Just five and a half months later, on 31 March 1982, he returned to work and called his generals for a meeting to discuss the current state of the corps and its activities, although, of course, he had kept himself well briefed in the meantime. The meeting was scheduled for the following day – inappropriately enough 1 April, given the forthcoming developments – and among the items to be discussed was the small detachment of Royal Marines in the Falkland Islands. Reports of some kind of military activity involving the Argentinians had been buzzing around, but inexplicably no one at the Ministry of Defence had found it necessary to impart any real intelligence to the officers of the Royal Marines, the only unit available for amphibious warfare. Major-General Jeremy Moore, who had deputised for the Commandant-General during his absence, recalled in a memoir for the Imperial War Museum:

At that meeting we did discuss the South Atlantic because of the corps' detachment. We had been aware from intelligence reports that something was cooking. [We did not know] the extent of the government's knowledge of how far it was going and what the plans were . . . but it was quite obvious that people were beginning to think of possible action to protect the islands or prevent an invasion, which was obviously seen as a possibility. A number of suggestions were put to us about what we might do about it. Could we provide a unit to go south? Of course we could. Various thoughts were being put . . . One was to recall a Commando from leave because they might be needed. But nobody must know about it. How do you recall 650 chaps from leave without their wives and local police and so on knowing? Another which tickled our sense of the ridiculous was that maybe we ought to send our air defence troop. It was a nice thought to consider how the Argentinians would view 54 young men with short haircuts and big boots, every single one of them carrying a double-bass case, because how else would you get missiles there through Buenos Aires airport, which was the only way to get to the islands? So the whole thing was not exactly out of the blue, but it had really been on a fairly low level.

Until, that is, 12 hours after the Commandant-General's return-to-work meeting concluded. That was when the Argentinians invaded the Falklands, and Jeremy Moore found himself in the driving seat, as divisional commander of the forces to be deployed to the islands to kick them out, an operation that in the event would be spearheaded by 3 Commando Brigade, the only British military unit equipped and capable of leading an opposed amphibious landing on distant shores. There was, of course, great irony in this statement, given that, just a few weeks before, the very question of the need for – and indeed the survival of – the Royal Marines was once again being discussed. The issue was raised, as it had been on many occasions in the past, when

Margaret Thatcher's government embarked on swingeing cost-cutting measures in which hapless Defence Secretary John Nott planned to take a machete to military spending. The theory behind the discussion went along similar lines to previous thoughts: that Britain no longer had any need for amphibious landings, and consequently had no need to maintain the Royal Marines, certainly not at the current level.

Financial constraints had already produced a Royal Navy – and indeed a military philosophy for Britain – that was almost exclusively geared to the Cold War, in which nuclear submarines had become the nation's capital ships. In company with her allies in Nato, Britain's fighting arms had become somewhat institutionalised by the procedures and rigidity of aligning their troops, air forces and ships to the overall East versus West battle scenario. The growth in the size and sophistication of the Soviet armed forces through the 1960s and 1970s, matched and beaten by the vast resources of America, left lesser nations – a category in which Britain now found herself irrefutably anchored – no choice but to accept a secondary role to the main players. At the time of the Falklands crisis – and possibly a trigger to it – John Nott was already in the process of defence cuts that originally included the possibility of selling off Britain's newest aircraft carrier, *Invincible*. In a plan for the future with the unoriginal title of *The Way Forward*, the thinking was once again reductive and primarily focused on Europe, where Britain and her Nato allies faced a great concentration of Warsaw Pact forces.

Four points were highlighted: providing an independent element of nuclear forces committed to the Nato alliance; defending the United Kingdom homeland; contributing major land and air forces to the European mainland; and deploying a major maritime capability in the eastern Atlantic and the Channel. This was a crucial statement that vividly came to be questioned when the Falklands conflict arose, which – along with events in later decades such as Iraq and Afghanistan – proved the folly of such thinking. By the beginning of the 1980s there was already considerable difficulty in terms of equipment and manpower in meeting the challenges of any major 'out-of-area' operations, a fact that the Ministry of Defence later admitted was highlighted by the Falklands War. Even so, what now began to unfold made the operation to meet Margaret Thatcher's demands for an immediate recapture of the Falklands all the more remarkable. The campaign, which was to test the British military as nothing else had in years, was launched after the sudden invasion of the Falkland Islands by Argentinian forces on 2 April 1982 – an event in part triggered by the publicity surrounding British defence cuts.

The Royal Navy's sole bearer of the White Ensign in the southern hemisphere, the ice-patrol vessel *Endurance*, was to be withdrawn in the summer, saving a mere £3 million a year in a budget counted in billions. In the belief that Britain no longer cared much about the Falklands and well aware of the small number of British troops stationed in the islands, the Argentinians sent over an invasion force consisting of a marine infantry battalion of just 680 men led in by Marines of the Argentine Amphibious Commando Company.

At the time the Falklands garrison was unusually large, because the detachments were just changing over, the new one, under Aden veteran Major Mike Norman, having recently arrived from England. Even so, the sum total was just 80 men. They were dispersed across the Falklands: three officers and 66 men of the garrison manning various positions, plus two officers and nine men aboard the Royal Navy's faithful old South Atlantic patrol vessel, *Endurance*. In the event of a fight, Mike Norman could enlist the aid of the local defence force – all 23 of them – plus a former Marine corporal, Jim Fairfield, who had met and married a local girl and had moved to Port Stanley.

Put up against the invading troops, they would be heavily outnumbered and outgunned. The Argentine Commando Company went straight to the Marines' barracks at Moody Brook, which was empty, but they trashed it anyhow, tossing phosphorus grenades in most of the rooms. They then moved on to Government House, where the bulk of the Marines had assembled to protect the Governor and his small staff.

By then, further elements of the invasion force were coming ashore, with armoured troop carriers and some heavy weapons. Lieutenant Bill Trollope's defiant group of eight Royal Marines were lying in wait at a point where the convoy would pass, and Marine Brown claimed a hit on one of the armoured vehicles with a 66-millimetre rocket that must have upset the 50 or so men inside. The group followed up with heavy bursts of machine-gun fire, and the Argentinians were temporarily halted. The Royal Marines garrison at Grytiken on the island of South Georgia, consisting of 20 Marines commanded by Lieutenant Keith Mills, also gave the landing parties a few shocks, first bringing down a Puma helicopter and then damaging a landing ship with their 82-millimetre Carl Gustav anti-tank rocket, the largest gun they possessed.

When the Argentinian navy started shelling them with its 100-millimetre gun, the Royal Marines had no alternative but to give up; there was nowhere on that inhospitable landscape to hide. Back at Port Stanley it was also decision time. Mike Norman reflected on that moment years later when he had retired from the Marines and was enjoying a more mundane life as a self-employed gardener.

Surrender, as far as we were concerned, was never an option. The men felt the same. But Rex Hunt, the Governor of the Falkland Islands, ordered me to do so, and he was commander-in-chief. I was devastated. My men knew the score. Although we were overwhelmed, they still wanted to fight on. I was terribly proud of them for that. The fact remains, we were not there to defend the Falkland Islands; that was impossible for such a small group. We were there to defend the seat of government and that was Rex Hunt. I gave him three options and none of them involved surrender. I told him we could carry on fighting, we could do a runner with him into the countryside and wage a guerrilla war, or he could negotiate a truce to give us some

289

breathing space. He told me: 'Mike, I want you to order your men to lay down their arms.' That decision undoubtedly saved our lives. I have to say, however, that the invasion was no surprise to us or to Rex Hunt. The captain of *Endurance* had been giving warnings for a year which were ignored in London. Mrs Thatcher and her government could have done better. They got us into that situation, and I told her so after I'd had a few drinks at a Falklands dinner a few years later.

But at least they were not being put in a prison camp. Hunt was told that he and his troops were being repatriated to England. They were shipped out of Port Stanley, quietly promising that they fully intended to return, and in due course they would, as Juliet Troop attached to 42 Commando. In the meantime, arrangements were made to send an RAF VC-10 to Montevideo, from where they were flown to Brize Norton.

There, apart from a large media presence, a whole range of military and intelligence people were waiting to debrief them, because by then Mrs Thatcher had demanded that a task force had better get down there pretty damned quick and reclaim the islands and return them to the British. In one remarkable top-level meeting between the suits and the uniforms, according to one of the latter who was there, 'some bloody fool [among the former] suggested making a very large bang in the area of Argentina'. For a while chaos reigned in the corridors of power, and the military planners were clearly working to a somewhat limited brief that incredibly amounted to no more than sending a token force (3 Commando Brigade) to make a landing in the Falklands in the hope of getting Galtieri to negotiate. General Moore recalled:

We were working on plans for a landing, but we were still not working on plans for repossessing the islands because [at that stage] that was not our stated mission. So you had the situation where it was perfectly possible and reasonable and right to plan on being able to make a landing with 3 Commando Brigade reinforced, which was what we had set forth and was assembling at Ascension Island. But as I sat and looked at this and saw the developing intelligence on the Argentinian build-up in the islands, it became apparent to me – no surprise, it was apparent to all of us – that one could not fight a battle to repossess the islands in all probability just with 3 Commando Brigade because I was going to be landing a force in the islands which was only half the size of the Argentinian garrison.

We all know that in any planned military operation you normally aim to have three times, in broad terms, the number of troops that the enemy has in order to overcome him if you're doing the attacking. So one began to think in terms of reinforcement. But since our mission was simply to make a landing, you couldn't justify reinforcement [and] here's the bit where people would say, 'Yes, but surely it must have been obvious?' It wasn't obvious . . . I think that the government sticking with just that as the mission we'd been given at that stage was perfectly reasonable because we all knew that if we were going to reinforce, a lot more shipping would have to be taken up from trade, which is a hugely expensive and disruptive business . . . So there was a pause where it was really quite difficult to get ahead from our angle. I and the commander-in-chief went to the Chiefs of Staff to argue the case for reinforcement [and] eventually that did happen . . . Our mission changed to: You are to repossess the islands.

Margaret Thatcher, the Supreme Commander, took charge and announced that a task force of 40 ships would be assembled to carry two reinforced brigades and a large assortment of top-quality supporting artillery, intelligence and reconnaissance units, not to mention the brilliant naval logistics and management teams – and in the Spearhead role would be 3 Commando Brigade, whose presence a few months down the line, incidentally, might not have been available had the cost-cutters persisted.

British warships and nuclear submarines were heading for the Falklands within 24 hours of the invasion as a preliminary to the main assault. This was in the hands of an Amphibious Task Force that sailed within a week carrying the whole of 3 Commando Brigade, including its own gunners and sappers and, of course, the Royal Marines band, which carried out a multitude of tasks in addition to boosting morale, plus the 2nd and 3rd Battalions of the Parachute Regiment, which was at the time described as forming the toughest fighting force in the world.

It would take five weeks for a convoy to reach the Falklands, but even as the troops began to embark the task force ships on 6 April it became apparent that Mrs Thatcher had called for an early response to the Argentinian invasion, well in advance of the arrival of the main force, and so a landing in advance of the main body of troops was given priority. Although it has often been written that virtually nothing was known about the coastlines and landing possibilities around the Falklands, this was not at all true. In fact, the Commandos had their own walking encyclopaedia, Major Ewen Southby-Tailyour, who had commanded the Falklands garrison in 1977. He had conducted an exhaustive study of the coastline and carried out the only detailed survey of many of the beaches and their approaches since the mid-eighteenth century. Barely three years after his return he found himself at the forefront of the planning team being drawn together by Brigadier Julian Thompson, commanding 3 Commando Brigade, for the move south. Utilising these skills, plans were drawn for a Commando-led landing ahead of the main assault, and the target area was on the island of South Georgia, 800 miles north-east of the Falklands and not actually part of them. It had a small Argentinian garrison but also possessed the most inhospitable landscape, with whirlwinds whipping up driving snow across treacherous glaciers. All Commando units had regular tough winter training in Norway for their Arctic role, and 42 Commando had not long returned from theirs. The

Commando was thus an obvious choice to provide the bulk of the force to be sent on ahead to capture South Georgia.

It was commanded by Major Guy Sheridan, second-in-command of 42 Commando, a very experienced snow and ice mountaineer who had only recently completed the first traverse of the Himalayas on skis. M Company, 42 Commando, commanded by Captain Nunn, was selected for the task, and he took with him two 81-millimetre mortars, a section of the Commando Reconnaissance Troop, a small logistic and medical party, two Gunfire Observer parties from 148 Battery, one SBS Section and an SAS Squadron: 230 men in total. They flew to Ascension Island on 7 April, embarked on the huge Royal Fleet Auxiliary tanker *Tidespring* and sailed south under the protection of the destroyer *Antrim* and the ageing frigate *Plymouth*. Two nuclear submarines shadowed the group, which reached the island on 21 April. It was to become a veritable nightmare of a job.

The SAS were first ashore, landing reconnaissance patrols on the hazardous Fortuna glacier against the advice of Sheridan. Within 12 hours they called for helicopters to evacuate them immediately because of appalling conditions and impossible terrain. Two Wessex Mk 5 helicopters from *Tidespring* were sent to extract them, but both crashed on the glacier when the pilots became disorientated and lost the horizon which merged with the sky in white-out conditions. An ancient single-engine Wessex 3 from *Antrim*, piloted by Lieutenant-Commander Stanley and flying in suicidal conditions, brought the SAS team and the crashed helicopter crews back to the ship, leaving the force's only two troop-lift helicopters destroyed on the glacier. The main body of M Company were on board *Tidespring* when reports of a prowling enemy submarine in the area sent them out to sea to hunt it down. The submarine *Santa Fe* was sighted on the surface five miles out from Grytiken by Lieuentant-Commander Stanley. He attacked her with machine-gun fire and depth charges, which stopped her from diving until two British missile-carrying helicopters arrived to deliver a more devastating blow. The sub was left badly damaged and listing heavily.

Although *Tidespring* was at that point miles away from him, Major Sheridan was determined to make the landing on South Georgia. He mustered a scratch force of 75 men from M Company headquarters, the Reconnaissance Section, the SBS and SAS aboard the destroyer *Antrim*. He was given permission to lead the group into attack, and with the backing of guns from the destroyer he headed for the target area on South Georgia. Before long the Argentinians ran up the white flag. The garrison consisted of 137 men who, on 26 April, became the first prisoners of war. Back in London, Mrs Thatcher dashed out of the front door of No. 10 Downing Street and in front of television cameras shouted: 'Rejoice, rejoice. South Georgia has been recaptured.'

Meanwhile, the task force was heading south after a stopover at Ascension Island to gather more troops and ships coming in from Gibraltar. Ahead of their arrival, SAS and SBS patrols were going ashore on the Falklands proper, inserted on 1 May to carry out the reconnaissance of enemy positions. With them were naval gunnery control officers who were to direct naval gunfire on Argentinian positions. Some of those units spent up to three weeks ashore, roaming across the windswept landscape gleaning intelligence. The advance shipping battle group was already giving the Argentinian positions a 'bloody good pounding' as the task force sailed to within sight of the islands.

On 13 May Brigadier Julian Thompson, boss of 3 Commando Brigade and overall commander of the ground forces, gave his first briefing to his unit commanders on board HMS *Fearless* on Operation Sutton, the codename given for the first stage of the repossession of the Falkland Islands. The meeting began with Major Southby-Tailyour, RM, providing the benefit of his extensive knowledge of the terrain the troops would face, followed by intelligence reports on the known locations and strength of the Argentinian troops. The SBS were to secure and mark landing beaches for the approaching landing craft and then deal with a potentially troublesome enemy position known as the Fanning Hill Mob. The main thrust of initial troop landings would involve 40 and 45 Commandos and the 2 and 3 Parachute Battalions, while 42 Commando would initially remain at sea as a floating reserve, to follow in several hours later. The SAS would provide diversionary action, flying ashore and weighing in with heavy firepower to keep the Argentinians occupied while the landings took place.

And so, just after midnight of 20 May, with the first 3,000 troops aboard, a fleet of 11 ships entered the narrows guarding San Carlos Water and by dawn the troop landing at San Carlos and Ajax Bay had been completed virtually undisturbed. The 3 Commando group – the only brigade with ancillary support groups in the British military trained in amphibious warfare and Arctic action – consisted of 40, 42 and 45 Commandos, the 29 Commando Regiment, Royal Artillery and sappers from 59 Ind. Commando Squadron, Royal Engineers. Others in the group included elements from the Logistics Regiment, an air squadron running Gazelle and Scout helicopters, an Air Defence troop, the 1st Raiding Squadron operating assault craft and the Mountain and Arctic Warfare Cadre. The 2nd and 3rd Battalions of the Parachute Regiment bolstered the infantry strength, and there were two troops of light tanks from the Blues and Royals and a battery of the Air Defence Regiment with Rapier anti-aircraft missiles. Following behind, to arrive a few days later, was the army's 5 Brigade with the Scots Guards, the Welsh Guards and the 7th Gurkhas.

The Rapier air-defence systems with 105-millimetre light artillery batteries were quickly established to provide a continual bombardment of the Goose Green airstrip to stifle Argentinian air activity, although by 9 a.m. the enemy air assault sprang to life with sorties flown from Port Stanley and from the mainland. A diary kept by Captain Ian Gardiner, commander of X Company of 45 Commando, makes fascinating if disturbing reading as he explores the sights and sounds of moving towards battle after coming ashore at Ajax Bay from the carrier ship:

We climbed over the guardrail down the scrambling net . . . One of the landing craft broke down somewhere [and we had to] cram the remaining people into three landing craft. Had there been any opposition at all, we would have taken a hammering. We secured our objectives and deployed to the hill. Nearing the ridge, I saw my first enemy aircraft. He whipped along the ridge line from north to south, very close to where I was. James Kelly, 1 Troop Commander, and I hit the deck. In a split second he was gone and was shot down soon afterwards. Our Rapier anti-aircraft missile detachment had by now arrived (late), but it was not in a position to deal with the four Mirages that had eluded the Harriers. One was shot down by a ship, but the other three pressed home their attack on HMS *Ardent*. I saw these aircraft as they whooshed over us and over our hill to strike *Ardent* in the Falklands Sound. Our Rapier fired one missile, but the missile failed to respond to the controls and missed badly. *Ardent* had not sunk but limped out of sight. We consolidated our positions and dug like little moles. That night, we froze. Our Bergens didn't turn up [bad weather halted their helicopter delivery service] . . . Early in the morning I sent Alastair Cameron, my artillery observer officer, to set up an observation post at the top of the hill. On arrival, he gave me a chilling description of *Ardent* burning and eventually sinking, stern first. The shock of actually being at war was beginning to sink in. I was to see things in the next few days that I thought I would never live to see, and hope I never see again.

As serious bombing by the Argentinian air force got under way, there were so many targets, with such a large number of ships landing forces and supplies, that in attempting to keep the Argentinians at bay the ships' gunners had to take great care to avoid hitting their own men and machines. On the following evening two more frigates limped into the bay. *Argonaut* came in steered by two landing craft. She had sustained damage to her steering mechanism but was otherwise fairly sound. The type-21 frigate *Antelope* was less lucky; she came in under her own steam and, although she was making smoke and had a hole either side of her hull forward of the funnel, to observers she seemed sound. But then, soon after sunset, an explosion ripped through her superstructure, followed by a number of secondary explosions, and helicopters appeared almost instantly to begin taking the crew off. The following day there were more exchanges as waves of Argentinian planes came in to be met by the task force gunners and Harriers in what Captain Gardiner described as 'a gladiatorial contest of the highest order . . . the navy certainly covered themselves with glory on this the most dramatic day I saw'.

After witnessing these preliminaries and consolidating their positions, the Commandos and paras received their orders to break out of the bridgehead on 26 May. First in action was 2 Para, destined to attack Goose Green in a now-famous battle against a considerably larger force in which their commanding officer, Lieutenant-Colonel H. Jones, led a vital assault as the attack seemed to be fading and succeeded in winning the position. In doing so, Jones was killed and was later posthumously awarded the Victoria Cross. For 45 Commando and 3 Para, a hellish journey lay ahead. They learned that no helicopters were available for the lift and the only alternative was a 30-kilometre 'yomp' across some of the world's most forbidding landscape in the dark, with Bergens on their backs, each weighing an average of 55 kilogrammes, and some carrying a good deal more.

The Commandos were given a route across East Falkland which consisted of every kind of ground from ankle-deep bogs to razor-sharp rocks. The paras took a southerly route, both to arrive at the same destination of the Teal Inlet. Meanwhile, 42 Commando had more luck. They stayed *in situ* to be flown forward when craft became available three days later, and 40 Commando remained for the time being in defence of San Carlos. Captain Gardiner recalling the 'yomp': 'It was 2 a.m. before the Commandos stopped for the night, only to discover that the plastic bags in which their sleeping bags were wrapped did not keep the water out and they were soaked. Furthermore, the makeshift bivouacs were simply waterproof groundsheets, supported by a small stick – totally useless under the conditions.' Given the vagaries of the equipment, said Gardiner, the Commandos 'refined our methods of living in this inhospitable place to such a degree that by the end we were like animals and almost preferred it out of doors. We could have gone on for ever'.

At first light they moved off in tactical formation in fighting order with X Company leading the way across the remaining seven miles to Douglas Settlement, which they reached at four in the afternoon and captured – unopposed. The men were tired, soaked and hungry and, having finished their rations at breakfast that morning, they had no food to replenish themselves nor, having advanced in fighting order, did they have even wet sleeping bags to climb into. Not for the first time, or the last, helicopters scheduled to collect and deliver their Bergens failed to appear.

The journey resumed on 30 May, and they could see Teal in the distance hours before they arrived there in the dark and where they spent a blissful night in a filthy, tick-ridden, beautiful sheep pen. The following day came orders for a general deployment into firm defensive positions around Teal itself behind 3 Para and 42, and they were subsequently to stand by to be flown by helicopter to a patrol base at Bluff Cove Peak. The weather closed in and flying was not possible, but by the time conditions improved no helicopters were available, so it was back to shanks's pony and a two-day march to Bluff Cove Peak, where a patrol base was set up on the rear slopes of Mount Kent.

For the next ten days Commandos and paras carried out extensive and continuous heavy patrolling while building up a detailed intelligence picture of enemy defences and positions. Royal Engineers and RM assault engineers surveyed and mapped the minefields, while gunners of 29 Commando Light Regiment and 4 Field Regiment gave enemy positions a pounding, in concert with naval gunfire. Finally, when every detail of the planning had been covered, the attacks were scheduled for 11–12 June. The battle plan put 3 Para heading for the northern feature of Mount Longdon, 45 Commando taking Two Sisters and 42 Commando awarded the southerly feature of Mount Harriett, with all units moving forward at the same appointed start time, with 2 Para and 5 Infantry Brigade coming in behind if necessary. Captain Gardiner recalled the final journey:

> The march to the forming-up point from which we were to start our assault was a near nightmare. I hadn't appreciated how much the man-packing of the Milan [a wire-guided anti-tank missile] would slow us down. Instead of covering the relatively easy ground, which had been recce'd in about three hours, thus giving us an hour to spare, we took six hours. A piece of rock or a small stream that a man in normal fighting order would never have noticed became a major obstacle when carrying his own kit plus a 14-kilogramme-weight round of Milan ammunition. We had something like 40 rounds, and the company was constantly being split as we stumbled and cursed our way over rocks and cliffs for half the night. I lost one man, a key signaller, who became ill in the middle of it all. We had to dispatch him to a nearby artillery battery, and one man knocked himself out falling down a very steep slope. By the time we reached the forming-up point, at least 2 hours had passed . . . and that was before the real work began.

The assault began just ten minutes after 45's arrival. After all the trials of the journey to the start-line, they were now confronted with what had to be a hair-raising dash across open ground:

> We could see, as we approached, the tracer from a heavy machine gun arching across towards a neighbouring hill from the top of our objective. While 2 Troop were moving up, I decided to see what the Milan could do and invited them to have a go. It would mean firing over our heads, and we were nearer to the target than we were to him [the Milan man], but it would fill the gap

299

before the artillery arrived. The round was fired. It must have passed about nine metres above us, and when it hit it produced a most satisfactory bang. Soon 2 Troop were ready and Chris Caroe had given his orders, but although mortars had given me one barrage of eight rounds, I could not, through Alastair Cameron, get any artillery at all. Poor Alastair was feeling very useless at not being able to provide at the critical moment. I don't really know what the problem was. All I remember is that when I really wanted the damned stuff, it wasn't available. I asked mortars to repeat their mission and ordered Milan to fire another two rockets. The rockets came but the mortars then failed me, too. Their base plates had disappeared into the soft ground, and they were only able to support us with one solitary mortar. So we forgot about artillery and mortars and Chris Caroe took his men up the hill regardless. It was an impressive performance. Not only were the enemy now using an anti-tank weapon, they were lobbing artillery shells at us, too. Caroe's men picked and clambered their way round, up and over the rocks towards the enemy position. It was almost like fighting in a built-up area. Two men covered while one man jumped over, leapfrogging all the way. When I saw the ground in daylight, my heart missed a beat. It was much more rugged than I had envisaged and I would have had serious doubts about their chances, but I would have had no alternative as there was only room for one group at a time.

At the top of the hill there was a ding-dong of a battle. They actually got on top but were forced off it by artillery. We then took our only casualty. Lance-Corporal Montgomery and Marine Watson were both some one and a half metres from the shell when it exploded. It picked them up and threw them several metres. Montgomery had broken or dislocated something in the shoulder and didn't know whether it was Tuesday or breakfast-time. Eventually, the leading section flushed the enemy out and we were secure on our objective. My headquarters was still being shot at in a desultory fashion by a half-hearted rifleman on a flank. We ignored him. But the shelling began more seriously now, and that was unpleasant.

From now until 36 hours later we underwent intermittent shelling, and the intermittent nature of this shelling added greatly to the danger and uncertainty. They were only using two guns, but over the period some 40 or 50 shells landed on our ridge among our positions, and the saddle between us and the rest of the unit became heavily cratered with many more. We received no casualties, but it is a disagreeable business being shelled. When I looked down the ridge and realised what we had done my spine froze. Potentially, the position was impregnable. The rest of the Commando had had their battles, too. They had secured their objectives after a spirited punch-up in which they lost four dead and 15 wounded.

We buried the enemy dead *in situ.* I myself supervised the burial of an unidentified officer and sergeant. They had both been shot at close range, probably by 3 Troop, on 9 June. We put them in a shallow grave, marked the spot carefully and made a record to submit to the authorities. I said a few words in prayer. We found a prodigious amount of ammunition, weapons, food and equipment on the position. Watching 2 Troop next day going through the camp at the top of the hill was strongly reminiscent of watching a family of tinkers picking over a rubbish tip. As it turned out, it was well that so much was there. Our Bergens again failed to turn up, and it froze that night. Without the Argentinian blankets and other clothing, we would have been extremely uncomfortable.

Elsewhere, a similar story unfolded as 42 Commando made their assault uphill and over open ground. Their battle commander had chosen a daring but ultimately very successful encircling movement, to hit the rear of the enemy on Mount Harriett, with the obvious advantage of going into the attack without having to face a full-frontal rebuff. It was a remarkable achievement. Tougher times were experienced by 3 Para, who were forced into a bloody battle on Mount Longdon, during which Sergeant Ian McKay was awarded a VC for his actions. But by dawn the three key Argentinian positions had been taken with minimal casualties. Captain Gardiner could sense that the worst was almost over:

By the 14th it became apparent that the enemy were crumbling towards Stanley and that a gap was appearing between Tumbledown and Sapper Hill. We were ordered to move at best speed to advance on Sapper Hill. It was a seven-mile gallop, but our spirits were high. We took the hill unopposed and were extremely surprised to find the Welsh Guards had turned up before us by helicopter. They would have taken a chopping if any enemy had met them. They were clean, well fed, and I thought they looked soft. It was later we heard of their marching fiasco. They had set off from Port San Carlos and the ground and the weather had been too much for them. They had turned back. We were not surprised. They were left behind to garrison the islands after we left, and I felt sorry for them. As we were advancing up Sapper, rumours started filtering through about a surrender. I think that it was the inner warmth supplied by that knowledge that kept me going that night. It was the bitterest of the war and the most uncomfortable of my life, and I slept not a wink. It was particularly bitter because although the navy could manage a victory flypast of helicopters, they couldn't find one to bring our Bergens up before we froze again!

But [next day] we marched into Stanley. It was an emotional hour or so. Naturally, having been in the field for a month, we would hardly have cut much of a dash in the Mall. But we were proud enough and I can think of few prouder experiences than walking into Stanley at the head of my company accompanied by Lance-Bombardier Ingleson carrying our home-made company flag. We were greeted by extremely happy civilians. Then the unbelievable happened. A pub was found open!

General Moore took the Argentinian surrender in Port Stanley at 9 p.m. that evening. More than 12,000 prisoners were taken and quickly repatriated to Argentina, while the Marines, the paras and the Gurkhas sailed home in the luxury and comfort of modern ships. The liner *Canberra* led the fleet home to a rapturous welcome at Southampton on 11 July. The cost was 255 British lives and 750 Argentinians lost. The Royal Marines had lost 26 killed and 86 wounded. The journey had been unusual and demanding but more or less resolved once and for all the hot–cold treatment of the Marines that had been going on since time immemorial.

CHAPTER SIXTEEN

Versatility, Flexibility

During the battle for the Falklands, the Royal New Zealand Navy temporarily took over a task in the Middle East, known as the Armilla patrols. These were set up by the Royal Navy in 1980 when a task group of frigates with Marines aboard was used to patrol the Persian Gulf and Indian Ocean to protect merchant shipping and other British interests in the region against what was described as 'belligerent activity'. The RNZN involvement had enabled ships to be released for service in the South Atlantic, but the RN/RM patrols resumed immediately after the Falklands issue had been settled and, indeed, were intensified at the height of the Iraq–Iran war when, during a two-year span between 1986 and 1988 alone, more than 1,200 ships were given this escort protection. At one point during that period, the Marines 'borrowed' the Royal Yacht *Britannia* in a quite dramatic rescue and evacuation of more than 1,000 British nationals during heavy fighting in the former British colony of Aden, by then known as the People's Democratic Republic of Yemen.

Tensions in the area remained high, especially in the period prior to the first Gulf War in 1991, and developments thereafter made it necessary to maintain the patrols well into the twenty-first century. A typical Armilla patrol deployment lasted six months, but longer for supporting Royal Fleet Auxiliary vessels which might spend up to a year in the area. Ships and patrols were reinforced in times of high tension and were substantially expanded during the first Gulf War, and then beyond it in association with the United Nations in an attempt to ensure that no unauthorised oil supplies were being smuggled out of Iraq.

Although originally planned as a temporary measure, the Armilla patrols were to remain a feature of naval life for many years, not only through the ongoing difficulties with Iraq, but also to take account of maintaining important links with Gulf states where trade and military alliances continued to be a vital aspect of British connections with the region. Indeed, from the early 1980s, when there was much talk of the proliferation of chemical and other weapons of mass destruction, 3 Commando Brigade had to include many new disciplines within its repertoire from an early stage of these developments as a specialist group at the forefront of Nato's constant state of readiness to meet all possibilities. Nuclear, biological and chemical warfare equipment, virtually unheard of in the 1970s, had become part of the regular training routines, especially after Saddam Hussein had tested his own capability by bombing Kurdish villages with mustard gas and other chemicals, killing 5,500 men, women and children. Recognised as the premier amphibious group anywhere in Europe, 3 Commando Brigade now had new battle criteria to meet.

On the home front, there was also a substantial widening of the areas of operation for the Marines and the SBS, particularly at the time of the expansion of Britain's nuclear assets and the proliferation of oil and gas installations off the coastlines of the United Kingdom. Their remote positions created the need for a permanent amphibious defence structure to protect them and other elements of national infrastructure, such as the nuclear plants, power stations and the Channel Tunnel, from potential terrorist action. Ongoing attacks on the British mainland by the IRA and the continuing rise of political and religious extremist groups merely heightened the necessity for amphibious cover around Britain's coast, with a Marine group maintained in a permanent state of readiness, prepared and trained for immediate action. These arrangements, first set in place in the early 1970s, needed to be constantly reviewed to meet both the arrival of new installations and the identification of methods of likely attacks by emerging terrorist groups. Coded plans, which could if necessary progressively involve the entire Commando Brigade, were in place to cover any attack situation.

Northern Ireland also continued to be a drain on British security forces' manpower, requiring an average of 16,000 men on permanent duty within the province. The Commandos took their place alongside the British army units in rotational duties, although some faced a residential posting lasting up to two years. For the most part, the Marines were non-residential, which meant they were separated from their families for long periods at a time.

The IRA continued to attempt to punish them for their involvement, and on 22 September 1989 11 Royal Marines musicians were murdered when a bomb was planted at the Royal Marines School of Music in Deal.

The fall of the Berlin Wall and a virtual end to the Cold War did little to diminish these specialist defensive requirements, although the collapse of Communism initially created some euphoria among the politicians as ushering in a new world order in which defence spending could be substantially reduced. Cuts in the whole of the British military structure were foreshadowed in the controversial document entitled *Options for Change*. To this, later, was added the possibility of a reduction of troops in Northern Ireland as the various peace initiatives got under way, and so substantial cuts in the UK's military manpower were achieved. But this time there were no calls for the Royal Marines to be disbanded and, indeed, manning levels were maintained and then stabilised at an establishment of around 7,000 men and women. Of these, the Commandos account for 5,000, including their support units – although there remained a very obvious and growing need for their specialist skills in so many areas which, like the paras, could not be duplicated by any other force.

Like their forebears in the Second World War, they could fight in the line when necessary, but when it came to the build-up for the first Gulf War in 1990 the Commandos were not required as a fighting unit, and in any event were already dispersed on other commitments, some in Norway and others completing a six-month tour of Northern Ireland. The Royal Marines did, however, provide numerous specialist teams whose activities were security-coded and received little publicity, not least among them the SBS. The Air Defence detachments joined the Royal Navy's Armilla patrols and were followed by the Marine Protection teams to provide naval boarding parties as the UN authorised economic sanctions. These events involved some spectacular raids, with teams using fast inflatable boats or roping down from helicopters to board ships, thus spearheading efforts to halt the delivery of proscribed goods. The Royal Navy also provided a substantial complement of officers and men for a varied number of tasks at Allied Headquarters, as well as security teams for the Royal Fleet Auxiliary. The Royal Marines Bandsmen, adopting the secondary role for which they were trained, provided the bulk of staff on board the Primary Casualty Receiving ships.

The Commandos were, however, mobilised to prevent a civilian catastrophe in the immediate aftermath of the 1991 Gulf War. While the coalition of international troops had been evicting Saddam Hussein's forces from Kuwait, a human tragedy of unimaginable proportions was unfolding in northern Iraq. Saddam's forces were switched to attack the Kurdish population in the northern part of the country. George Bush senior, playing golf in Miami, refused to commit his troops to getting involved in what he described as a civil war. In fact, it was an ongoing campaign of genocide against the Kurds as a whole. Fearing another chemical weapon massacre by the Iraqi leader, the Kurds began fleeing their homes. Within a week, the situation was desperate. Television pictures around the world showed the Kurds massing on the mountains, their suffering caused by the cruelty of Saddam Hussein and the dithering of the West, and Bush in particular, who had the power but not the will to resolve the problem. It was left to British Prime Minister John Major to devise a 'safe haven' plan for the Kurds, to force Saddam to allow them to rest above the 36th parallel without fear of attack, and 3 Commando Brigade, along with elements of other British troops, were dispatched at once to provide the protective measures against Saddam's forces. They were then to involve themselves in the international relief operations under the banner of the United Nations. The Commandos forced the Iraqis back behind a 'line drawn in the sand' 20 miles south of the town of Zakho. Any Iraqi aircraft overflying the safe haven area would be shot down and any troops on the ground would be forced back to the 36th parallel. Matthew Cawthorne, then a young officer in 45 Commando, which had just returned from a six-month period of patrolling in South Armagh, recalled: 'We hadn't actually perceived our role as protector of the Kurds. The only possibility that we did envisage was in going out to help the withdrawal in the south as soon as the main battles were over. But there is no question: they badly needed a force that could deploy quickly and be capable of operating in appalling conditions.'

Apart from the protective patrols to encourage the Kurds to return to their villages, the Commandos played a major role in the international efforts to provide food, tents, fuel and medical supplies. The Kurdish leaders, meanwhile, were keen to know what arrangements were being made to curtail the activities of the remaining secret police and how long the protective forces would remain. There were also delicate discussions about the setting up of their own community administrative structures to enable the UN troops to pull out as soon as possible, given that the threat of trouble was already looming elsewhere. Even as the Commandos were returning home, a crisis was unfolding in Yugoslavia, where the ill-fitting jigsaw of nations held together since the end of the First

World War was coming apart and finally burst into a horrendous and brutal series of wars that were to continue for the remainder of the century.

Fighting between Croatia and Slovenia in the north-east of the country lit the fuse for an explosion of hostilities across the whole region. British, American and European troops would be engaged first under the banner of a UN force to resolve the murderous battles in Bosnia, while the British military provided a newly created Rapid Reaction Force under the command of Major-General David Pennefather. He took with him 74 officers and men of the Royal Marines along with members of the SBS. They remained *in situ* during the Bosnia-Herzegovina troubles, acting as liaison officers and UN observers.

Later, as new crises emerged, the Marines were back into the Balkans, where they had won much respect from the Americans for their restraint and patience in the unravelling of the Bosnian conflict. Their delicate handling of powder-keg situations on the ground became an intrinsic ingredient in the move towards the peaceful resolution in Bosnia that Yugoslav president Slobodan Milošević hated. Now, Milošević had embarked on parallel lines of conflict in the province of Kosovo, attempting to ethnically cleanse the towns and villages of the Albanian Kosovars.

Like many elements of the three services, 3 Commando Brigade supplied specialist teams and manpower in support of the allies' effort throughout the Balkans crisis and again as the horrific situation in Kosovo began to unfold. After Nato's 67-day bombardment of Yugoslavia and the eventual arrest of President Milošević, the whole of 3 Commando Headquarters, supported by its Signal Squadron, deployed to Kosovo to take command of the Multi-National Brigade Centre, with the task of supporting the Nato and UN missions in restoring order when endemic violence erupted as the ethnic communities began settling scores with each other in the aftermath of the conflict. The HQ had 18 units under command, including the Commando Logistics Regiment, Swedish, Finnish and Norwegian battalions and elements of 45 Commando that had just returned from six weeks' jungle training in Belize.

Barely had that situation been calmed when new conflicts emerged that would keep the Royal Marines fully engaged for the first half of the new century. The first occurred in May 2000, at the very moment when the Commando Brigade had joined exercises as part of an Amphibious Ready Group aboard *Ocean* and *Fearless* and other support shipping. In fact, the title could not have been more apt, because their 'readiness' was called on even as the exercise got under way when the former British colony of Sierra Leone was in danger of collapsing into turmoil. A UN peacekeeping force had been unable to quell the bitter, bloody conflict between government and rebel troops. As the fighting worsened, scores of British aid workers and expatriates became trapped by the fighting and more than 500 UN soldiers were taken hostage by the rebels.

Britain dispatched what its military strategists believed to be the model of modern strike-power for such situations: a three-pronged force totalling 1,600 men made up of an SAS squadron for clandestine operations and intelligence-gathering, 700 lightly equipped men from the rapid response spearhead battalion of the Parachute Regiment, and 42 Commando. The Commandos were already aboard the helicopter assault ship *Ocean*, fully equipped with helicopters and landing craft, which set sail at the head of a small flotilla of three support ships and a frigate, *Chatham*. The British aircraft carrier *Illustrious* was also diverted towards Sierra Leone carrying 16 Harrier aircraft and three helicopters.

The Marines had a substantial inventory of equipment with them for the exercise: two Lynx helicopters equipped with anti-tank missiles, six Sea King helicopters and four RAF Chinook transport helicopters. Their heavy equipment included a battery of six 105-millimetre Royal Artillery guns, plus BV-206 tracked vehicles, trucks and Land Rovers carried on the support ships *Sir Bedevere*, *Sir Tristram* and *Fort Austin*. In the event, the British government maintained its stance of a non-assault role and the Commandos completed their mission in good order and were withdrawn on 15 June 2000.

It was, however, an example of their modern capability when the need arises. British troops, minus the Commandos, were back in Sierra Leone in August when 11 British soldiers, part of the UN peace-keeping force, were captured and held to ransom by a notorious 300-strong militia known as the West Side Boys, a ramshackle pro-government army of men, women and children run by self-styled 'Brigadier' Foday Kally. The hostages were subsequently freed by a specially convened force of Britain's finest – a team from each of the SBS and the SAS and A Company Group of 1 Para Battle Group – after a tough fire fight.

That first year of the twenty-first century saw new units formed, following the ending of the practice of having detachments aboard Royal Navy warships – the very reason why the Royal Marines were formed in the first place. They were to be replaced by what was termed a Fleet Standby Rifle Troop consisting of six-man teams with a four-man headquarters unit, available to support fleet operations worldwide. At the same time the teams were linked to the Comacchio group whose own workload was expanded considerably. The unit was moved to purpose-built accommodation at the Faslane naval base in Scotland and given a new title of Fleet Royal Marines Protection Group. These changes came as a result of a study of general aspects of security of both civilian and naval sites and in recognition 'of the changing role of the navy as underlined by the concept of Littoral Warfare and the increasing inventory of specialist amphibious shipping'.

On 7 October 2001 American ships and bombers and British submarines began their bombardment of Afghanistan after the ruling Taliban refused to hand over Osama Bin Laden in the wake of the 11 September attack on the World Trade Center in New York. The main cities of Kabul, Kandahar and Mazar-e Sharif all felt the

American wrath, and in an address to the US nation President George W. Bush said strikes by US and British forces were also taking place against training camps and military installations of the al-Qaeda network in Afghanistan, and that they had been carefully targeted.

All elements of British Special Forces – including a hundred members of the SBS – were engaged in various operations and actions as the campaign in Afghanistan moved towards its conclusion, at least in terms of defeating the Taliban. Over the course of the many weeks of bombing, the Americans switched from dropping so-called smart bombs used to attack Taliban installations and cluster bombs to hit their troops, often with little accuracy, and instead turned to 5,000-pound bunker-busting bombs to hit the networks of caves and bunkers, again generally called down by US or British Special Forces who had provided the coordinates from close surveillance. They radioed back to US air controllers at the US Special Operations Command in Tampa, Florida, who in turn sent in the US bombers with their bunker-busters.

Much of the bunker-bombing was in preparation for the arrival of ground forces that would include 3 Commando Brigade before the coalition of nations began to fall apart in the face of increasing criticism of the bombing and the deaths of so many civilians. In March 2002 a second group of 60 Special Boat Service personnel flew into Bagram, paving the way for the arrival of the Royal Marines. Within a month they launched Operation Snipe to clear out al-Qaeda forces along the Afghan–Pakistan border. The US Green Berets, who had been training in Uzbekistan for two weeks, also moved into the region through Bagram, while the Northern Alliance, assisted by members of the 10th Mountain Division, took control of the high ground around the airfield to secure the airfield as a base for tactical air strikes by USAF F15 Strike Eagles and RAF Tornado GR4 ground-attack aircraft.

The Pentagon also confirmed that elements of the SBS and SAS were in the vanguard of a bloody fight to flush out hundreds of Taliban

313

and al-Qaeda fighters making a last stand in eastern Afghanistan. They were part of a 3,000-strong coalition force engaged in the largest land battle of the war in clearing well-defended caves at Shah-e-Kot, near the town of Gardez. Fierce fighting ensued, and the coalition troops took some of their highest casualties of the war, with many wounded being ferried away by helicopters. Some evacuated from the area told of a gruesome fight against a well-covered enemy and of facing Taliban fire for up to 18 hours at a time in atrocious conditions.

They became dizzy from the thin air and loss of blood as they dodged from one hiding place to another to avoid mortar fire before darkness fell and they could be rescued. 'They appear to have no discernible command structure, with small groups of up to 20 fighters dispersed in bunkers or natural features suitable for defending their ground,' said one officer. 'It is not clear whether they were protecting their leaders or had simply been hiding out in the hope that American troops would abandon the fight in Afghanistan and move on to other targets.'

The significance of the SBS contribution, however, was evident from its eventual recognition when the NCO in charge of the SBS patrol was awarded the Congressional Medal of Honor, America's equivalent to the VC, the first time it has been awarded to a living foreigner. Four of his colleagues received a Presidential Citation. Their operations paved the way for the American-led Operation Anaconda to flush out Taliban groups who were proving difficult to track. In any event, large numbers of Afghan troops had simply gone to ground, to avoid being captured so that they could return to the fight later.

Many were known to have trekked to the relative safety of Pakistan's Tribal Areas in the North-West Frontier province, while some Afghans have simply returned to their homes and merged into the background. It was into this arena that elements of 3 Commando Brigade arrived for their tour of duty as the task of tracking down al-Qaeda and the Taliban became harder. The Royal Marines force was led by 45 Commando, whose presence was especially requested by the American general because of their specialisation in mountain and Arctic warfare. They were supported by 7 Battery of 29 Commando Artillery Regiment, equipped with light 105-millimetre guns, as well as Royal Engineers and logistics troops. The deployment brought the total number of British military personnel in Afghanistan in the spring of 2002 to about 6,400.

On arrival, the Marines lost little time in deploying to Operation Ptarmigan, which was aimed at flushing out terrorists and destroying any cave complexes that could be used as bases or arms dumps. The Marines were based at Bagram, north of Kabul, and when they moved to their mission areas they were operating at about 10,000 feet above sea-level. It was harsh, rugged terrain, very hot and windy with a tendency to snow at night, when temperatures plummeted. They were carrying their own Bergen rucksacks weighing 80 to 90 pounds, which, with low oxygen levels, seemed a lot heavier. As they went to work, Adam Ingram, the Armed Forces Minister, told the Commons: 'This is a very specific mission, of which there will be more, to achieve that overall broad objective of dealing with residual Taliban and al-Qaeda forces which remain in Afghanistan.'

There was a good deal of media speculation that the Commandos were off in search of Osama Bin Laden, but few in the brigade felt that this was high on the list of probabilities. In fact, the whole operation became something of an anticlimax for the media, and especially for the troops engaged. There were few contacts with terrorists and following the American-led Operation Anaconda the previous month, intelligence sources believed that the Taliban and their foreign allies had split into small, mobile groups, so difficult to track. Hundreds were believed to have fled Afghanistan for the relative safety of Pakistan's Tribal Areas in the North-west Frontier province, while some Afghans simply returned to their homes and merged into the background. So the task of tracking down al-Qaeda and the Taliban became harder and the Marines made few contacts with their quarry. At the end of their tour, 3 Commando Brigade commander, Brigadier Roger Lane insisted that the mission had been a great success and that it had been unrealistic to have expected the Marines to return with 'Osama bin Laden's head on a plate'.

After Afghanistan, the build-up of military force in the Gulf region was a remarkably swift affair, further fuelling the accusations that, come what may, America and Britain were going to war and that the orders were out long before Hans Blix, head of the UN inspectors searching Iraq for weapons of mass destruction, had presented what proved to be his final report, and long before the shenanigans at the UN were played out to their conclusion. Blix had said he did not believe Saddam Hussein had any weapons of mass destruction. George W. Bush did not believe him and Tony Blair, for reasons best known to himself, agreed.

The principal nations were pretty well split down the middle about whether war should be declared, the Yes vote seriously influenced by the spin surrounding weapons of mass destruction and claims that Saddam could launch a chemical warhead within 45 minutes. Unless he was hiding a large stock that Hans Blix and his team had been unable to find, Saddam possessed only four ballistic missiles capable of carrying ballistic warheads beyond the Iraqi borders, but they would probably drop well shy of Israel.

Within the rest of the Nato partner countries, few believed that the alternatives to war had been fully explored. That didn't stop the military build-up, which the British and American spinners said was to put further pressure on Saddam in the hope of convincing him to comply with 'international obligations'. Sceptics said it had more to do with timing, i.e. that Bush would be running for re-election in November 2004 and he wanted it all over and done with long before that. Blair raised no objections and placed the British forces at the Americans' disposal. Just before Christmas 2002, all leave was cancelled for most of those serving with 3 Commando Brigade. They were subsequently told that they would probably be going to Iraq, and by mid-January most of the ships associated with the Royal Marines had sailed, allowing a little time for some hasty training at

Cyprus and later in the Gulf region. The Naval Task Group and Amphibious Ready Group with the Marines aboard arrived in the Gulf on 12 February, integrating with US and coalition maritime forces to commence operations by 15 February. A UK force of four Mine Counter-Measures had conveniently been 'in theatre' since November on a 'routine training deployment'.

In fact, the actual planning for what eventually became Operation Telic had begun in September 2002 and at first only a single Commando and an Amphibious Ready Group had been included in the British military line-up. However, as intelligence on the Iraqi force numbers was disseminated, the Americans asked the British to take on greater responsibility. This in turn led to the commitment in early December 2002 of 3 Commando Brigade, minus 45 Commando. The latter were committed to Operation Telic but not to the brigade, and in the event W and X Companies played vital roles elsewhere in the operation.

The brigade deployed to the holding areas in the Middle East by sea and air: 40 Commando Group went with the amphibious group on 16 January 2003 and the remainder, including 42 Commando, went by air direct to Kuwait between 20 January and 15 February and began acclimatisation to the conditions and training for their particular roles. By 18 March, 46,000 men and women from the British services and their equipment had been deployed over 3,400 miles to the Gulf in ten weeks, half the time it took in 1991. Of the total personnel, 15,000 were engaged purely on logistics, a considerable undertaking, using 670 aircraft sorties and 62 ship journeys, up to the point of deployment. Four C-17 aircraft and other air transport were used 24 hours a day to carry more than half the personnel and stores, the rest going by sea. Vehicles shipped to theatre alone, if laid end to end would have stretched the 82 miles from London to Southampton, while general stores and equipment, normally measured in lane metres rather like supermarket shelves, would have covered 77 miles. Thereafter, the daily operational requirement necessitated the daily delivery of

254 metric tonnes at its peak. The speed at which this pre-war move-ment of stores had to be carried out was little short of a logistical nightmare, but by and large the exercise was completed on time and in good order.

In the event, 3 Commando Brigade had once again drawn the short straw in that when the land offensive began on 20 March the men were to lead the southern invasion of Iraq with a complex opposed assault on to the Al Faw Peninsula at night. Their objective was to seize the oil infrastructure intact and to provide flank protection to the main body of troops clearing the Khawr Abd Allah waterway to Iraq's only deep-water port, Umm Qasr.

Flight ceilings were imposed on the Commando helicopters because of the prolific T-Lam operations from American ships and Royal Navy submarines in the Gulf and Red Sea. They were using a flight path above that of the helicopters so that they had a clear path en route to their targets in Baghdad. Elsewhere, RAF Tornado GR4s took off from the Ali al-Salim air base in Kuwait to join the assault with US air force F15 Strike Eagle and US navy FA18 Hornet ground-attack aircraft. The Commando Brigade took the US 15 Marine Expeditionary Unit under command while US jets, A10 tank busters and AC130 Spectre gunships flew in support of the first assault. American MH 53 Sea Stallion helicopters landed the first men of 40 Commando on to the muddy wastes of the Al Faw Peninsula.

The advance itself was covered by a massive assault from 32 AS90 155-millimetre self-propelled guns of the 3rd Regiment, Royal Horse Artillery, while the Royal Navy ships *Marlborough*, *Chatham* and *Richmond* and the Australian frigate *Anzak* provided heavy bombard-ment cover. This was the first use of naval gunfire support by the British forces since the 1982 Falklands War and the first for Australia since the Vietnam War. The artillery attacks were coordinated by the SAS and SBS, whose presence inside Iraq was confirmed by Geoff Hoon, the Defence Secretary, in the Commons in what was a complete diversion from the normal noncommittal descriptions about the activ-ities of the Special Forces. The Commandos' reconnaissance force was also out, pinpointing tasks for both the artillery and the oncoming troops.

The results were incredibly accurate. When, for example, the Royal Navy began firing at an Iraqi bunker complex that was pinpointed for *Marlborough* by the recce troops, from six miles away her shells reached the target 25 seconds later with deadly accuracy. The first rounds were fired short to give the troops the chance to surrender, and then after ten rounds had been fired and the white-hot shrapnel had burst into the bunkers, an onshore spotter radioed back: 'Possible white flags being raised.'

The early objective to seize the Al Faw Peninsula, to secure access to the strategically important port of Umm Qasr, was led in by 40 Commando while 42 Commando launched the amphibious assault on the peninsula, landing in helicopters from the UK's Joint Helicopter Command and a variety of landing craft, covered by the guns of the three Royal Navy frigates. As they made final preparations for the assault in the tactical assembly area, they were fully expecting a chemical attack and for the helicopters to be engaged by air defence artillery. They had to assume strong resistance from the outset and, although the chemical threat did not materialise, they were to meet determined and fanatical fighters, and as they began their movement north 40 Commando would be involved in some of the heaviest action seen by British forces in the initial phases of the war. The operations towards their final objective of capturing the port of Basra began when 40 Commando, supported by Lima Company of 42 Commando, was involved in a day-long battle that also involved tanks and attack helicopters at Al Khasib, on the approach to Basra from the south.

Given the complexities of the operation and the opposition strategically positioned in well-covered areas, the Commandos pursued rigidly their prearranged strategy of forward movements to take predetermined positions en route towards Basra, and it worked almost to the letter. For Bravo Company this entailed a 15-kilometre yomp with Bergens, Milan missiles and heavy machine-gun ammunition to reach their next location. During these operations, more than 5,000 rounds of the Royal Marines' own mortars were fired, most covering 40 Commando's advance to its objectives.

The initial advance was facilitated by a blocking movement at the Al Faw Peninsula by 42 Commando before the troops began their own push forward beyond Umm Qasr, towards Umm Khayyal, to take over a position from the US Marines. In this period, in dire conditions in the sand-blown evening dusk, tragedy struck during otherwise brilliantly executed manoeuvres. An American CH-46 Sea Knight helicopter crash-landed on to the desert, killing 14, including eight men of 3 Commando Brigade's reconnaissance group. One Marine was also killed in a rocket attack on an LCVP (Landing Craft Vehicle, Personnel).

At Umm Khayyal, where the SBS had been operating, 42 Commando received intelligence concerning Ba'ath Party headquarters, the local centre of Saddam Hussein's government. As the men came closer, there was a definite hardening of opposition fire, and it soon became apparent that Saddam's most loyal Fedayeen troops in their black uniforms backed up by local Ba'ath Party militias were lodged here in strength. There were snipers on many buildings, and certain buildings logged as targets were given names linked to the James Bond movies. What now emerged was a hard-fought guerrilla action as the teams advanced under their own mortar fire and smoke to give them cover. The arrival of the Royal Scots Dragoon Guards in their Challenger II tanks provided some welcome additional firepower that blasted the most steadfast opposition from their positions as the Commandos followed on behind the mayhem. By the end of March, 42 Commando, under Lieutenant-Colonel F. H. R. Howes, had cleared to the north of Umm Qasr and Umm Khayyal to launch a full company attack against Fedayeen positions, while 40 Commando had reached the southern reaches of Basra. The commanding officers of the two Commandos subsequently met up at Saddam Hussein's summer palace in the city, their task virtually wrapped up. The Commando group's role in the success of the coalition operation in Iraq was pivotal and profound. In a two-week period of intense operations, it secured key oil infrastructure, cleared a large expanse of enemy-held terrain and defeated a major enemy stronghold on the periphery of Basra, killing over 150 Iraqi soldiers and taking 440 prisoners.

The invasion of Iraq, or at least the main combat phase, was completed in 25 days at which point the country was – in theory at least – under the control of the coalition forces. Of course, the hopes of the main sponsors of Operation Enduring Freedom that the fall of Saddam Hussein would enable a rapid and peaceful transfer of power to a duly elected government proved to be a pipedream. The Royal Marines, along with most of the premier units of the British military would be called upon to return to Basra and the British-controlled areas time and again as other nations withdrew their troops from the pool of forces available to 'manage' the so-called peace. The ongoing cost in terms of casualties among the coalition forces, and of course to the Iraqi population at large, continued to mount. It will be left to history to eventually confirm – or not – the wisdom of this enterprise.

Meanwhile, duty called in other areas as it became clear that the Taliban in Afghanistan were intent on a revival, that region once again demanding a considerable boost in the presence of Nato forces, of which America and Britain were to provide the main body of troops. The Marines, from 42 Commando Royal Marines, were the first combat troops to deploy to southern Afghanistan following the decision in January 2006 to commit around 3,300 British troops as part of Nato's planned expansion. The Marines formed part of an 850-strong advance party deployed to Afghanistan which included engineers from 39 Regiment, Royal Engineers and three CH-47 Chinook helicopters. The Marines carried out the vital function of protecting army and RAF personnel as they built the infrastructure critical for the follow-on deployment of 16 Air Assault Brigade in the summer. The full deployment followed in the long hot summer of 2006, with the British-led Provincial Reconstruction Team taking up positions at Lashkar Gar, the capital of Helmand province, one of the most dangerous areas of Afghanistan, initially staffed and protected by 16 Air Assault Brigade.

Later in the year, 3 Commando Brigade took over in a wholesale deployment of its units and support groups. They went *en masse* to Helmand province despite being promised a rough reception by the Taliban commanders there. The main body of Commandos arrived in late September 2006 with a mandate to assist attempts by local government to rebuild the province after 35 years of war, strife and destruction, and to provide a measure of security to the local people. In all, 2600 members of 3 Commando Brigade deployed to the province, along with 800 Naval Air Squadron, rotational army units and somewhat limited air support from the RAF. They were joined by peace-keeping forces from Estonia and Denmark.

After completing what was described as a 'robust training package in the UK', the Commandos hit the ground running and continued where the Paras left off, taking up position in a number of District Centres in the north and providing a round-the-clock protection force for the provincial capital of Lashkar Gah and the main town of Garmsir in the south. Their prime task was to ensure that the Taliban did not regain a foothold in these far-flung outposts. But this, in turn, resulted in continuous, hard-fought battles. In Garmsir, as the advance approached, Taliban fighters launched a ferocious and organised attack with heavy weapons and attempted to outflank the British via a network of tunnels and defences around the town, making fighting particularly difficult. Major Andy Plewes, commanding Zulu Company, 45 Commando who led the assault, said the troops had expected resistance: 'What we didn't know was how strong it was. We don't currently have enough forces in the area to hold ground completely and that has to be done by Afghan security forces.'

A further example of the key tasks that stretched the resources of the Royal Marines was that faced by M Company, 42 Commando, led by Major Martin Colin. The company was clearing villages where Taliban fighters were embedded around Kajaki, in the north of Helmand province. Codenamed Operation Clay, this began in the early hours of New Year's Day and ran for four days as a party of 110 troops, comprising Marines, Royal Engineers and members of the Territorial Army, carried out various operations around the town and the site of a major hydroelectric dam. Major Oliver Lee, 3 Commando Brigade's Operations Officer, commented: '42 Commando carried out a very focused and targeted military operation intended to gain ownership of the key high ground around Kajaki. In the process of that operation we understand that a Taliban commander was killed.'

The operation was deemed a success because of its wider implications – it allowed significant development in the area, and possession of the Kajaki Hydroelectric Dam, built in 1953, and part of the largest USAID programme in Afghanistan. By securing the area around Kajaki, contractors were able to carry out repairs to the dam and so resume electricity supplies for 1.8 million Afghans across southern Afghanistan.

The Commandos also set about the potentially dangerous task of clearing a series of caves, used by Taliban forces to the north-east of Kajaki. The operations seemed to be going smoothly when, in the final stage of the clearance, M Company was stung by heavyweight fire from a much larger force of enemy troops. They had been grouped in specific compounds in the heart of the village. Typical of the numerous fire-fights that were continually testing the Marines was that led by Second Lieutenant Burty Kerr, 11 Troop, M Company, who commanded his men towards a compound deep within Kajaki Olya. As the troop approached the form-up point to begin the assault, they came under enemy fire, targeted with small arms fire and rocket-propelled grenades. They responded with pinpoint attacks using heavy machine gun fire, 81mm mortars and hand-held missile launchers, until they had established a foothold within the compounds. At this point 10 Troop came forward to assist with the systematic clearing of the buildings. Still under fire, the Marines gradually made their way towards the Taliban training compound. Major Colin, reporting on that day's events, said: 'From troop level downwards, the mission command was excellent and the young guys in particular all performed their jobs very, very well with an immense amount of enthusiasm and professionalism. I couldn't ask any more of them.'

In three of the British areas of operations, a succession of suicide

323

bombers brought additional security problems. Almost three-quarters of the 105 suicide blasts reported in Afghanistan in 2006, killing 217 Afghans and 17 foreign soldiers, were in the Kandahar area. At one point, Royal Marines commanders had to enforce a 'lock-down' for the troops in barracks and fortified positions until a strategy for dealing with this rash of deadly attacks had been rolled out. It resulted for the first time in Afghanistan in the deployment of the new Viking armoured vehicles, costing £1 million each, capable of travelling up to 65mph on roads and firing up to 300 grenades a minute. Tactics learned and used in Iraq were also adopted where any vehicle approaching a military vehicle at speed is given a succession of warning signals to try to slow it down or stop it, using mini flares fired into the air. Warning shots follow and, if the driver still refuses to slow down, troops are authorised to fire into the engine block. Under the military's rules of engagement, soldiers are allowed to kill the driver if he continues on towards them.

The ongoing operations in Afghanistan as described above were judged by military analysts as some of the most intense and courageous fighting by British troops since the Korean War. It was not without cost. At the time of writing, six Marines had been killed, bringing the total number of deaths among British servicemen to 35 since May 2006. Nor were casualties among the Commandos restricted to the Afghan battles. During the same period, various special units and elements of 45 Commando were on particular duties in Basra and southern Iraq where they faced an ever-present threat of attack. One Marine from 45 Commando, attached to 539 Assault Squadron, was among four British servicemen killed and three others 'very seriously' injured when a makeshift bomb exploded near their boat as they patrolled a river in Basra. Other members of the patrol came from the Royal Signals and the Intelligence Corps.

CHAPTER SEVENTEEN

A Force for the Future

As will have become evident from preceding chapters, the position of amphibious forces within the British seagoing inventory has been famously challenged at various stages in the history of the Royal Marines, often and ironically at the end of some great effort and sacrifice. In spite of these many contributions to the nation's military and naval prowess in times of dire straits, the question arose with predictable regularity, even into modern times: are they really necessary? The fact was that the Marines came close to becoming extinct on a number of occasions. Only the foresight and steadfastness of senior officers at various points in their history prevented their demise. Towards the end of the twentieth century, however, when no more could be done to prove their viability, the years of inter-service wrangling and rivalries, political intrigue and budgetary concerns were finally set aside with the recognition that the Royal Marines possessed the skills, flexibility and the know-how gained from years of experience to spearhead the most vital British military missions in the demanding world of twenty-first-century emergencies.

Specifically, 3 Commando Brigade, with its various RM support units, was to be revamped and upgraded in readiness to move anywhere in the world to confront threats to British interests, or in conjunction with allies or Nato armies. The key to the overall vision for the Commando role was envisaged by the RM planners themselves in their studies and papers on the demands of the future. Long before 9/11, they had been plotting a course into the post-Cold War scenario in which terrorists and rogue powers were seen as the potential enemy in their battle plans and exercises. Again, their various elements had long experience of dealing with such matters, and what now emerged largely at the behest of the Royal Marines themselves was the foundation of what they describe as a 'unique national capability: independently or as an integrated part of a maritime contribution to a joint force . . . [with] utility in all phases of a campaign, from benign presence to the conduct of forced theatre entry combat operations'.

The first steps towards this began in the 1990s, when the brigade was reorganised to become a key element in the British government's Rapid Reaction Force. From these beginnings, the Royal Marines began moving towards a revolutionary experiment in battalion reorganisation to point the way in which the British military prepares to meet the challenges of the first two decades of the twenty-first century. Up to that point, Commando units were organised in the manner of army battalions, a structure that had basically remained unchanged since the Second World War.

As mentioned in the prologue, the new concept was to be introduced under the title of Commando 21, in which the Commando units were to be reorganised from the ground up so that the basics of the new force were built around the Marines themselves. Each one was to become part of a four-man team, and the teams represent what is described as the 'building blocks' of all Commando operations. The Marines in the field will remain in their team throughout, living together, training together, travelling together and working together. Training routines would be expanded so that all specialisations could be experienced in an intense programme covering the whole gamut of possible deployments, ranging through hot and arid desert conditions to jungle warfare or cold mountainous conditions. Training areas that all Marines will experience include the Middle East, the jungle of Belize, Norway and elsewhere. A further vital element in training includes preparations for assignment at sea to the Amphibious Ready Group (ARG), which, as the title suggests, is designed to operate virtually as a complete entity in itself, capable of immediate deployment anywhere in the world.

The ARG is based around the star asset of the Commando organisation, HMS *Ocean*, the pivotal machine among other specialist vessels, and the whole amounts to a highly mobile amphibious force concentrated on the Commandos and supporting units, ranging through fast boats to helicopters that can be kept at high readiness, 'in waiting' to move swiftly to any emergency situation and achieve the rapid landing of an assault force by helicopter and landing craft. *Ocean*, designed and built to accommodate a complete Commando unit and all its stores, weapons and aircraft, was commissioned in 1998. The hull design was based on the design of the *Invincible*-class aircraft carrier with a modified superstructure. The ship carries a crew of 255, an aircrew of 206 and 480 RM Commandos. An additional 320 Marines can be accommodated in a short-term emergency, and in reality *Ocean* is capable of transporting and sustaining an embarked military force of up to 800 men equipped with artillery, vehicles and stores. The ship also has the capacity to carry 40 vehicles as well as four versatile LCVP Mk 5 (vehicle and personnel landing craft) on davits.

The ship also has facilities for 12 EH101 Merlin and six Lynx helicopters, and landing and refuelling facilities for Chinook helicopters. With a 170-metre-long flight deck, it also has the ability to carry 20 Sea Harriers, although they would require ground facilities for support. *Ocean* is also equipped with eight Sea Gnat radar reflection infrared-emitting decoys, developed under a Nato project with the USA, Germany, Norway, Denmark and the UK, for protection against anti-ship guided missiles. Thus protected, the amphibious flotilla provides a hugely diverse combination of options, not least of which is the ability to operate in international waters without infringing territorial boundaries, with the ability to 'poise' offshore almost indefinitely.

The Commando 21 concept also introduces equipment and weaponry designed specifically for the amphibious forces in their new modus operandi. The suite of new vessels, aircraft, vehicles and intelligence assets surrounding *Ocean* will be enhanced over the coming years to carry the force well into the twenty-first century. Other equipment and weaponry will be progressively introduced into the Commandos, including a new long-range rifle, a heavy machine gun and a Light Forces anti-tank guided weapon (LFATGW). Among the new vehicles is the Viking, an armoured all-terrain vehicle that will provide units with protected mobility.

Meanwhile, the 'building blocks' for Commando 21 – i.e. the teams of Marines manning the various elements of the Commando forces and supporting assets – will emerge from an infantry training regime that is without doubt one of the most demanding anywhere in the world. The first step on this journey begins at the Commando Training Centre at Lympstone, Devon, where new recruits are introduced to the well-tried and well-tested training programme. It is a stiff and prolonged trial of strength to hone fitness, endurance and military skills; once the programme is completed, recruits are rewarded with the famous green beret and the Royal Marines Commando flash for the uniform.

The Commando Training Centre trains all Royal Marines recruits, as well as army and navy personnel who volunteer to serve with Royal Marines, such as seamen, artillery support and engineers. All must get through the infamous Commando course and, while certain minimum standards are set for what is described as the 'pass ethos', there is also a built-in self-selection process in the preliminaries, in that the minimum required levels of determination, commitment and physical ability are more demanding than in any other branch of the British military establishment outside of the SAS and SBS.

A large percentage of hopefuls in fact never get past the preliminary tests. Those who succeed will normally join one of the three Commando units: 40 Commando based at Norton Manor, Taunton, Somerset, 42 Commando at Bickleigh, Devon, and 45 Commando at Arbroath, Scotland. The three Commandos provide the core fighting teams of the brigade and represent its main combat capability. Each is 700-men strong and each one can deploy as a Commando group, including its elements from the combat support units.

Apart from the artillery and engineer elements provided by the army, the Commando brigade is otherwise a completely self-contained force with its own Command, Control and Communications and computing teams, along with Intelligence, Surveillance, Target Acquisition and Reconnaissance (ISTAR) linked to the Permanent Joint Headquarters in Northwood. The Communications Squadron is manned by RM signallers and provides communications for the brigade HQ to its units to and from any location in the world.

Other highly trained specialists include the Brigade Patrol Troop, which is usually deployed ahead of any amphibious landings to provide a full range of intelligence on the terrain and the enemy. There is also a heavy reliance on Y Troop, the brigade's electronic warfare specialists trained in communications equipment that can find and intercept enemy transmissions.

The Commandos also have the support of their own dedicated Logistic Regiment, which consists of a Headquarters Squadron and four specialist squadrons providing logistics, medical and other services for the brigade, and the 539 Assault Squadron, Royal Marines, operates landing craft, raiding craft and hovercraft, providing additional mobility to the assault force. Finally, the Commando Helicopter Force provides the aviation support to the brigade. This consists of two squadrons of support helicopters, equipped with Sea King, and a squadron of light helicopters, equipped with Lynx and Gazelle.

In line with the changes envisaged under Commando 21, the RM recruitment and training process was also updated and brought under one controlling administration. It is a gruelling procedure that begins initially with a three-week Foundation Module designed to help recruits make a successful transition from civilian life. Individual training covers a wide spectrum of skills, such as weapons training, field craft, physical training, close-quarter combat, map-reading, first aid, radios and individual Nuclear, Biological and Chemical Defence (NBCD) drills. The first 15 weeks concentrate on physical preparation, which is merely a taster for the challenging training schedule ahead.

The sheer exertion and future demands may be seen from the fact that a unit known as Hunter Company is on permanent stand-by. The company specialises in the treatment and rehabilitation of recruits who suffer serious injuries or illness during their training. Given the robust nature of the course, injuries sustained in training are not uncommon. It is a long-established system, but during the past decade it has developed a deservedly high reputation within the British military as a whole for its work.

The first phase of training requires recruits to pass exercises in field craft, map-reading, navigation, signals, first aid and NBCD, as well as demonstrating physical and mental robustness in passing a four-mile speed march carrying 32 pounds of equipment, including their weapon, in 40 minutes and an eight-mile march also carrying equipment. Training then moves into the second phase, which covers a more intensive programme of military skills in which recruits begin to discover more of the tactical side of military operations.

Then they move on to amphibious and cliff assault training and the Commando Course. The latter provides what the Royal Marines describe as 'the ultimate in progressive physical challenges', leading the recruits finally towards the final stages of qualification: Test Week. This represents the grand finale in the assessment of the recruits' performance in every aspect of their training. It will include a number of disciplines that have to be undertaken and passed within an eight-day period, including amphibious landings, helicopter assaults and the famous Royal Marines' physical endurance trials, such as a 12-mile load-carry test with a 69-pound Bergen and weapon, a nine-mile speed march, the 'Tarzan' Assault Course and a 30-mile 'yomp' across Dartmoor.

But, of course, this is only the beginning . . .

APPENDIX I

Victoria Cross Awards

CORPORAL 1. PRETTYJOHNS, RM, at the Battle of Inkerman, 5 November 1854, successfully led a section that dislodged Russian marksmen from some caves.

BOMBARDIER T. WILKINSON, RMA, at the Siege of Sebastopol, 7 June 1855, repaired damage to the advanced battery's revetments while under heavy fire.

LIEUTENANT G. D. DOWELL, RMA, at the Baltic, 13 July 1855, rescued the crew of a rocket boat under intense grape and musketry fire.

CAPTAIN L. S. T. HALLIDAY, RMLI, at the Siege of Peking, 24 June 1900, led the way into burning legation buildings under heavy small-arms fire.

LANCE-CORPORAL W. R. PARKER, RMLI, at Gallipoli, 30 April 1915, for displaying conspicuous bravery in rescuing wounded in daylight under heavy fire.

MAJOR F. J. W. HARVEY, RMLI. Posthumous award for action at

the Battle of Jutland, 31 May 1916, when he saved his ship by ordering the flooding of his turret's magazines, although he himself was mortally wounded, having lost both his legs.

CAPTAIN E. BAMFORD, RMLI, for actions during the Zeebrugge raid, 23 April 1918, when he led his company with initiative and daring in the face of great difficulties (nominated for the award by ballot).

SERGEANT N. A. FINCH, RMA, at the Zeebrugge raid, 23 April 1918, when he maintained continuous covering fire from the exposed foretop, although severely wounded himself.

CORPORAL T. P. HUNTER, RM. Posthumous award at the Battle of Comacchio, 3 April 1945, for advancing alone over open ground to save his troop by offering himself as a target.

APPENDIX II

Sources and Bibliography

Imperial War Museum Sound Archive

Bethel, Horace (accession number 9003), RM colour sergeant; enlisted as a bugler, 1888.

Branscome, Alfred F. (7078), 41 Commando, Salerno, 1943.

Cawthorne, Matthew (12407), Operation Safe Haven, 45 Commando, 1991.

Chappell, Ernest (00997), 9 Independent, then army Commandos, captured at St-Nazaire.

Coote, Leslie (14964), served aboard HMS *Ramilies*, North Atlantic, 1940–42; HMS *Glasgow* during Normandy landings; Korea.

Cosgrove, Henry (10177), 45 Commando.

Dowell, Howard R. (18576), Landing Craft (Flak), 1944.

Durrant, William (9018), RM corporal, gunner in North Sea operations 1914–18.

Ferguson, Richard Gerald (17990), Royal Marines, Malaya, Aden, Borneo etc.

Hill, Edward John (4691), RMNBDO, captured at Crete, 1941.

Horner, Edward William (007473), RM, 1938 aboard HMS *Calypso* (sunk), then RMBPD and SBS, 1938–45 and beyond.

Horton, Vincent (23141), RMNBDO, Crete, 1941.

Instance, Howard (11904), seaman, 1939–45.

Jenkins, William (21288), 43 Commando, Yugoslavia, Italy, 1944–5 and beyond.

Johnson, John Adair (20516), 44 Commando, Far East, 1943–5.

Kelly, James A. (11281), 41 Commando, Salerno, D-Day, North-West Europe etc.

Langton, Henry (16761), 41 Ind. Commando, Rhine Squadron, SBS, 1952–6.

Napier, John (113222), seaman aboard HMS *Exeter* in *Graf Spee* encounter and beyond, 1938–56.

McAlester, William (12957), 40 Commando, Falklands, 1982.

Maindonald, G. (16627), 41 Ind. Commando, Korea, 40 Commando, Palestine and beyond.

Moore, Major-General Sir Jeremy (10482), Falklands, 1982.

Richards, George Richard (9860), 42 Commando, Libya, 1947, Palestine, 1948.

Shale, Samuel (941), aboard HMS *Ajax* in Atlantic and Mediterranean, 1939–41.

Smith-Hill, Philip (11739), HMS *Vernon*, 1915, Murmansk, 1919 and beyond.

Smithson, Ivor (20990), 40 Commando, Sicily, 41 Commando, Walcheren and beyond.

Sparks, William E. (8397), paddler to Major H. G. Hasler, RMBPD, on Operation Frankton.

Storie, David (11139), 45 Commando, Cyprus, helicopter pilot, Indonesia, 42 Commando, Northern Ireland and beyond.

Vaux, Nicholas (11142), 45 Commando, Suez, Northern Ireland, 1970.

Warburton, Kenneth (19941), guard at Quebec and Potsdam conferences, 1944–5.

Imperial War Museum Department of Documents

Badenoch, A. C. (box ref: 04/34/1), memoir written shortly after return from Normandy, 1944, serving with RM.

Chater, A. R. (66/202/1), MS account of his service with RM, 1913–20, including Antwerp and Gallipoli.

Couldrake, H. T. (01/39/1), diary written during service with RMLI 1916–18.

Empson, R. H. W. M. (95/16/1), transcript of letters written autumn 1914 during service with RMLI; killed in action at Gallipoli, May 1915.

Hines, A. E. (92/27/1), account of service with RM, including Salerno and Walcheren 1939–46.

Horne, H. (80/44/1), junior officer 1st Batt. RM, in 63rd Royal Naval Division, 1916–19.

Rhodes, N. F. (77/137/1), transcript of brief diary kept during service with RM on battleship HMS *Canopus* and firing first shot in the Battle of the Falklands, 1914.

Sinclair, R. (92/18/10), three letters written to members of his family while serving as captain RM in the battle cruiser HMS *Inflexible*, December 1914.

Royal Marines Museum

A Short History of the Royal Marines, 1664–2002, published by the Royal Marines Historical Society.

45 Commando in South Arabia: Synopsis of Events, 1960–67.

45 Commando: Report on Patrol Action, Sha'ab Gatana, 2 September 1964.

45 Commando: Aden History: An Account.

42 Commando: Borneo Campaign, Log of Action, 1962–6.

Middle East Command: Report: Last British Troops Withdraw from Little Aden, dated 16 September 1967.

R. W. Madoc, notes of lecture to the Royal Naval War College, on the Suez Crisis, dated 10 June 1958.

Lieutenant-Colonel T. M. P. Stevens, report on patrolling in Aden, dated 12 May 1964.

335

Published Sources

Billière, General Sir Peter de la, *Storm Command: A Personal Account of the Gulf War*, HarperCollins, London, 1992.

Brooks, Richard, *The Royal Marines: 1664 to the Present*, Naval Institute Press, Annapolis, Maryland, 2002.

Calvert, Michael, *Chindits: Long-Range Penetration*, Ballantine Books, London, 1973.

Chinnery, Philip D., *March or Die: The Story of Wingate's Chindits*, Airlife Publishing, Shrewsbury, 1997.

Churchill, Randolph S., *Young Statesman (1901–14)*, Heinemann, London, 1967.

Churchill, Winston S., *The World Crisis, Volumes I-IV*, Odhams Press, London, 1938.

Fortescue, J. W., *History of the British Army* in 20 volumes, Naval and Military Press, 2002.

Geraghty, Tony, *Who Dares Wins: The Story of the Special Air Service, 1950–1980*, Arms and Armour Press, London, 1980.

Gilchrist, Donald, *The Commandos: D-Day and After*, Robert Hale, London, 1992.

Harclerode, Peter, *Secret Soldiers*, Cassell, London, 2000.

Jerrold, D., *Royal Naval Division*, with foreword by Winston S. Churchill, Hutchinson, London, 1923.

Kitson, Frank, *Low-Intensity Operations, Subversion, Insurgency and Peacekeeping*, Faber and Faber, London, 1971.

Ladd, James, *Commandos and Rangers of World War II*, Macdonald, London, 1978.

Lockhart, Robert-Bruce, *The Marines Were There: The Story of the Royal Marines in the Second World War*, Putnam, London, 1950.

Lodwick, John, *The Filibusters*, Methuen, London, 1947.

Moulton, J. L., *Haste to Battle: A Royal Marine Commando at War*, Cassell, London, 1963.

Parker, John, *SBS: The Inside Story of the Special Boat Service*, Headline, London, 1997.

Parker, John, *Commandos: The Inside Story of Britain's Most Elite Fighting Force*, Headline, London, 1998.

Rhodes-James, Robert, *Gallipoli*, Batsford, London, 1965.

Thompson, Julian, *Royal Marines: From Sea Soldiers to Special Force*, Sidgwick and Jackson, London, 1988.

Ziegler, Philip, *Mountbatten: The Official Biography*, Collins, London, 1985.

INDEX

NEWBURY COLLEGE LRC